W9-AAT-523

DEFEAT IS AN ORPHAN

MYRA MACDONALD

Defeat is an Orphan

*How Pakistan Lost
the Great South Asian War*

HURST & COMPANY, LONDON

First published in the United Kingdom in 2017 by
C. Hurst & Co. (Publishers) Ltd.,
41 Great Russell Street, London, WC1B 3PL
© Myra MacDonald, 2017
All rights reserved.
Printed in the United Kingdom by Bell and Bain Ltd.

Distributed in the United States, Canada and Latin America by
Oxford University Press, 198 Madison Avenue, New York, NY 10016,
United States of America.

The right of Myra MacDonald to be identified as the author
of this publication is asserted by her in accordance with the
Copyright, Designs and Patents Act, 1988.

A Cataloguing-in-Publication data record for this book
is available from the British Library.

ISBNs: 9781849046411 hardback

This book is printed using paper from registered sustainable
and managed sources.

www.hurstpublishers.com

For Hannah

CONTENTS

ACKNOWLEDGEMENTS

Having first arrived in Delhi as Bureau Chief of Reuters in March 2000, this book is the product of so many years of engagement with India and Pakistan that it is impossible for me to acknowledge individually everyone who contributed. First and foremost then, I would like to thank the many people from India and Pakistan, and from Jammu and Kashmir, who helped over the years. In the period since I began covering the region, India and Pakistan came close to war on at least one occasion, and tantalisingly near to a peace agreement on Kashmir on another. By the second decade of the 21st century, peace remained as elusive as ever, and the chances of a settlement on Kashmir had become vanishingly small. The most striking change, though, was that India had emerged as a rising power while Pakistan floundered. After leaving Reuters, I decided to go back over recent history, much of which I had covered myself as a journalist. My aim was to review what had happened without the pressure of daily news, pulling at the threads that are often overlooked in the urgency of the moment. *Defeat is an Orphan* is the product of multiple viewpoints gathered from around the region and around the world, in part during my years as a reporter, in part more recently. This included interviews with both serving and retired officials on both sides of the border.

My particular thanks are owed to Shashank Joshi for reading an early draft and providing an essential critique of its content and structure. Fiona Leney edited a later draft with professional ruthlessness. Siddiq Wahid in Srinagar has been particularly helpful on the history of Jammu and Kashmir and a long-standing source of inspiration. Liz

ACKNOWLEDGEMENTS

Harris provided insight on the situation in the Kashmir Valley. Zalan Khan opened a window into the various perspectives of Pashtuns from Pakistan's north-west. I should also thank Ayesha Siddiqa in Islamabad and Praveen Swami in Delhi. Among the many former colleagues at Reuters who helped me over the years, I should mention Sanjeev Miglani in Delhi, Zeeshan and Kamran Haider in Islamabad and Sheikh Mushtaq and Fayaz Kabli in Srinagar. Officials and former officials in London, Washington and Paris added their perspective. The vast majority of my interlocutors, however, were in South Asia. My thanks too to my publisher, Michael Dwyer, for taking on the idea and helping to refine it, and to all his colleagues at Hurst.

Finally, my daughter, Hannah, has shown remarkable fortitude since first being dragged out to India at the age of nine. Her sense of humour and joie de vivre have been a constant source of joy, all the more needed when writing about a conflict that often leaves little room for optimism.

I recognise that in such a polarised environment as exists in South Asia, my book, or elements of it, will be criticised in many different ways. I hope, however, that it contributes to further critical thinking, particularly on the vexed question of Jammu and Kashmir. I should add that all mistakes in *Defeat is an Orphan* are my own, as are the views expressed in it.

PROLOGUE

THE SPIDER'S WEB

The Hijacking

Indian Airlines Flight IC-814 had just taken off from Kathmandu when the cabin crew began the scramble to serve the food and drinks. It took less than two hours to reach Delhi and the plane was full of first-time flyers anxious for their free whisky-and-soda or beer, an illicit pleasure on international flights since alcohol was banned on domestic routes. It was Christmas Eve 1999, the last month of the old millennium. Many passengers were returning from a brief holiday in Nepal. A few couples were coming back from their honeymoon. Others had been given a paid break by their employers as a reward for meeting sales targets. For many Indians, Kathmandu at the time was as exotic a place as they could afford. The seat of a crumbling royal dynasty, the splendour of its magnificent palaces and temples belied the desperate poverty of the countryside where a rural Maoist insurgency held sway. With its cheap hotels and basement casinos, it was also a perfect getaway for lower middle class Indians. It was one of the few places where the Indian rupee bought more than it did at home and where shops were stocked with consumer goods then still hard to find in India. This was the world's only Hindu kingdom, a country frozen in time and trapped between Asian giants China and India. Like Vienna during the Cold War, Kathmandu teemed with political intrigue and the whisperings of intelligence officers. India's external intelligence agency, the

1

Research and Analysis Wing (R&AW), had a big presence, working to counter the influence of China. Pakistan's Inter-Services Intelligence (ISI) agency, taking advantage of lax security along the long porous border between India and Nepal, worked out of Kathmandu too. It was a useful base to push jihadis, spies and counterfeit money into India. On the return flight, the passengers were celebrating a holiday well spent, their duty-free purchases crammed into the overhead lockers above. The plane was an old Airbus-300, relatively roomy even in economy class. Those in window seats could see the Himalaya disappearing into the dusk as the plane approached Indian airspace.

In the cockpit, Captain Devi Sharan was looking forward to time away in Sharjah with his wife and two daughters. This was his last day at work before the holiday and it had been frustratingly long. He had started early in the morning from Hyderabad in southern India. In Kathmandu he had been held up for hours waiting for permission to take off. Nepal's Tribhuvan International Airport had been as chaotic as ever, with no sign of security. He had noticed that one woman who was meant to be looking at the monitor screen attached to the baggage X-ray machine was knitting a sweater. Now he was tired after his long day and glad to be heading for home. He asked senior flight purser Anil Sharma to bring him a cup of tea and set course for the Indian border. He began to relax and to chat, grumbling about the late take-off. He had 178 passengers on board along with eight cabin crew and the three flight crew.[1]

In seat 1B, at the front of Business or J-Class, was passenger Romi Grover. Unlike most of the other passengers, he was a regular visitor to Nepal for his company's import-export business. He had been lucky to get on the plane. At Kathmandu he had been running late and might have missed the flight had it not been delayed. The airport that day had been "at its absolute, absolute worst," he recalled. "I walked into the airport with my boarding pass, went through immigration and security in less than five minutes. Officials were not interested in anything." He eased off his shoes and began his meal.[2]

From his seat at the front, Grover saw the flight purser come out of the cockpit and stand for a moment facing the passengers. Behind him, two men in balaclavas appeared from the toilets on either side. One was holding a holding a pistol and a grenade; the other a pistol and a dagger. Since Sharma had his back to them, he did not immediately notice the two men. "The first thought that came to my mind was 'this is a prank Indian Airlines is playing, wishing passengers a Merry Christmas,'" Grover said. Then one of the men tapped Sharma on the shoulder and said, "This flight is hijacked."

* * *

Afterwards, when the different witnesses to the hijacking recounted their ordeal, many of the details they gave contradicted each other. India never held an official public enquiry into the event; it made no attempt to unravel differences over crucial questions such as how well armed the hijackers were or what language they spoke. Over time, the story fell victim to lapses of memory; to the chaos of fear and emotion; to individual perspectives. Grover recalled the hijackers talking in a mix of Hindi and Urdu, but using the English word for hijack. The pistol he saw one of the hijackers wielding was polished and finished. Other accounts suggested their guns were rough-hewn, of the type easily available in Nepal. What is clear is that the hijackers moved quickly to establish control. First they ordered the passengers in J-Class to move to the back of the plane. Grover still had his food tray in front of him. He had just begun putting on his shoes when one of the hijackers lunged towards him and flung the tray off the table. One of the gunmen went into the cockpit, while another moved towards the back of the plane, joining three other hijackers waiting in the rear. All the hijackers—as it turned out later—were Pakistani nationals. In economy class, they made the passengers lean forward in their seats and told the cabin crew to help blindfold them using the cloth covers on the seat backs. Food and drinks were pitched into trolleys which the cabin crew hurriedly pushed away. Passengers were shuffled around to separate them from their families, isolate them and break their will to resist. Then they sat stiffly with their heads bowed, barely daring to look up to check on their relatives. Several men were selected for "special treatment" and moved up into J-Class. "It was very well-planned and perfectly executed," said Grover.

In the cockpit, the lead hijacker, a man the others called "Chief", pushed his gun into the back of Captain Sharan's neck. "Fly west," the Chief ordered. Beyond Delhi, towards Lahore in Pakistan. One-by-one, four of the five hijackers filed into the cockpit. Between them they had at least two to three grenades and possibly more, three to four

3

revolvers and a knife. Captain Sharan tried to persuade them that he did not have enough fuel to fly beyond Delhi. But at least one of the hijackers, a man who identified himself as Burger, knew about flying. He spoke English and could read fuel gauges and the central instrument panel, along with the Jeppesen charts used for navigation. "What is your alternate?" Burger asked, using a phrase rarely known to the layman for the alternative choice of landing should an emergency or bad weather force the destination airport to close. Captain Sharan had to admit that his alternate was Bombay—meaning he had enough fuel to fly beyond Delhi. Burger had come prepared with knowledge about planes. "Somewhere he told us, 'I have done some simulator training on the A-300,'" Captain Sharan said.[3]

Over the intercom, Captain Sharan announced to the passengers that the plane had been hijacked and asked them to cooperate with the hijackers. He set his transponder to a code that would tell Indian civil aviation authorities his plane had been hijacked and allow them to track Flight IC-814, and then persuaded the "Chief" to let him inform Air Traffic Control. He continued to argue about fuel while the plane flew west. Indian Airlines had never held training for a hijacking, but its standing instructions were to do what the hijackers asked and leave decisions about how to handle the crisis to authorities on the ground. Captain Sharan was certain he did not want to fly to Lahore. India and Pakistan had fought a bitter border war in Kargil on the Line of Control dividing Kashmir that year and the wounds were still raw. In October, General Pervez Musharraf, the architect of the Kargil War, had seized power in a military coup.

Captain Sharan slowed the plane down to give Indian authorities more time to plan a rescue operation. Helped by a decision by Pakistan to shut its airspace to the hijacked plane—whatever Pakistani involvement in the hijacking there was, it did not extend to having Flight IC-814 land on its territory—Captain Sharan finally convinced the hijackers that the aircraft's fuel situation was desperate. Reluctantly, they let him land for refuelling in Amritsar, the city in Indian Punjab nearest to the Pakistan border. He breathed a sigh of relief. The plane was on Indian territory. Now would be the time to send special forces to storm the plane and rescue the passengers and crew.

* * *

In Delhi, the government was struggling to decide what to do. Right from the outset, it suspected the involvement of Pakistan which for decades had supported non-state actors to destabilise India and try to wrest control of Kashmir. The US and Saudi-funded jihad run by Pakistan against the Soviet occupation of Afghanistan in the 1980s had given the ISI all the more muscle to challenge India. Then when a separatist revolt against Indian rule erupted in Kashmir in the late 1980s, Pakistan diverted some of the jihadis it had trained to fight the Russians towards its eastern border. By the time of the hijacking, Pakistan's proxy war against India was at its peak. In Afghanistan, run since 1996 by the Pakistan-backed Taliban, the ISI organised training camps for militants to fight in Kashmir. Pakistan's possession of nuclear weapons, confirmed by nuclear tests that followed those of India in May 1998, deterred Indian retaliation for fear of triggering a bigger war. The Indian government needed to act before the hijacked plane somehow reached Pakistani territory. India had the capability, and sometimes the will, to act ruthlessly in its own defence. It was in Amritsar, where the hijacked plane was awaiting rescue, that Prime Minister Indira Gandhi had sent troops into the Golden Temple, the Sikhs' holiest shrine, to dislodge the leaders of a Sikh separatist rebellion in 1984. The Indian authorities had at their disposal the means to storm the plane using the elite troops in the National Security Guard (NSG) who were permanently on standby at their base outside Delhi. Yet the Indian government, then led by the nationalist Bharatiya Janata Party (BJP), fumbled. Prime Minister Atal Behari Vajpayee was travelling and his plane was in the air when his government was told about the hijacking. His National Security Adviser, former diplomat Brajesh Mishra, who had the reputation of being one of the most able men in the government, failed to muster a coherent response. According to a reconstruction published by former Punjab police chief KPS Gill, Air Traffic Control (ATC) in Delhi first received a warning about the hijack at 4.52 pm. Four minutes later, the captain told the ATC the hijackers were armed and the destination was Lahore. After a scramble to find the right telephone numbers, the information was passed on to the government's Crisis Management Group (CMG) of senior officials and ministers.[4] Yet according to Gill, it was not until after Vajpayee had landed that the prime minister called a crisis meeting of senior ministers. They met shortly before 6 pm, more than an hour after ATC had been alerted about the hijack.

Flight IC-814 landed in Amritsar at 7.01 pm. No preparations had been made for holding up the plane. The government in Delhi told the authorities at Amritsar that all efforts should be made to prevent it from taking off again. Yet during the forty-eight minutes that the plane was on the ground, no specific instructions were given about how this should be done. National Security Adviser Mishra, who died in 2012, later claimed the government had told local forces in Amritsar to hide a sniper in a fuel tanker who could shoot to disable the plane.[5] Not only did this not happen, but such was the confusion that no one thought to check the elite commandos of the NSG had been sent from Delhi.[6]

No one knew at the time what the hijackers wanted or what kind of people they were. Passengers interviewed by the Indian media after their ordeal described them as amenable to reason and even showing occasional flashes of humanity. "When the children and some others started crying they assured us that they would not harm us," said one passenger. "They had asked us not to speak to each other. I was speaking to my child who was crying. One of them walked up to me and asked why he was crying. When I said he was hungry, they got him some milk," said Geeta Baisla, the twenty-five-year-old wife of an employee at the Indian embassy in Kathmandu.[7] These were not like the hijackers on 9/11 for whom survival was neither possible nor intended. The men who had taken over Flight IC-814 appeared to inhabit a greyer area—a bridge between the twentieth-century hijackings inspired by political disputes and offering the possibility of negotiation, and the nihilistic violence of al-Qaeda.

During the hijacking women were treated with respect and nobody was robbed. "They knew they had a job to do," said Grover. Had India acted fast enough at Amritsar, it might have found the space to storm the plane with few, if any, casualties. Five years earlier, during another hijacking which also began on Christmas Eve, passengers and crew on board an Air France flight hijacked from Algiers survived when French troops stormed the aircraft while it was on the ground in Marseilles. But the slowness of the Indian government response left no time for the NSG commandos to reach Amritsar from their base outside Delhi. According to Gill, the commandos received information of the hijack at 6.10 pm; they were ready for take-off on an Indian Air Force plane at 7:05 pm but then delayed by a further half-hour by the failure of trained negotiators from intelligence agencies to reach the airport in time. Meanwhile, authorities at Amritsar had yet to realise they needed to find a means to prevent the plane from taking off. Wrongly, they assumed that merely because the pilot had said he was running out of fuel—his excuse for landing in Amritsar in the first place—he would not be able to take off again. It was a fatal error of judgment that stemmed in part from their reluctance to take action without clearer, specific instructions from Delhi. "Everyone was scared of taking a decision," said one former senior Indian intelligence official.[8]

* * *

On board Flight IC-814, the passengers had little idea where they were. Heads bowed and eyes blindfolded, they knew only that that the plane had landed but was taxiing on the runway and the hijackers were nervous. "We were moving constantly," said Grover. "I had the sense we were on home soil because the panic (among the hijackers) was intense." The five hijackers, in t-shirts, jeans and balaclavas, had by this time identified themselves as Chief, Burger, Doctor, Shakir and Bhola. Fearing a commando raid at Amritsar, they told Captain Sharan they would start killing the passengers if the plane was not refuelled and sent on its way. Captain Sharan made increasingly frantic calls to Amritsar Air Traffic Control (ATC) to send a refuelling bowser. ATC stalled, claiming that Indian Oil was closed at that time, a plausible enough excuse given the lateness of the hour. Captain Sharan kept trying to calm the hijackers.

At some point he switched off the engines. He told ATC to bring a refuelling bowser in front of the plane—not because he wanted fuel, but because he wanted them to block his exit. But his pleas went unanswered. Even when the fuel truck finally arrived, it was not parked in front of the aircraft. "It was very far and at the side of the runway, which was not benefitting me at all," he said. The flight engineer now brought him terrifying news. The hijackers had begun to kill the passengers who had been brought to sit in the business class cabin. Rupin Katyal, a young man returning from his honeymoon, was stabbed multiple times. His new wife sitting back in economy class did not know

7

what had happened. Another man sitting with him in business class was also stabbed, though less badly wounded. Captain Sharan relayed to ATC what he was told by his flight engineer—that his passengers were being killed one-by-one. According to the standard instructions given out by Indian Airlines, a pilot's first priority was to his passengers. "We have to follow the instructions of hijackers. We are told not to argue with them. The work will be done by the government." Captain Sharan thought frantically about what to do. Lahore was about thirty miles away and he had just enough fuel to get there. "I had to make a decision," he repeated. "To stop the killing, I had to take off from Amritsar." He took off and set course for Pakistan.

The elite commandos from the National Security Guard reached Amritsar at 8:15 pm—twenty-six minutes after Flight IC-814 had taken off, one hour and fourteen minutes after it landed at Amritsar, and a full three hours and twenty-three minutes after the first information of the hijack had been received by Air Traffic Control in Delhi.[9] Captain Sharan would not get another opportunity to land on Indian territory. In the long days that followed, the BJP-led government came under increasing criticism from angry relatives and the media for failing to stop the plane at Amritsar. The loss of confidence in the government dogged it throughout the hijacking, complicating all the more the decisions it was forced to make. India would pay a very high price for the fumbling at Amritsar. For the passengers on board Flight IC-814, the worst of their ordeal lay ahead.

* * *

Pakistani authorities still wanted nothing to do with the hijacked plane. Throughout the 1990s, Pakistan had come under increasing pressure from the United States to end support for Islamist militants after Washington belatedly realised the error of funding them to fight the Russians in Afghanistan. The ISI had responded to the American pressure by covering its tracks better and loosening its links with jihadis enough to ensure operational deniability. By 1999, Pakistan, with its nuclear weapons, support for Islamist militants and military coup, was in serious danger of becoming an international pariah. Whatever Pakistan's exact role in the hijacking of the Indian Airlines plane, it could not be seen to have any link with it.

As Flight IC-814 headed towards Lahore, Pakistan switched off the navigational lights at Allama Iqbal International Airport to prevent it from landing. Indian diplomats say they are convinced Musharraf was by then fully in control of Pakistan's response. Air Traffic Control is normally run by civilians even when Pakistan is under army rule, but in the case of a hijacking it is taken over by military authorities under the supervision of the local corps commander. He in turn reports to the army chief. By the time the hijacked aircraft approached the airport it was dark and the plane was running worryingly short of fuel. Captain Sharan circled above the city unable to land and without enough fuel to fly elsewhere. In desperation, he thought about looking for an open space for a crash landing. He made a feint at a busy road, terrifying his co-pilot who thought he had mistaken the string of lights from cars for a runway. Captain Sharan said he was trying to scare ATC in Lahore into letting him land. Either way, it worked. Pakistan opened up the airport and allowed the aircraft to land.

By this time, Rupin Katyal was bleeding to death. Captain Sharan tried to convince the hijackers to let him and the other wounded passenger leave the plane, along with the women and children. At the same time, the Indian government called on Pakistan not to let the plane take off again. India's High Commissioner to Islamabad, G. Parthasarathy, asked for permission to fly to Lahore—Indian diplomats, then, as now, faced severe restrictions on their movements inside Pakistan. "I kept desperately asking for me to go to Lahore and I said 'hold the plane at Lahore, don't let it proceed'. They stalled," he said.[10] The Pakistanis took hours to provide a helicopter for him. Inside Flight IC-814, according to Captain Sharan, the hijackers agreed to offload some passengers, including women and children. But the Lahore ATC refused. "They did not want to be involved in this hijacking, so that the world should not say, 'OK, Pakistan has helped them'," Captain Sharan said. All they were willing to do was to refuel the plane and send it on its way. By the time High Commissioner Parthasarathy was sitting in a helicopter about to fly to Lahore it was too late. The plane had been refuelled and was once again in the air.

* * *

Initially, said Captain Sharan, the hijackers wanted to fly on to Kabul. He had to convince them that landing such a big plane in Kabul in the dark—in a hilly area, with a runway in bad shape, and with no night-landing facilities—would be impossible. But that meant Flight IC-814 had nowhere to go. "Nobody wanted to get involved," said a retired Indian ambassador. At that time, most countries in the region tried to stay out of the India-Pakistan conflict. If the nearby Gulf States were to let the plane land, they would be faced with the choice of taking sides and possibly sending troops to storm the plane. One by one, they shut down their airspace to the hijacked plane.

Eventually the United Arab Emirates (UAE), possibly under American pressure, agreed to let the aircraft land, though it was directed to Al Minhad Air Base, a desert airstrip run by its military. "The Americans were very helpful ...the US role was extremely important," the retired Indian ambassador said.[11] But in an era before the September 11 attacks, the United States was not willing to become too heavily involved. Nor was the UAE. In 1999, it was one of only three countries that had recognised the Taliban in Afghanistan—the others were Pakistan and Saudi Arabia. In Indian eyes, it enjoyed a deliberately ambiguous and symbiotic relationship with Islamist militants, allowing them to use Dubai as a base for the transfer of money provided they did not attack it. When it came to Flight IC-814, the UAE would be as helpful as possible. But it would not storm the plane. That would be to cross an invisible line.

At Al Minhad Air Base, the Emiratis worked to convince the hijackers to release some of the passengers in exchange for fuel while also trying to buy time by delaying the arrival of the refuelling bowser. As had happened at Amritsar, Captain Sharan and his crew again hoped for rescue, believing that commandos might storm the plane and end their ordeal. The Indian government appealed to the UAE not to allow the plane to leave. The fuel-for-passengers exchange offer worked—the hijackers allowed twenty-seven passengers, mostly women and children, off the plane. Conditions were chaotic. Those on board were separated at random so that in one family, a mother left with one child, leaving her other child behind with her husband. The hijackers also offloaded the body of Rupin Katyal. Sitting in economy class, his wife still did not know he was dead. Seeking to delay the plane further, the Emiratis sent catering trucks with food for the passengers and crew. But the hijackers were becoming increasingly nervous and ordered

Captain Sharan to take off again. He did so, only barely clearing the catering trucks that the Emiratis had left out on the runway. He was unwilling to take the risk of deliberately crashing the plane on take-off. If he had done so, the wing would likely break and since the fuel was stored in the wing, it would catch fire. "For these things, you should have authority," he said.

Once again, Flight IC-814 was in the air. The hijackers again demanded to be flown to Kabul but the Afghan authorities said that instead the plane should land at Kandahar, in southern Afghanistan. There could hardly have been a worse destination for a hijacked Indian plane. Like most countries, India had no diplomatic relations with the Pakistan-backed Taliban. Moreover, it was actively supporting the sole remaining domestic opponent of the Taliban. Along with Russia and Iran, India backed the Northern Alliance, whose most prominent leader Ahmad Shah Massoud continued to hold out against the Taliban from his base in the Panjshir Valley to the north. Now, on Christmas Day, 1999, the Indian Airlines flight was heading right into enemy territory. "There is no way you are going to get out of Kandahar," said the retired Indian ambassador. "You are right in the spider's web."

* * *

Captain Sharan brought his plane down in Kandahar's small and derelict airport. It was barely suited for landing such a big passenger aircraft; the tarmac was pot-holed and cracked. He still had 162 people on board including the crew; it was some seventeen hours since the plane had been hijacked and he was exhausted from the physical and mental stress. The Taliban approached in an open-topped jeep, some carrying rocket launchers. "They just waved towards the chief hijacker and the chief waved ... like they were recognising each other," Captain Sharan said. His spirits sank watching the Taliban on apparently friendly terms with the hijackers. Ordered by the hijackers to leave the cockpit while they talked to the Taliban on the ground, Captain Sharan was able to see for the first time the conditions inside the passenger cabins. Food trays lay all around, forks and spoons on the floor. The business class cabin was empty save for hand luggage that had been thrown there early in the hijacking. In the darkened economy class cabin, passengers sat with their heads bowed, still using seat covers as blindfolds. Some had dozed off from hunger and exhaustion. After about twenty minutes, the captain and flight crew were called back into the cockpit and told to taxi in the aircraft. Captain Sharan could see some damaged fighter aircraft on his right; all around were turbaned Taliban carrying rifles and grenade launchers. He parked in front of the shabby terminal building. Then for the first time, the hijackers relaxed.

At first the passengers were unaware of where they were. They knew the plane had landed several times; someone had whispered during one such landing that some women and children were being allowed off. Now the hijackers let them sit up. They were served tea with a small packet of biscuits. Grover examined the biscuits with the dazed intensity of a man who had not eaten for hours—this was the first food they had been given. The packets were labelled in several languages, including Urdu, and the passenger sitting next to him suggested they might have landed in Bangladesh. But Grover was sure they had not flown east. As soon as the hijackers let smokers go to the rear of the aircraft, he looked out the open door and saw a man in Afghan dress. "He had a rocket launcher slung on one side and an AK-47 on the other side and another in his hands." It was then Grover realised they were in Afghanistan. The enormity of their predicament was summed up by Captain Sharan. "We were in a hostile country," he said. "Inside are hijackers; outside are terrorists."

* * *

In Delhi, the government was under fire for failing to stop the plane at Amritsar. Wild rumours circulated about the number of passengers who had already been killed and about how the hijackers had managed to board the aircraft with weapons. The Indian government, stumbling to explain its inaction in Amritsar, alternated between saying the hijackers were highly dangerous and claiming they were poorly armed. According to one government source quoted by the Indian media "the hijackers appeared to be hardened and cunning professionals who managed to cow the 178 passengers and 11 crew by merely brandishing knives and antique pistols."[12]

Initially, the Indian government was unsure whether it would get any cooperation from the Taliban. It had little doubt that the hijacking had been masterminded by the ISI, and that the plane had been deliberately manoeuvred to land at Kandahar, not far from the Pakistan border.[13] But the Taliban were internationally isolated and under severe censure for sheltering Osama bin Laden. Would it be possible to muster enough international pressure to convince the Taliban to help bring the hijacking to an end? India subsequently decided the Taliban were helping the hijackers, but its immediate problems were practical. "We had no diplomatic representation in Taliban-held Afghanistan, obviously, therefore, we had no representative in Kandahar either," Foreign Minister Jaswant Singh recalled.[14] "I had no telephone contact in Kandahar, no officers there, no other way of knowing what was happening." The earliest contacts, with Afghans in Air Traffic Control in Kandahar, proved particularly frustrating because they either could not, or refused to, speak English. As Singh called his counterparts around the world, the Indian government scrambled to send in diplomats and negotiators, as did the United Nations. India managed to get a diplomat from its Islamabad embassy to Kandahar—though since the political counsellor was female, it had to send her husband, the commercial counsellor, instead. Three senior officials were also to fly from Delhi, though this took longer to organise since Pakistan delayed in allowing overflight rights for their plane. Then the Indian government received word of the hijackers' demands. They came via ATC in Kandahar and were sent by fax. The hijackers listed the prisoners they wanted released from Indian jails. Top of the list was Masood Azhar, a Pakistani militant who had been arrested in Kashmir in 1994.[15]

* * *

Born in Bahawalpur in south Punjab in 1968, Azhar had risen through the jihadi ranks thanks to his intelligence and oratorical skills. The son of a headmaster in a government school, he had been sent to study at the Binori mosque and seminary in Karachi, a centre of support for the anti-Soviet jihad in Afghanistan. It was at Binori that he joined the Harkat-ul-Mujahideen (HuM), a militant group with close ties to al-Qaeda and the ISI. Though too late to fight the Russians by the time he graduated in 1989, he was nonetheless sent to a camp in Afghanistan. He was ill-suited to physical activity and failed to complete the mandatory forty days training. But thanks to his literary skills he was asked instead to bring out a monthly magazine for HuM promoting its activities in Afghanistan.[16] He was soon travelling far and wide to promote the jihad globally. In the early 1990s, he went to Britain to seek support from the Pakistani diaspora—preaching to packed audiences in mosques and raising both funds and recruits.[17][18] He was reputedly so inspiring that British jihadi Dhiren Barot compared him to Abdullah Azzam, the Palestinian scholar and ideological father of al-Qaeda.[19] Like most militants motivated by international jihad, Azhar's interests did not directly correspond to those of the Pakistani state. But he was careful with the ISI. The intelligence agency provided funding for the Harkat ul-Mujahideen and could make life difficult if he strayed too far off course. In turn the ISI found him useful as a go-between because of the respect he commanded amongst militant groups. In 1994, he flew to Delhi from the Bangladesh capital Dhaka using a stolen Portuguese passport that he had acquired in Britain.[20] He had instructions to make his way to Kashmir to restore order among the different militant groups fighting Indian rule so that they could be more easily controlled by Pakistan. Within a month he was arrested, and might have continued to languish in an Indian jail were it not for the hijacking of Flight IC-814. The lead hijacker, the man they called "Chief", was his brother.

Along with Azhar, the hijackers demanded the release of a British-Pakistani who had spent five years in jail in India for organising a kidnapping in an earlier failed attempt to free him. Omar Sheikh would later become better known as the man who masterminded the kidnapping of American *Wall Street Journal* correspondent Daniel Pearl in 2002, luring him to his death. At the time of the hijacking, he was just another young man drawn into militancy in the febrile 1990s when the influences of the anti-Soviet jihad in Afghanistan were spilling out around the world. Born in 1973, Omar Sheikh was the son of first-generation Pakistani immigrants, and grew up in Wanstead, an unprepossessing suburb of east London. Even as a boy, he spoke fervently and often of "my country" and praised Pakistan's then military ruler, General Mohammad Zia ul-Haq. He loved chess and spent his lunch breaks pouring over a chess board with a group of friends who were mainly from Sri Lankan, Indian or Bengali families, according to a former school-friend who had first known him at the age of eleven. His other great love was arm-wrestling and he would often be found in smoky pubs—drinking only milk—competing with his team.[21] Wary of England's influence, Omar's father sent him to study at Lahore's elite Aitchison College. He returned a junior boxing champion and full of stories of contacts with organised crime, gun battles in the ghettos of Lahore and visits to brothels. At the age of sixteen, he was fascinated with girls and shocked at the liberal relations between young girls and boys in England, his former school-friend said.[22]

Omar would follow in the footsteps of many young British Pakistanis drawn to the twin poles of international jihad and Kashmir. The two causes were never identical—the young Kashmiris who launched the separatist revolt in the late 1980s were interested in winning freedom from India, not global jihad. But for a while the two causes became intertwined, helped by persuasive orators like Azhar. British Pakistanis, many of whom traced their roots to the Pakistani side of the divided state, were particularly susceptible. Their sympathies for the Kashmir cause and family ties to Pakistan would also bring them into the orbit of al-Qaeda, in what became known as "the Kashmir escalator". After throwing himself into the cause of Muslims in Bosnia, Omar dropped out of his studies at the London School of Economics, and is believed to have then gone for training in the militant camps of Afghanistan and Pakistan's tribal areas.[23] At some point along the way he met Azhar. When his mentor was arrested in Kashmir, it fell to Omar to try to force India to release him. He did so by kidnapping westerners in Delhi.

Using the same charm and guile that would later fatally deceive Daniel Pearl, Omar kidnapped three British and one American tourist in Delhi in 1994, keeping them prisoner in a house outside the capital. The hostages were freed after an Indian police raid, and Omar was imprisoned in Delhi's Tihar jail. Indian investigators concluded that he had been trained by Pakistan and that he would not have been able to carry out the kidnapping—which required both money and weapons—without the help of ISI officers based in the Pakistan High Commission.[24] The appearance of his name on the list given by the hijackers was for India yet more evidence of the involvement of Pakistan in organising the hijacking.

* * *

On December 27, a top-level Indian negotiating team finally reached Kandahar from Delhi. They were led by Vivek Katju, then Joint

Secretary in the Ministry of External Affairs, accompanied by Ajit Doval, head of the domestic Intelligence Bureau (IB) and C.D. Sahay, his counterpart at India's external intelligence agency, the Research and Analysis Wing (R&AW). They brought with them a large team of doctors, engineers and emergency support staff along with intelligence officers who had served in Pakistan, and signals intelligence personnel to intercept conversations. But the limits on their options were made clear the minute they landed, when the Taliban took up offensive positions against their plane. "There were a lot of Taliban on the tarmac with their weapons," said Doval. [25]

The negotiating team made another discovery when they landed. Two ISI men were on the tarmac and others soon joined them. One was a lieutenant-colonel and the other a major, said Doval, who had spent many years serving in Pakistan. To make matters worse, the Indian officials realised the hijackers were communicating directly with ISI officers in Kandahar. "We were getting very good intelligence about all that was happening," Doval said. With backing outside the plane, the hijackers were far less susceptible to being worn down by negotiations. "If these people were not getting active ISI support in Kandahar, we could have got the hijacking vacated," Doval said. "The ISI had removed all the pressure we were trying to put on the hijackers." Even their safe exit was guaranteed, so they had no need to negotiate an escape route. "Normally that is not the way hijackers talk. Normally the biggest fear is how to get out," he said.

Pakistan has consistently denied involvement, while insisting the Taliban had no choice but to let the plane land at Kandahar since it could otherwise have run out of fuel and crashed. One retired Pakistani ambassador also noted that the ISI had a big station in the nearby town of Quetta, capital of Pakistan's Balochistan province, and could have sent officers from there to find out what was going on, with the Taliban then doing what they could to ensure the hijacking ended peacefully. [26] Another version provided by the researchers Alex Strick van Linschoten and Felix Kuehn, based on their own contacts with the Taliban, suggests they were indeed torn over what to do about the hijacking, but were under pressure from Pakistani militant groups and figures within the ISI to cooperate with the hijackers. [27] India dismisses descriptions of the Taliban as helpless onlookers, saying they had been pushing Delhi to give the hijackers whatever they wanted. The Taliban had good reason to be hostile to India, given its backing for Afghan opposition fighters in the Northern Alliance. "I am not suggesting they were slaves of the ISI but there was a convergence of interests," said a former senior Indian official who had been involved in the handling of the crisis.[28] The Taliban expressed public discomfiture about the presence of IC-814 on Afghan soil but did nothing to help the Indians. The United Nations sent a negotiating team, but there was little it could do. Nor was the United States in much of a position to help. Having first hoped the Taliban might bring stability to Afghanistan when they seized power in 1996, Washington had become increasingly frustrated with their failure to expel bin Laden. After American embassies in Tanzania and Kenya were bombed by al-Qaeda in 1998, President Bill Clinton had ordered cruise missile strikes on a camp in Afghanistan the CIA believed bin Laden was visiting. They missed bin Laden, but did manage to kill ISI officers and Kashmir fighters at the camp—proof, if needed, of how closely al-Qaeda, the ISI and the Kashmir-focused Pakistani jihadi groups were interlinked at that time.[29]

Pakistan did not even try to explain why it was not offering to help end the hijack. Instead Foreign Minister Abdul Sattar suggested that India's intelligence service had staged the hijacking itself to discredit the military-backed government installed after Musharraf's October coup. Pakistan supported its allegation by leaking to the press something it had discovered, or known all along. Among the passengers on the hijacked plane was an officer from R&AW stationed in Kathmandu.[30] It failed to explain why R&AW would choose to fly a plane full of Indian passengers including one of its own men into the heart of Taliban-controlled territory.

With no help forthcoming from the Taliban, Pakistan or the outside world, India was well and truly trapped. It either had to release the prisoners demanded by the hijackers or risk the lives of its passengers and let its own officer fall into the hands of the Taliban, Islamist militants or the ISI. It had already sacrificed lives rejecting an earlier attempt to force it to free Azhar and his young British acolyte.

* * *

Back in July 1995, four westerners, two Americans and two Britons, had been kidnapped while trekking in Kashmir. One American managed to escape, prompting the kidnappers to seize two more adventure tourists, a Norwegian and a German. The kidnappers demanded the release of Azhar, Omar Sheikh and other prisoners held in Indian jails. The government in New Delhi refused, and the westerners remained captive, much to the anguish of their families waiting for news. The Norwegian, Hans Christian Ostroe, was found beheaded in August 1995. The others were never found and are presumed dead. Responsibility for the kidnapping was claimed by the hitherto unheard-of "al-Faran", which India said was a front for Azhar's Pakistan-based militant group. The details of the kidnapping remain murky and contested. One account suggests the western hostages were sold onto a militia who worked for Indian security forces after the kidnappers failed to win their demands.[31] Indian authorities, according to this version, had then decided against rescuing the hostages to discredit Pakistan. The assertion has been dismissed by Indian officials. One thing was clear however. After two attempts to free Azhar—the kidnapping of westerners in Delhi and in Kashmir—failed, Pakistan was determined to achieve its goal. In June 1999, another attempt was made to free him by digging a tunnel into the high-security jail where he was held. When Azhar tried to escape, he was reportedly too tubby to squeeze through the narrow tunnel. Months later, in a letter purportedly written from jail, Azhar praised Musharraf's coup. Paying "glowing tribute" to the Pakistan Army as the guardian of Islam and Pakistan, he said the coup had rescued the country from disaster and turmoil.[32]

"He (Azhar) was extremely important for them," said Doval. By forcing Delhi to free him, Pakistan would regain a valuable asset while also embarrassing India. "Azhar was close to (Taliban leader) Mullah Omar and Osama bin Laden. He was hard, hard core," said one former Indian ambassador. "There must have been a strong section of the ISI who wanted him back."[33] By 1999, Pakistan was finding it harder and harder to keep on top of the different militant groups its security establishment had spawned. It had to manage the competing impulses of militants who wanted to fight in Kashmir, those drawn to global jihad and those ready to turn their guns on the Pakistani state itself. It had loosened links down through the chain of command to ensure operational deniability only to discover this also eroded its control. Azhar had been the ideal go-between, linking the ISI with militant movements across the spectrum. "The man in between is very important, extremely important," said Doval. Azhar was a link with the Taliban and al-Qaeda, nearer ideologically to the latter, and close to the ISI. Omar Sheikh was useful to the militants, who were always looking to recruit educated foreigners both for their ability to operate without suspicion and to show the strength of the movement. But of the two, Azhar was by far the most important. "Azhar was extremely close to the ISI. Omar Sheikh was supported by them but not that close," Doval said. In his view, they were not ISI agents as such, but had become "ISI-sponsored terrorists. Therefore any task has their approval." Doval had spent years of his career shadow-boxing with the ISI, having served at the Indian High Commission in Pakistan and run counter-insurgency in Kashmir. Now he faced them directly at Kandahar airport.

* * *

On board Flight IC-814, the passengers and crew had greeted their arrival at Kandahar with mixed feelings. The Taliban sent food—chicken and bread with potato chips and an orange. The cold air of the Kandahar winter swept into the plane as the supplies were delivered. With the hijackers now visibly more relaxed, the passengers no longer had to sit hunched over and blindfolded. Some tried to engage the hijackers in conversation in the hope they would not be harmed. With their hectic flight around the region now ended, some even dared to look forward to the arrival of an Indian negotiating team in the expectation their release would be quickly secured. But as the days dragged by, their optimism dissipated. A rancid smell spread throughout the aircraft as the toilets clogged up and began to overflow. "At one point the carpet under my seat was wet with overflowing toilets," said Grover. The crew had to lay the curtains used to separate cabins along the corridor because the carpet was so wet. People stopped eating so they could avoid having to use the toilets. One day the Taliban sent in cleaners with buckets but the cleaning was very superficial. The hijackers became very nervous when the cleaners came in, suggesting they did not have full confidence in the people outside the plane. No one else came into the aircraft; the caterers stopped at the plane door.

Days blended into one another, the sheer boredom rivalling the passengers' and crew's anxieties about their fate. "People used to just sit in the seat and speak to each other. Some people used to sleep. Some people used to walk," said Captain Sharan. It was bad, he said, lowering his voice so that the memory came across all the more powerfully as he described it nearly fifteen years later. "It was very bad; very bad." Although the temperature outside dropped to minus 12, the doors of the plane were often kept open to ease the stench from the overflowing toilets. With so many passengers inside the plane, it never became impossibly cold, but it was terribly uncomfortable. The passengers were not dressed for it; they had no blankets and no woollens. Grover, wearing a half-sleeved T-shirt, slept with his feet tucked under him and his jacket over him in a desperate effort to keep warm. Some of the passengers confronted the ordeal with remarkable courage, he said, among them the women and children. One Japanese woman from Osaka stood out for her casual grit. She had been so determined to make a trip to India that after failing to find a direct flight, she had booked a ticket from Osaka to Tokyo to Bangkok to Kathmandu to Delhi just for the sake of an eight-to-ten day trip. "She was a very spirited woman," said Grover. At the back of the plane were two to three trolleys full of beer cans, left over from that moment at the start of the hijacking when the cabin crew were serving drinks. "She would go and take a beer, go into the toilet, and smoke a cigarette and come back," he said. But others were panicking. Among them was a man who had been rewarded by his company with a short break in Kathmandu for meeting his sales targets. "One day a chap got hysterical and started howling," said Grover. "Why did I hit the target?' he was screaming." The plane was also carrying people returning from a medical conference in Kathmandu and one female doctor had been particularly brave in trying to help Rupin Katyal after he was stabbed. By the time the plane was sitting in Kandahar, however, she had begun to lose her nerve from the strain and had a near breakdown. Another passenger was a Hindu Pandit who had been asked by the others to predict the future and tell them when they would get out of the plane. "When his prediction turned out to be wrong, everyone then made his life hell—they were being vicious," said Grover.

The worsening conditions were matched by the growing confidence of the hijackers who had brought up a fresh supply of weapons and ammunition from the hold, loaded, according to some Indian versions, in Lahore; in other versions in Nepal. "One day at 3 am they made us open the cargo compartment…they got one case from there. We think more weapons came from that suitcase," Captain Sharan said. Every now and then the hijackers suggested to him he should be prepared to fly for another five hours. The implication was that if their demands were not met, they could force the plane to take off again and blow it up in mid-air, possibly over an Indian city. A former senior Indian official said he was not convinced the hijackers were serious about blowing up the plane; rather it was a ruse to put pressure on the Indian government.[34] But whether or not they were serious, the threat darkened the mood even further.

As the days went by, the stench became nearly unbearable. "All the physical discomforts of sitting in one place, hunger, thirst, being dirty, had turned into a numb weariness," Captain Sharan recalled.[35] Some passengers struggled with claustrophobia. Others complained of real or feigned illnesses to try to get off the plane. One man sitting next to Grover said he had a severe stomach ailment and was allowed off briefly to go to a hospital nearby. "When he came back you could see cold fear on his face," Grover said. "He was really, really rattled." Then there was the psychological torture from the highs and lows of the negotiations. At one point it looked like thirty-five passengers, mainly women and children, were to be allowed off. But then they were told they would have to stay on the plane after all. At another point the hijackers said that negotiations had come to a standstill and they would now decide whether to blow the plane up or shoot the passengers one-by-one. "It's time you started saying your last prayers," Grover remembered them saying. "You could hear a pin drop ten miles away."

Outside the plane, the negotiating team tried to wear down the hijackers. Normally, said Doval who had been involved in ending previous hijackings, when you talk about negotiations with hijackers, you are really talking about tactics. You needed to make sure they did not harm the passengers. You needed to tire the hijackers out while gaining time and information. But aside from the ISI involvement, the Indian team faced another problem—time was not on their side. The new millennium was approaching and the Indian government wanted the hijacking over by then. Usually it would be the hijackers who feared running out of time while trained negotiators remained calm, following an unofficial rule book put together from years of internationally pooled experience. "In a normal hijacking, the stop-clock is for them," said Doval. Time to wear the hijackers out; time to prepare and execute a plan. Infinite patience. It should, he implied, be the hijackers losing their nerve. Instead, it was Delhi. "We could have tried a little more," he said.

* * *

When the fax with the hijackers' demands first arrived in Delhi, they had been unanimously rejected by the cabinet, according to Foreign Minister Jaswant Singh.[36] At first the hijackers had asked for the release of thirty-six prisoners, including Azhar and Omar Sheikh, along with $200 million in ransom. Every demand was dismissed outright. But the government's will began to crack under public pressure. India was getting no help from outside. The Taliban insisted they wanted no bloodshed, ruling out any possibility of commandos from India or other nations storming the plane. The United States too said the hijacking should be brought to an end with no loss of life. Relatives of the passengers were holding street protests or angrily interrupting government briefings, their demands for a quick resolution of the crisis amplified by the noisy television media. The public mood was approaching a kind of collective hysteria.

The government was worried too that the plane might take off again and be blown up mid-air. "Deliberations on our options were agonising, prolonged and extremely testing," Singh recalled.[37] Prime Minister Vajpayee decided that India would concede to some of the hijackers' demands. A leader who operated by consensus, Vajpayee won the backing of his cabinet for his decision, though later some ministers would distance themselves, claiming they personally would have refused all concessions. On December 31, National Security Adviser Brajesh Mishra announced that India would hand over three prisoners—Azhar, Omar Sheikh and Kashmiri militant Mushtaq Ahmed Zargar—in exchange for the release of the passengers and crew.[38] Zargar was a former fighter with the pro-independence Jammu and Kashmir Liberation Front (JKLF) who, according to India, had been used by the ISI early in the Kashmir insurgency to form a splinter group that would be more in favour of Kashmir joining Pakistan. Before he was captured, he had a reputation for executing suspected collaborators by exploding grenades tied to their bodies.[39] Singh decided to fly to Kandahar with the three prisoners, his presence acting as a guarantee that nothing would go wrong. It was a remarkable climb-down for the BJP-led government. Afterwards it said public opinion had left it no choice. "What if we had said, 'fine, we wash our hands of it'?" asked National Security Adviser Mishra. "The public would not have allowed us to do that. We had been asked to negotiate and once you negotiate, this is what you get."[40]

"It was not easy to decide to go to Kandahar," recalled Singh, who was later ridiculed by his political opponents for doing so. His aim, he said, was to provide the Indian negotiating team with someone who could make decisions on the spot should the exchange of prisoners for passengers and crew run into any unexpected obstacles.[41] The disbelieving prisoners were hastily gathered from their different jails and put on Singh's plane. After three failed bids to spring him from captivity, Azhar was finally going to be free.

Singh was received at Kandahar by Taliban Foreign Minister Wakil Ahmed Muttawakil, and drove with him in a brand new Toyota out of the airport and along a dirt track to a concrete building. There the two men held a stilted conversation over a spread of canned juices and cola and biscuits. They returned to the airport to make a brief statement to the waiting press, mainly Pakistani and some foreign journalists. The agreement with the Taliban was that first the prisoners were to be identified; following that the passengers would be allowed off the plane and only then would the freed men be handed over to the hijackers. The agreement, however, according to Singh, was violated at the very last minute: India was forced to release the prisoners before the passengers and crew were freed.[42] The hijackers and released prisoners hugged on the tarmac and then were whisked off in cars supplied by the Taliban, driving towards the Pakistani border. The released prisoners would later be shown on Pakistani television celebrating their release at the Binori mosque complex in Karachi.

Inside the plane, the passengers and crew were suddenly left alone. The hijackers had been unusually polite at the end, telling everyone to leave the aircraft as early as possible—perhaps fearing a bomb hidden on the plane might explode at the last minute. "We don't want that anybody should die," Captain Sharan remembered one of them saying. The evening before, the passengers had been served a feast, with burgers in food boxes brought from a city in Pakistan, said Grover. But when one passenger said something a hijacker did not like, he hit him, so the atmosphere was still tense. There had been so many false hopes that even when the final announcement came, nobody quite trusted it. They had heard Singh's aircraft land in Kandahar. They waited. And then it was over. "These guys were simply gone," said Grover. People got very excited, among them the first-time flyers, pulling duty-free Black Label whisky from the overhead lockers to celebrate. Someone suggested that drinking alcohol in a strict Muslim country might not be such a good idea. It was chaotic. "We Indians are not easy to organise," said Grover.

Captain Sharan handed over the plane to another pilot who was to fly it back to Delhi and the passengers and crew were then divided into a relief aircraft and the one which had brought Singh for their flight home. They clapped as they took off from Kandahar. Some thanked the foreign minister; others berated him. A young Frenchman cried endlessly, said Singh, recalling his interaction with the passengers on the flight home. A mother who had been supposed to meet her children at the railway station after they travelled by train to Delhi demanded to know if anyone in the government knew what had happened to them. Nobody did. "Then that overwrought young mother, still trembling with anger and suppressed fear—she came up to me in the aircraft and with her tiny hands, grimy because they had been so confined for eight days, had clutched at my throat and yelled as loudly she could, 'Why have you come so late? Where were you all this time? You have betrayed all of us. Where are my children? Where is my family?"[43] Singh tried to keep the passengers happy by offering around cigarettes and the use of his cellphone, Grover said. He made sure no newspapers were distributed on the plane, since Rupin Katyal's wife had still not been told of her husband's death. The plane landed at 9.30 pm on December 31, just in time for the new millennium and to wild greetings of relief by the relatives of the passengers. Rachna Katyal would not learn her husband was dead until she returned home. "We broke the news after she reached home last night," her uncle said. "I think she already had her suspicions. She kept saying, 'Where is he? Why isn't he here to see me?' "[44]

* * *

The minute the passengers landed in Delhi, they were forgotten. Some wandered around the airport for hours, unsure what to do. When their luggage finally arrived from Kandahar, it would not be delivered to their homes. Instead they received a curt phone call telling them to come to the airport to collect it. There would be no counselling to help them process their ordeal, though some would meet in small groups for years afterwards to try to make sense of what had happened. Indian intelligence agencies held their own private investigations, of which the only outcome was intense pressure on Nepal to improve border and airport security. Several years later, Kathmandu airport remained chaotic and it was still possible to find crossings on the India-Nepal land border where, with the right connections, you could slip in amongst the crowds and the donkey carts to travel between the two countries without proper paperwork or visas. Indian domestic security arrangements barely changed, and the commandos from the NSG continued to be limited to a single base outside Delhi—leaving India as exposed as ever when ten gunmen landed by sea from Pakistan to attack Mumbai in 2008.

The three released prisoners lived openly in Pakistan. When the United States put pressure on Pakistan to arrest both them and the hijackers, its ambassador to Washington, Maleeha Lodhi, promised her country would take action.[45] Nothing was done. Azhar went on to found a new Pakistan-based militant group, the Jaish-e-Mohammad. He also returned to Afghanistan to visit Mullah Omar in February or March 2000.[46] The group was blamed by Delhi for an attack on the Indian Parliament in December 2001 which brought India and Pakistan to the brink of war. In January 2002, Omar Sheikh lured Daniel Pearl to his death.

The Taliban saw their image further tarnished internationally. While their exact role in the hijacking remains disputed, the fall-out made it all the harder for the more pragmatic members of the movement to establish relationships with the outside world. Instead the Taliban became even more isolated. This would prove particularly damaging both before and after the September 11 attacks when they failed to grasp the implications of refusing to hand over bin Laden. India became more hostile to the Taliban than ever. Angered already by the Taliban's behaviour during the hijacking, Delhi had been incensed by their insistence on checking the hold of the hijacked plane, then still full of the passengers' baggage, before it was returned to India. They checked every red suitcase until they found one belonging to the hijackers that Indian officials believed may have contained explosives intended to blow up the plane, along with their original passports. The Taliban refused to return the suitcase, or to meet again with India's remaining diplomat in Kandahar, who eventually left for Islamabad on a UN flight.[47] It was, as far as India was concerned, an act of complicity too far. Delhi also came away further convinced that the international community was failing to pay enough attention to the threat of terrorism emanating from Pakistan. "The US and the UK in particular played a terrible role. Their strategic thinkers were simply blinded," said the former senior Indian official. "We kept telling them what's emerging in the belly of Pakistan is serious. They wouldn't listen."[48]

In the short-run, Pakistan appeared to have scored a major victory over India by springing the prisoners from jail. Yet the hijacking—a twin success for the ISI and Islamist militants—also meant that Pakistan's agenda, and its fate, were becoming increasingly entangled with international jihad. The hijacking coincided with unrelated millennium plots planned or carried out by al-Qaeda elsewhere in the world. But this was not an al-Qaeda operation. It was, somewhat terrifyingly, one that linked the ISI's interests with al-Qaeda. In bringing back their go-between from India, Pakistan's premier intelligence agency showed how far the different battlefields of Kashmir and Afghanistan had become intertwined. It also hinted at something else that went less noticed. In its desperation to repatriate Azhar, the ISI revealed an anxiety that it dared not admit in public—by needing him so badly, it showed it was no longer fully in control. Nobody was. Nobody controlled the jihad. Pakistan would, as it had done for years, continue to allow different strains of militancy—of ISI-cultivated Islamist militants and global jihadism—to run in parallel. But as it would discover to its cost, neither strain was manageable. The nuclear tests in 1998 had given the Pakistani security establishment a false confidence that it could run an undeclared war against India without fear of retaliation.

"We'll absorb this," the former senior Indian official recalled saying when the prisoners were handed over during the hijacking.[49] Pakistan had no such ability to absorb the militants it had created.

SETTLING A SCORE

FROM 1947 TO THE NUCLEAR TESTS

This is the story of how Pakistan lost the "Great South Asian War". The causes were deeply rooted in its history. But the policy choices it made after India and Pakistan declared themselves nuclear-armed states in 1998 showed it was not merely a victim of circumstances. The hijacking of Flight IC-814 was only one chapter, but it drew together many threads of that story. The nuclear weapons that were celebrated throughout Pakistan as putting it on par with India instead accelerated its downfall—by giving it a false sense of inviolability under which it unleashed militant forces that it could no longer fully control. Insecurity fed on itself, keeping the country in a state of siege and the military-dominated elite in power even as Delhi exploited its own nuclear-armed status to gain greater international standing. As a praetorian state, Pakistan had always prioritised military over diplomatic and political solutions. The nuclear weapons that made it stronger militarily only accentuated that imbalance. India's success, in contrast, was based on an approach that was largely diplomatic, political and economic. The possession of nuclear weapons was, at most, a complement to its strategy. As Prime Minister Vajpayee had foreseen when he announced the nuclear tests to the world, India won recognition from the United States as an ally and rising power. It was not so much that

India won the Great South Asian War but that Pakistan lost it. A process that had begun in 1947 accelerated after 1998.

Eighteen months before the hijacking, on May 11, 1998, Vajpayee had arrived without fanfare at a news conference hastily convened in the garden of his official residence in Delhi. Behind the dais where he stood, an aide had wheeled out the Indian flag. Vajpayee, in white *dhoti-kurta* and blue waistcoat, pulled out his glasses from a top pocket as he began to speak. "I have to make a brief announcement," he said. "Today, at 1545 hours, India conducted three underground nuclear tests in the Pokhran range." He spoke in English, eschewing the Hindi oratory for which he was famous. He was matter-of-fact, almost casual, as though to suggest that here was India merely claiming its natural place at the top table of big powers. He gave brief technical details on the tests and reassured the public there had been no leakage of radiation.[1] The journalists sat stunned as Vajpayee completed his statement and walked off, with no time for questions. Then they ran, past the security guards and the peacocks, to the gate where they had left their cellphones in order to report the news: India had become a declared nuclear weapons state. It followed up with two more tests on May 13.

Just over two weeks later Pakistan Prime Minister Nawaz Sharif addressed the nation on television. His appearance, in formal black *sherwani*, was sombre; his tone mournful. Unlike Vajpayee, who had directed his announcement both to his country and the outside world, Sharif spoke in Urdu. He had been under intense pressure from the United States not to match India's nuclear tests with Pakistan's own and he sought to reassure his countrymen about the international sanctions that were sure to follow. His message was one that summoned up decades of grievance against India and presented Pakistan as a victim of Indian provocation. "Today, we have settled a score and have carried out five successful nuclear tests," he said.[2] He would go on to say that India's "reckless actions" had left Pakistan no choice.[3]

The nuclear tests were a pivotal moment in South Asian history. For half a century, Pakistan had defined itself in opposition to India, nursing its wrath over a dispute about the former princely state of Jammu and Kashmir. The two countries followed different trajectories: India a lumbering secular democracy, Pakistan a militarised state. They fought three full-scale wars, two over Kashmir. When East Pakistan broke away from

West Pakistan with Indian help to form the independent state of Bangladesh in 1971, Pakistan lost its raison d'être as a homeland for Muslims. Opposition to India expanded into an increasingly aggressive use of Islamist militants to counter Indian influence from Afghanistan to Kashmir. To justify its actions, Pakistan pleaded insecurity about India, hard-wired into the Pakistani system from the early years.

The nuclear tests offered the possibility of a reset to zero. The two countries had been quietly developing nuclear technology for years, acquiring a covert nuclear weapons capability that according to India had already emboldened Pakistan's support for Islamist militants. In 1974 India had carried out a crude test of a device which it disingenuously called a "peaceful nuclear explosive". But with the 1998 tests, India and Pakistan proved they had mastered the technology and publicly declared themselves nuclear-armed powers. The nuclearisation of South Asia provided the strategic parity that Pakistan believed it had always lacked against its bigger neighbour. India could no longer risk an invasion without fearing an escalation into nuclear war. As veteran Pakistani politician Sartaj Aziz, then finance minister, remarked, the Pakistani tests "effectively countered Indian doubts about Pakistan's nuclear capability and by restoring the strategic balance between the two countries improved the prospects for peace and meaningful negotiations..."[4]

It did not work out that way. Far from taking advantage of the new strategic parity to put its own house in order, Pakistan remained as insecure as ever. It relied on the protection of the nuclear umbrella to pursue its proxy war against India. No longer forced to adapt to the threat of external invasion that might compel it to disarm its Islamist militant proxies, it clung to them ever more tightly. It continued to do so even in the face of intense pressure from the United States following the September 11 attacks and subsequent war in Afghanistan. In other words, it became sealed within its own dysfunction. In the years that followed the nuclear tests, Pakistan lost ground to India economically, politically and strategically. Its reputation became that of a near-failing state while India emerged as a rising world power. Whatever appeal it once held for the people of Kashmir was dissipated by Pakistan's own domestic problems, weakening its claim to the disputed region. Its influence in Afghanistan, high at the time of the nuclear tests when the Taliban were in power, dwindled to the point that it could only be maintained by subterfuge and the use of force. It sacrificed the lives of thousands of its own citizens by not-so-secretly backing the Taliban after their 2001 overthrow to curb Indian influence in Afghanistan. After Pakistan's dismemberment in 1971 it had recovered and even thrived compared to India. But after 1998, it lost so decisively that its downward trend relative to its eastern neighbour, a country Pakistan had once aspired to match or outshine, appears irreversible.

* * *

After the subcontinent was partitioned into Muslim Pakistan and Hindu-majority but secular India in 1947, leading to communal bloodshed in which at least one million died, both countries nursed a deep but very different sense of insecurity. Pakistan, famously dismissed by Salman Rushdie as "insufficiently imagined", had emerged as an idea only in the 1930s and 1940s. Arguably demanded initially by its founder, Mohammad Ali Jinnah, as a negotiating tool to secure the rights of Muslims within a federal and united India, it had no chance to grow organically. Established in two wings, East and West Pakistan, separated by more than a thousand miles of Indian territory, beyond a shared religion Pakistan had nothing to unite its diverse peoples, among them Pashtuns, Punjabis, Sindhis, Baloch and Bengalis. If much of the drive for Pakistan had come from the Urdu-speaking elite in the old Mughul heartland in Delhi and Agra, the state was set up on land already occupied by other ethnic groups, some of whom had actively opposed its creation. Jinnah died in 1948, leaving adrift the new country he had willed into existence. Opposition to India became the glue that was meant to bind Pakistan together.

Indian insecurity was more diffuse. Domestically it was too big to be managed efficiently. Externally, its sheer size meant that, rather like Russia, it was exposed across a much wider front. It shared with China the longest disputed border in the world, outright enmity with Pakistan, and varying degrees of awkwardness with its other neighbours. If in Pakistan Partition had anachronistically "proved" that Muslims could not be safe in India, in Indian eyes it had weakened the natural geographic defences of the subcontinent, while the communal bloodshed pointed to the folly of the decision. India refused to see itself in direct competition with Pakistan, preferring to pair itself with a neighbour of comparable size, namely China. But it also disguised in quietest rhetoric an aspiration for regional hegemony, an ambition repeatedly frustrated by Pakistan. This, along with the rancour of inti-macy, meant Indian policies were far more influenced by rivalry with Pakistan than it cared to admit. Pakistan's obsession with India, and India's less acknowledged competition with Pakistan, would help drive the development of nuclear weapons.

So too would the dispute over Jammu and Kashmir (J&K), though its influence was lopsided. If Pakistan insisted on the centrality of the dispute, India regarded it as an irritant. J&K was the largest of the semi-autonomous princely states in British India and geographically contiguous to both India and Pakistan. It was a sprawling, diverse king-dom that included the Kashmir Valley, its political heartland, the remote mountain regions of Ladakh, Gilgit and Baltistan, and Jammu, which ran from the foothills of the Himalaya down into the plains of Punjab. As Independence Day passed in August 1947, the Hindu ruler of the Muslim-majority state was unable to decide whether to accede to India or Pakistan or try to remain independent. Pakistan discreetly began helping his rebellious pro-Pakistan subjects in the west of the state, while also supporting an invasion of the Kashmir Valley by a tribal militia. When the maharajah panicked and appealed for Indian help, Delhi persuaded him to sign an Instrument of Accession to India as a condition for its support. On October 27, 1947, India airlifted Indian soldiers to the capital, Srinagar, to secure the kingdom. With Pakistan then sending its own soldiers to support the rebels, the two countries began their lives as independent states at war.

When the fighting stopped with a ceasefire in 1948, some two-thirds of the territory of J&K was in Indian hands, including the Kashmir Valley, Ladakh and much of Jammu. Pakistan held Gilgit and Baltistan, along with a strip of land it called Azad (Free) Jammu and Kashmir. At the height of the crisis, India had approached the United Nations for help, leading to a UN Security Council resolution recommending a plebiscite. This called on Pakistan to withdraw all its nationals from J&K first, followed by Indian moves to reduce its own troops to the minimum needed to maintain law and order. The people of J&K would then be asked whether they wanted the state to join India or Pakistan. The princely state was to be treated as a whole, rather than disaggregated into its constituent parts, and independence was not offered as an option.[5] The conditions for a plebiscite were never met. J&K would remain divided through all the wars between India and Pakistan, the source of a dispute that was both territorial and ideological. As a signifier of national identity, Pakistan saw possession of Kashmir as confirming its role as a natural homeland for Muslims, while India viewed it as evidence of its secularism. Neither country had any interest in letting J&K reunite as an independent state. This dissonance over Kashmir fed into broader assumptions about national security that informed the way both countries approached nuclear weapons. Pakistan claimed innocence, insisting its nuclear weapons programme had merely been a response to India's efforts to acquire nuclear bombs. India downplayed the influence of Pakistan on its own decisions. In reality, both played catch-up with the other at different points in time.

* * *

In a now legendary quote about the nuclear arms race in South Asia, Pakistan's then Foreign Minister Zulfikar Ali Bhutto remarked in mid-1965 that, "If India builds the bomb, we will eat grass or leaves, even go hungry, but we will get one of our own."[6] This quote would come to define Pakistan's view of its nuclear bombs, bolstering its conviction these had been forced upon it by a threatening larger neighbour. It was one that encapsulated its foundational assumptions—that Pakistan was an inherently peaceful nation rendered insecure as a result of relentless targeting by India. The reality was somewhat different.

India had indeed started a nuclear programme at independence, but its primary aim was to generate nuclear power for what its first prime minister, Jawaharlal Nehru, hoped would underpin economic self-sufficiency and a state-driven expansion of industry. Pakistan had soon followed suit. When Bhutto made his comment, India's interest in turning this programme to military uses was driven not by Pakistan but fear of China. India had lost a border war to China in 1962 and its anxieties about its powerful neighbour to the north multiplied when Beijing held its own nuclear tests in 1964. However, it was deeply ambivalent about nuclear weapons, calling instead for international disarmament. That ambivalence would remain for decades, producing in India a hesitant approach to its nuclear weapons programme that would not finally cohere until the 1990s.

If Bhutto's portrayal of Indian intentions was misleading, so too was his projection of the balance of power between India and Pakistan that caricaturised the former as a confident aggressor and the latter as desperately insecure. At the time, India had more reasons to feel insecure than Pakistan. Defeat by China in 1962 had been followed by Nehru's death in 1964, depriving India of a political giant who had piloted the country through independence. Then serious rioting by Tamils in early 1965, after Delhi had declared Hindi as the official language, raised fears about whether India could hold together as a united country. Compared to India, Pakistan was flourishing. Bhutto had just successfully exploited tensions between Delhi and Beijing to lay the foundation of an enduring security relationship between Pakistan and China. Pakistan was a member of two US-backed multilateral treaty organisations, the Southeast Asia Treaty Organization (SEATO) and the Central Treaty Organization (CENTO), giving it the international support that non-aligned India lacked. The Indian economy was in trouble, dragged down by Nehru's idealistic state socialism. Pakistan had seen its economic growth climb to 6.7 per cent per year, industrial production had risen to 12 per cent and investment to 14 per cent per year.[7] For the first time since independence, the Pakistani rupee stood higher on world markets than the Indian rupee.[8] Pakistan appeared to be doing so well politically that its president, Ayub Khan, was dubbed an Asian de Gaulle. Such was the position of both countries in 1965 that the projection of an Indian threat had as much to do with tub-thumping populism. At the time Bhutto was trying to make his mark by mixing left-wing policies promising "bread, clothes and shelter" for the poor with a heavy dose of right-wing nationalism. Indeed, far from being threatened by India, it was Pakistan that initiated conflict. Soon after Bhutto's comments about eating grass, Pakistan tried to wrest control of Kashmir from India—leading to a full-scale war that ended in a stalemate.

Six years later, West Pakistan became embroiled in a civil war with the Bengali-speakers of East Pakistan. India intervened and forced the surrender of the Pakistan Army at Dhaka on December 16, 1971, taking 90,000 Pakistani prisoners of war. Bhutto became president of what remained of Pakistan within days of the humiliating surrender. He turned to what he knew best to revive and reunite the people—nationalism. It was a manufactured nationalism that aimed to transcend

Pakistan's ethnic divisions by projecting it as a strong country, bullied by India but inspired by Islam. The possession of nuclear weapons would both burnish this nationalism and shield Pakistan from further dismemberment. On January 24, 1972, just over a month after he took office, Bhutto held a secret meeting with Pakistani scientists in the town of Multan at which Pakistan committed to obtaining a nuclear bomb.[9] He then went on to sign a far-reaching settlement with India, agreeing to a framework for lasting peace, including over Kashmir, in return for the release of the Pakistani prisoners.

The Simla Agreement was signed on July 2 1972 by Bhutto and Prime Minister Indira Gandhi and named after the Indian hill town where they met. In the accord, the countries agreed to settle their disputes bilaterally. The ceasefire line dividing Jammu and Kashmir since 1948 was to be renamed the Line of Control (LoC) and formally mapped. In the Indian telling of the story, this agreement superseded the UN resolutions on Kashmir by excluding external intervention by third countries.[10] India also saw the demarcation of the LoC as a prelude to making it the international border and settling the Kashmir dispute once and for all. That Mrs Gandhi did not insist this be made more explicit was attributed to her desire to avoid imposing too humiliating a settlement on Bhutto, hoping instead to encourage civilian rule in Pakistan.[11] It proved to be an error on her part. The treaty did not explicitly repudiate the UN resolutions and left just enough ambiguity for Pakistan to resume its demands for a plebiscite. It would nonetheless become the bedrock on which future Indian diplomacy rested.

Bhutto was not alone in pushing nuclear weapons in tandem with his peace-making at Simla. Later that year, Gandhi authorised an acceleration in the development of what India called a "peaceful nuclear explosive" (PNE), a label that suggested it could be used for the purposes of civilian engineering. On May 18, 1974, India exploded a nuclear device, nicknamed "Smiling Buddha", only half-bothering to obfuscate its military applications. Since Indian decision-making about the country's nuclear weapons is tightly controlled within the Prime Minister's Office, Gandhi's motivation in authorising the test remains unknown. It has been variously viewed as a delayed reaction to China's 1964 tests, a response to Pakistan's own nuclear programme,[12] or a means of boosting her own domestic political standing at a time of economic recession.[13] Others have suggested Gandhi had resented American support for Pakistan during the 1971 war—the United States sent its Seventh Fleet to the Bay of Bengal in a failed effort at gunboat diplomacy—and resolved that India had to boost its military strength. Whatever the truth, an analysis of notes written by Gandhi's advisers at the time showed that a presumed threat from Pakistan figured prominently in India's security thinking. The notes show that in between 1973 and 1974, Indian decision-makers did not consider a Chinese invasion of India as a real possibility, nor did they see the possibility of China using nuclear weapons against India as credible. The primary threat continued to be seen as a surprise attack by Pakistan, albeit with tacit support from China and the United States.[14]

Significantly, India made no attempt to acquire the means for delivering a nuclear weapon at the time, either with aircraft or by developing nuclear-capable missiles.[15] Thus the device tested had no immediate military use, suggesting that 1974 should be seen as a one-off rather than a stepping-stone in a coherent plan to build a nuclear capability. After 1974, India's efforts to develop nuclear weapons were shelved, in part due to international opposition. Pakistan, however, rushed to match what it presumed were India's hostile intentions. In 1976, Bhutto secured Chinese support for the development of a Pakistani bomb[16] and Pakistan went on to identify a test site in its Balochistan province. Bhutto did not live to see the completion of the programme he had initiated. He was overthrown in a coup by General Mohammed Zia ul-Haq in 1977 and hanged in 1979. China continued to help Pakistan. In doing so, it could keep India tied down in a permanent state of conflict with Pakistan while securing the latter as an ally without the expense of providing the kind of security umbrella that the United States gave to its closest allies in Europe and Asia. In 1982, China flew highly enriched uranium to Pakistan while also providing expertise in weapons design.[17] According to an Indian intelligence assessment, by 1981–82 Pakistan had enough weapons-grade highly enriched uranium to make one or two cores for uranium-based weapons.[18] Gandhi responded by seriously considering another Indian nuclear test in 1983. She called it off under US pressure, but that same year, India established a programme to develop ballistic missiles—a clear sign it was considering pursuing nuclear weapons since putting anything other than nuclear warheads on such inaccurate missiles made little sense. China in turn provided missiles to Pakistan.[19]

Assessments of which country obtained nuclear weapons first are contested and murky, not least because the process of developing nuclear bombs is one that moves along a spectrum from being able to explode crude nuclear devices, to turning these into a form that can reliably be used as a weapon, to designing the means to deliver them, whether from aircraft or nuclear-capable missiles. Neither country had signed up to the Nuclear Non-Proliferation Treaty (NPT), thus shielding them from the kind of scrutiny that NPT members like Iran later faced. But in the 1980s, Pakistan appears to have been the first to "weaponise", a process that requires working out how to adapt a nuclear device for use in a bomb by miniaturising it and keeping it reliably stable until it is exploded.

In 1983, Pakistan carried out a "cold test"—exploding a nuclear-capable weapon without the fissionable core. It followed up with about two dozen cold tests over a number of years.[20] By 1986 or 1987, Pakistan is believed to have weaponised its nuclear programme.[21] In 1987, a crisis triggered by a large Indian military exercise on the Pakistan border prompted Indian diplomats to report that Pakistan was privately threatening to use its nuclear weapons if India did not back off.[22] Pakistan has always denied making that threat over the military exercises known as Operation Brasstacks.

Pakistan was also ahead of India in finding the means to deliver its nuclear weapons. In 1988, Pakistan started perfecting its designs for dropping nuclear bombs from fighter aircraft, although it could have used its bombs a year or so earlier by dropping them from cargo aircraft in what may have been a one-way mission for the pilots. In 1990, it cold-tested an aerial device, dropping it from a modified F-16 aircraft.[23] For most of this time, the United States turned a blind eye so long as Pakistan did not keep its weapons in an assembled state or conduct a hot test. Then in 1990, a year after the Soviets withdrew from Afghanistan, President George Bush announced that he could no longer certify to Congress that Pakistan did not have nuclear weapons, triggering non-proliferation sanctions. By then it was too late.

As for India, Rajiv Gandhi, who had become prime minister after his mother was assassinated in 1984, did not give the weaponisation order to the country's nuclear scientists until March 1989. The process of adapting the device tested in 1974 had been put on ice before that. It was not until the early 1990s that India had weapons ready for assembly and 1995–1996 before it had the means to deliver these reliably from fighter aircraft. It would be another five years or so before India and Pakistan were able to mate nuclear warheads to nuclear-capable missiles with similar confidence.[24]

By the 1990s, both India and Pakistan were going through a period of turbulence. Pakistan felt abandoned by the United States after the Soviet withdrawal from Afghanistan and was facing sanctions over its nuclear programme. General Zia's death in a plane crash in 1988 ushered in a period of shaky and spiteful democracy. India faced if anything more severe problems. Having followed state socialist policies since independence, its economy had stagnated into what became known as "the Hindu rate of growth". Standards of living trailed heavily behind those in Pakistan, whose readiness to align itself with the west combined with its greater openness to foreign investment had produced a more buoyant economy. Thus in 1990, for example, income per capita measured in terms of purchasing power parity was roughly the equivalent of $1,850 in India compared to $3,000 in Pakistan.[25] Since India had fallen largely within the Soviet camp during the Cold War, the 1991 collapse of the Soviet Union deprived it of diplomatic support and a source of weaponry. In 1990–91, it faced a severe balance of payments crisis as the spike in oil prices caused by Iraq's invasion of Kuwait hit its weak and unproductive economy. It began a crash course of economic liberalisation that would only slowly begin to yield results. Politically, India was on edge, running through a series of unstable governments in the course of the decade. In 1992 senior BJP leader Lal Krishna Advani led a protest march against a sixteenth-century mosque in the northern town of Ayodhya that Hindu hardliners said had been built over the birthplace of the Hindu god Ram. When they reached the site, a mob of Hindu zealots tore down the mosque, known as the Babri Masjid. The demolition triggered communal riots in which more than 2,000 people died and a series of revenge bombings in Mumbai in March 1993 whose organisers India linked to Pakistan. Political upheaval was accompanied by an intensifying separatist revolt in the Kashmir Valley that was quickly backed by Pakistan.

By then, the nuclear weapons programmes were beginning to shape the behaviour of the two countries and their view of each other. When Pakistan began to train, fund and arm men to fight in Kashmir, some in India believed it was relying on its nuclear capability to deter Indian military retaliation. Already in August 1990, according to an Indian official report, the Indian government had received information "from a sensitive intelligence source" that in any future confrontation, Pakistan might use nuclear weapons as a first resort.[26] Their nuclear weapons programmes remained covert, however, as they followed a policy similar to that still exercised by Israel, of seeking deterrence through an unacknowledged nuclear-weapons capability.

The final push for nuclear tests came from India. Throughout the 1990s, the strategic community in Delhi—most of whose members supported nuclear tests—built up political pressure. For these advocates, the current system dividing the world into those who had nuclear weapons and those who were denied this right was unacceptable nuclear apartheid. While a nuclear-armed China and Pakistan was always at the back of their minds, they framed the debate as one that was anti-West, portraying western powers as trying to box an independent, proud India into a corner. So shrill was the crescendo of noise through the 1990s that it was hard to find anyone who dissented. The one or two who tried to resist the tide were branded as being on western payrolls, or overly influenced by the "non-proliferation ayatollahs" in Washington. The "bomb lobby", as it came to be known, was also worried that global non-proliferation regimes were closing in on India. The NPT had been extended indefinitely in 1995, despite objections, particularly from India, over its discriminatory structure under which only the five permanent members of the UN Security Council could have nuclear weapons while the others renounced them in return for civilian nuclear energy assistance. More critically, the Americans were pushing hard for a Comprehensive Test Ban Treaty which would close off all options to conduct nuclear tests. The test of a single device in 1974 was nowhere near enough to build the necessary expertise; indeed as the bomb lobby pointed out, the Americans, the French and even the Chinese had conducted dozens of tests to build their capability. Some dismissed the 1974 test as a physics experiment.

By then, the idea of holding more tests had cross-party support, though the right-wing tried to push the pace in order to portray itself as a champion of national security. For the BJP, still in opposition but rising on a wave of Hindu revivalism, the nuclear debate provided a perfect opportunity to burnish its credentials. The economy was also slowly reaping the benefits of the economic reforms launched in 1991. Indian standards of living still lagged behind those in Pakistan, and would do so for many years to come. But the economy, still less open than that of Pakistan, was strong enough to withstand the international sanctions that were expected to follow nuclear tests. Pakistan, in contrast, having depended on international aid that had since dried up, and with a more open economy, was more vulnerable to sanctions.

In 1995, under Congress Prime Minister Narasimha Rao, India began preparations for tests. But with less than 72 hours to go, India backed down under US pressure when Washington confronted it with satellite imagery of activity at its Pokhran test site in the Rajasthan desert.[27] Its ballistic missile programme was briefly suspended, again under US pressure, and then resumed. After that, sometimes India would change the dates of its missile tests so as not to embarrass a visiting US dignitary or sour the mood of an Indian official delegation to the United States. Such was the atmosphere instigated by the bomb lobby that even such temporary delays provoked outcry that the government was caving in to American pressure.

In May 1996, the BJP led by Vajpayee was asked to form a government after it won the largest, but minority, share of seats in an inconclusive election. After campaigning for nuclear weapons, Vajpayee quickly moved to order nuclear tests. Three devices were brought to the Indian test site and placed in tunnels. The preparations came within about a day of being completed,[28] when it became clear Vajpayee's government was not going to win a vote of confidence in parliament. Vajpayee cancelled the tests and his government collapsed after just thirteen days.

Two years later, in March 1998, the BJP was re-elected. Again its campaign platform had included a commitment to nuclear weapons and this time it succeeded in putting together a ruling coalition. Determined to press ahead with nuclear testing as quickly as possible, Vajpayee established that the earliest practical date would be in May.[29] Quietly, India flew its nuclear devices from their vaults at the Bhabha Atomic Research Centre (BARC) in Mumbai to Jaisalmer in Rajasthan and then sent them by truck to the test site, where preparations were made at night to avoid detection by US spy satellites. On May 11, scientists waited for the wind to die down to make sure any radiation leakage was not blown into inhabited areas. Nuclear scientist A.P.J. Abdul Kalam, who would later become president of India, telephoned Vajpayee at his official residence at 3 pm to tell him conditions were good and the tests could be conducted during the next hour. At 3:45 pm, India began its nuclear tests.

* * *

Pakistan Prime Minister Sharif was in Uzbekistan on an official visit when the first set of Indian tests were conducted. He cut short his trip and returned the next day. Almost immediately, Pakistan came under intense pressure from the United States not to follow suit, with President Bill Clinton—desperate to shore up the non-proliferation regime—telephoning Sharif to offer promises of aid if he desisted. A meeting of the Defence Committee of the Cabinet on May 13, chaired by Sharif and including senior ministers, the heads of the army, navy and air force, and Pakistan's nuclear scientists, among them AQ Khan, weighed up the options. Its assessment, later recounted by then finance minister Sartaj Aziz, was that India wanted to become a de facto member of the nuclear club without signing the NPT, and that its new status would strengthen its claim, over time, for permanent membership of the UN Security Council. India would also be able to adopt a more aggressive stance on Kashmir. The meeting agreed that Delhi aimed to force Pakistan into testing at a time when its economy was vulnerable. If this were to happen, said Aziz, "the deepening economic imbalance will bring about a decisive shift in the balance of power between India and Pakistan." In Aziz's telling, Pakistan had not yet fully decided to hold its own tests after that meeting. Some advocated that Pakistan hold off testing and instead move to isolate India while taking advantage of the economic sweeteners on offer, including debt relief. It could continue to rely on Pakistan's covert nuclear weapons capability as a deterrent. But Pakistan did immediately begin preparations for nuclear tests, while drawing up an economic contingency plan to deal with the expected sanctions—suggesting that the decision was tilting heavily in favour of matching India.[30]

Domestic pressure mounted with other political leaders, including Benazir Bhutto, demanding that Pakistan give a strong response to India. India also goaded Pakistan into holding its own tests in order to force its nuclear capability out into the open. BJP hardliner Advani, by then Home Minister, taunted Pakistan. "Islamabad should realise the change in the geo-strategic situation in the region and the world [and] roll back its anti-India policy, especially with regard to Kashmir," he said at a news conference. Vajpayee's declaration that India intended to build nuclear weapons, Advani said, "has brought about a qualitatively new stage in Indo-Pakistan relations" and "signifies—even while adhering to the principle of no first strike—[that] India is resolved to deal firmly with Pakistan's hostile activities in Kashmir."[31] The goading was probably unnecessary. At a practical level, Pakistan needed to neutralise any technical advantage India had gained through its tests, while politically, its entire identity was built on competition with its neighbour. Sharif's position as prime minister was strong—in the 1997 elections he had won an unprecedented two-thirds majority in the National Assembly. His position was not, however, so impregnable that he could take the risk of not testing. Bhutto called on him to resign if he failed to order nuclear tests.[32] The Pakistan Army might have overthrown him in a coup had he refused.

The United States and its allies continued to pile the pressure on Pakistan, hoping it could still be won over. With a smaller and less self-reliant economy than India and with just over $1 billion of cash reserves—enough to cover only six weeks of imports—Pakistan would suffer the impact of international sanctions almost immediately.[33] But Washington's intelligence was also suggesting its arm-twisting would fail. According to one account, on May 18, 1998, Sharif summoned the chairman of the Pakistan Atomic Energy Commission to his office and told him to carry out the tests.[34] If so, Advani's comments made on the same day goading Pakistan into testing made no difference other than to provide Pakistan with a pretext to claim it was responding to Indian aggression.

After India had announced its own tests, Pakistan had sent two teams of scientists with support personnel and equipment to the test site at a granite mountain in the Ras Koh range in the Chagai district of Balochistan, where, fifteen years earlier, an L-shaped, 1 km long tunnel

41

had been drilled into the rock. They prepared the nuclear devices and established a command and observation post at a safe distance. The test tunnel was sealed on May 25. The next day, the prime minister was informed that everything was ready.[35] By May 27, the US government reported that Pakistan had been observed pouring cement to seal the test shaft, the final stage before an explosion could be conducted. The same day, Clinton made one last plea to Sharif, imploring him not to conduct a test. It was the fourth presidential call to the Pakistani prime minister since May 11 and as unsuccessful as the others.

Before dawn on May 28, Pakistan cut the communication links for Pakistani seismic stations to the outside world and put its military installations on alert. Soldiers and officials preparing the test site were withdrawn to the observation point. A young scientist, Muhammad Arshad, was selected to operate the trigger mechanism. With a cry of "Allahu Akbar", at exactly 3:16 pm, he pushed the button.[36] The result was shown on Pakistani television, the colour, cynics said, touched up for dramatic effect. Footage shows the jagged barren ridges of a mountain, peaceful against a clear blue sky. A sudden burst of bright yellow dust spreads across the ridgeline and envelops the mountain so that it appears as though a huge chunk of rock is disintegrating. Another shot from a different angle begins with the crack of what sounds like thunder, followed by the mountain lighting up. It looks as though the granite itself is turning white from the explosion.[37] This was intended as Pakistan's finest hour and May 28 was henceforth celebrated every year as "Youm-e-Takbeer", a day of greatness. None bar a few dared openly question the tests. "I saw on television a picture more awesome than the familiar mushroom cloud of nuclear explosion. The mountain had turned white," the left-wing journalist Eqbal Ahmad wrote. "I wondered how much pain had been felt by nature, God's most wondrous creation."[38]

When he announced the tests, Prime Minister Sharif whitewashed Pakistan's own pursuit of nuclear weapons, claiming that the nuclearisation of South Asia should be blamed entirely on India. Pakistan, he insisted, had sought for thirty years to convince the international community to pay attention to India's nuclear programme while itself exercising the utmost restraint. "We pursued in all earnest the goal of non-proliferation in South Asia," he said.[39] His attempt to portray Pakistan as an aggrieved victim sat uncomfortably with a national mood of jubilation that the country had made it into the big league, the world's seventh declared nuclear power. People poured out into the streets to celebrate and distributed sweets and unfurled the national flag outside their houses. Like India, Pakistan had shown the West that it would not take orders. Two days later, Pakistan exploded another device. In the euphoria, nobody thought to check on the impact on the people who lived in the area. Though the immediate vicinity of the desert test site is inhabited only by nomads, an estimated 410,000 people lived in the broader Chaghai district, none of whom had any warning about the tests. The only reports that leaked out subsequently suggested a disproportionately large number of people were suffering from skin diseases and damage to the thyroid glands. Surface and ground water could also have been contaminated and the water table reduced, harming farming.[40] But this was Balochistan, Pakistan's least populated but biggest province where an on-and-off separatist insurgency had made travel and independent reporting extremely difficult. Baloch separatists, fighting for independence from Pakistan, afterwards complained about the damage done to their homeland. But in urban Pakistan, few of those celebrating in the streets cared about Balochistan. In time, it became important to them only as the scene of a separatist insurgency that Pakistan said was backed by India.

* * *

In India, popular reaction to its own tests was overwhelmingly positive. Gone was the sense of inferiority that had accompanied the sluggish economic growth of the post-independence years and the humiliation of colonisation. Just as Pakistan had ignored the impact in Balochistan, nobody questioned whether people in Rajasthan had been affected. The rhetoric was of asserting India's place in the world. The political benefits went primarily to the BJP, which had made the transition from a large but fringe Hindu nationalist movement into a party of government. In the years ahead, the BJP would steadily become more central to Indian politics, both reflecting and encouraging a transformation of society into one that was more unashamedly Hindu and less secular.

In time, India would win the approval of Washington for its nuclear status. As the sole superpower, only the United States had the clout to acknowledge India's bid for a seat at the high table of international relations. The tests, however, also brought unwelcome interest in Kashmir as the United States and other big powers fretted it could become a flashpoint for a nuclear war. The UN Security Council condemned the tests, urged India and Pakistan to resume talks, and stressed the need to tackle the root causes of tensions, including Kashmir.[41] Delhi, which resented outside interference on Kashmir, would have to expend a great deal of diplomatic energy over the coming years fending off suggestions that if only it were willing to settle the Kashmir dispute, it might transform Pakistan and convince it to drop support for Islamist militants.

As for relations with Pakistan, India had underestimated how far the nuclearisation of South Asia would embolden its neighbour to cling to its militant proxies. India's energies had been focused not on Pakistan, but on what it saw as a hypocritical Western stance that preached nonproliferation to others. It assumed nuclear weapons would stabilise the balance between India and Pakistan by preventing a traditional conventional war and—if accompanied by confidence-building measures—open the way to a permanent peace settlement.[42]

Instead, Pakistan discovered that its overt possession of nuclear weapons acted as an insurance policy against pressure from the United States and India to disarm its Islamist militant proxies. Problematically for Pakistan, Islamist groups knew this too and were among the most vocal in welcoming the world's first "Islamic nuclear bomb". As Maulana Fazlur Rahman Khalil, a Pakistani militant leader with close ties to al-Qaeda, said, "Pakistan's nuclear capability does not belong to Pakistan alone but to Muslims everywhere for defending themselves and their rights."[43] According to Maulana Sami ul-Haq, a Pakistani cleric close to the Taliban, "Western countries conspire and help each other. Similarly we Muslims should not hesitate. It will be a matter of great joy if all Muslim countries get nuclear weapons."[44] By making itself impregnable, Pakistan was doing the equivalent of locking itself inside a house on fire.

The impact of the tests would become clear only over time. India and Pakistan did not become nuclear powers overnight—they had an undeclared capability before 1998 and would spend years improving it afterwards. As a milestone in the Great South Asian War, the tests even appeared in the short-run to favour Pakistan. With nuclear weapons, Pakistan neutralised India's advantage in terms of size even as India remained weak relative to China. But as India and Pakistan would go on to demonstrate, nuclear weapons in themselves did not make a country weaker or stronger. That depended on how these weapons were perceived, how the threat of using them was manipulated and the wider political, diplomatic and economic context.

In the short run, hopes ran high in the region that nuclear weapons would bring peace, rather in the same way that they had prevented open conflict between the United States and the Soviet Union during the Cold War. Both Vajpayee and Sharif also saw their personal standings raised by the tests and thought they could afford to take risks. Sharif would ultimately become the first victim of the illusory power of Pakistan's nuclear weapons. Buoyed up by the success of the tests, he became more autocratic, going as far as to take on the Pakistan Army chief. General Jehangir Karamat had suggested the formation of a National Security Council made up of political and military representatives to stabilise the political system. But Sharif insisted the army had no business saying how the country should be run. Karamat, seen as relatively well disposed to democratic rule, was forced to retire early and Sharif looked for a new army chief. In October 1998 he appointed a man who was third in line for the top job, an outsider from Karachi with fewer connections in the Punjab-dominated army establishment, someone he thought would never be able to oust him in a coup. It was a year before Sharif realised how badly he had miscalculated in appointing General Pervez Musharraf.

Vajpayee made an equally impulsive decision, though one that would have less drastic consequences for his personal standing. He would stake his reputation on a bid for permanent peace with Pakistan.

* * *

At a meeting on the fringes of the UN General Assembly in September 1998, Vajpayee and Sharif agreed that the Indian prime minister should visit Pakistan.[45] It would be the first visit to Pakistan by an Indian prime minister in ten years. The two countries had been working on a framework for peace talks since 1997 when Sharif had been elected on a promise to improve relations with India. The two prime ministers settled on a plan that would be as dramatic in form as they hoped it would be in substance. Vajpayee and Sharif had already agreed to set up a direct bus service between Delhi and Lahore. With symbolic flourish, Vajpayee would travel on the inaugural bus on February 20 1999. Rather than start out from Delhi, Vajpayee boarded the bus at Amritsar just across the land border from Lahore. Before Partition, these cities had been near neighbours, barely 50 km apart. Nowhere was the bloody division of the subcontinent more keenly felt than the region they both dominated, now separated into Indian and Pakistani Punjab. Vajpayee's bus journey, dripping with emotion and symbolism, was meant to bury the past, reopen borders and allow the leader of the Hindu right in India to show his embrace of Pakistan.

Vajpayee and his accompanying ministers duly flew to Amritsar and boarded the bus, accompanied by an eclectic collection of dignitaries, editors and film stars. "The mood was truly, irrepressibly infectious," recalled Foreign Minister Jaswant Singh.[46] Crowds lined the route, waving and cheering, as Vajpayee and his entourage travelled the short distance to the border crossing at Wagah, where the gates were thrown open for him. Waiting on the Pakistani side of the border were Prime Minister Sharif and his brother Shahbaz Sharif, then Chief Minister of Punjab province. The seventy-four-year-old Vajpayee was the first to alight from the bus, walking stiffly down the steps at the front before embracing Sharif in an awkward and apparently unexpected hug.[47] As his visit proceeded to rapturous public enthusiasm on both sides of the border, only one jarring note disturbed the mood. The Islamist political party, the Jamaat-e-Islami, declared it a black day and organised big street protests. Sartaj Aziz, by then Foreign Minister, noted that there were reports the Jamaat-e-Islami was encouraged by certain "agencies"—the word used in Pakistan for its intelligence services—opposed to the peace process.[48] Otherwise the Pakistani hospitality was typically exuberant: a banquet in Lahore Fort, tables piled over-high with different meat dishes in classic Punjabi cuisine, too many guests, and musicians playing sentimental old Hindi film songs. "A bit kitsch," said Foreign Minister Singh, but "sheer unrestrained Punjabi enthusiasm".[49]

During his visit, Vajpayee tried to put to rest lingering Pakistani suspicions that the BJP had never accepted Partition by visiting the Minar-e-Pakistan, the monument marking the spot where Muslim leaders had called for the creation of Pakistan in 1940. He was rewarded with an agreement which appeared to offer a sound basis for continued peace talks. In the Lahore Declaration, the two prime ministers promised to step up efforts to resolve all issues, including over Kashmir, a concession to Pakistan. They also made a commitment to "implementing the Simla Agreement in letter and spirit"—a concession to India, which set great store by the accord signed after the 1971 war.[50] Musharraf did not join the talks in Lahore. The official reason given was that he was required to attend a meeting with the Chinese defence minister scheduled before Vajpayee had decided on his visit.[51] His opposition to peace would become painfully apparent to Vajpayee within months. For now, both prime ministers believed they had put the tensions of the nuclear tests behind them. The agreements reached at Lahore also included a Memorandum of Understanding signed by their foreign secretaries promising India and Pakistan would give each other advance notice of ballistic missile tests, abide by moratoriums on further nuclear testing, and improve communications on their nuclear doctrines to avoid conflict and the risk of nuclear war. But even as Vajpayee and Sharif promised lasting peace, the storm clouds of the next war were gathering. In April, the BJP-led government was defeated in parliament by just one vote and Vajpayee called mid-term elections. He stayed on in a caretaker capacity and a month later, India and Pakistan were at war.

2

"A BRILLIANT TACTICAL OPERATION"

PAKISTAN'S DEFEAT IN THE KARGIL WAR OF 1999

For a crucial link between two of India's most strategic regional capitals, the road from Srinagar to Leh is also one of the most treacherous. It starts out gently enough, heading up the slopes of the Kashmir Valley through fields of lush green rice and villages of mud-and-brick houses with sloping corrugated roofs, half-hidden behind the trees. Further up, the road follows the course of a river fed by glacial streams that in the spring turn into a torrent. Beyond is Sonamarg, an Alpine meadow ringed by the mountains of the Himalaya. This road was once a pony track used by traders travelling from Kashmir up into the high Tibetan plateau and along the tributaries of the old Silk Route to Central Asia and Tibet. On their return journey, they brought the pashmina wool obtained from goats that thrive at high altitudes for weaving into Kashmir shawls. It is now the only direct road joining Srinagar and Leh, a two-day drive between the capitals of Kashmir and Ladakh. It is also an important link for the Indian Army, joining two centres where it maintains a significant military presence, the former to check any advance by separatist insurgents, the latter to guard India's borders against encroachment by China.

It is after Sonamarg that the road begins its perilous ascent into the Tibetan plateau. Here the collision of continental plates that thrust up the Himalayan mountains millions of years ago has left Ladakh perched high above the Kashmir Valley. The two regions, one a fertile valley, the other a high cold desert, are so different that they seem improperly put together. They were forged into the princely state of Jammu and Kashmir in the nineteenth century. Along with the Jammu region which runs into the plains of Punjab, they make up the Indian state of Jammu and Kashmir. The road narrows into a bumpy metalled track that winds up through a series of corkscrew switchbacks etched into a barren cliff. On one side of the car, solid rock rises near-vertically above. On the other, the crumbling edges of the track sheer away into grey-and-brown scree. The pass, called the Zoji-la, climbs to a height of 11,575 feet. It is not the highest in India, but it is one of the steepest.

At the top, the road levels off to follow the floor of a highland valley until it reaches Dras, a small town of one- and two-storey houses strung out along the main street and crouched beneath barren snow-flecked mountains. It is here that the road runs closest to the Line of Control (LoC) which runs through the high mountains above, separating Ladakh from Baltistan, in the Pakistan-held part of the former princely state of Jammu and Kashmir. Dras and the district capital Kargil, more than an hour's drive further along the road, have been hard hit by the division of the state that severed links with their neighbours in Baltistan. Dras also has the reputation of being the coldest town in India—temperatures can drop as low as minus 45 degrees in winter. Some of its houses are gaily painted in bright blue and turquoise, but overall Dras has the subdued look of Himalayan hill towns that comes from the ferocity of the weather and the shabbiness of poverty. The mountains looming above are dark, forbidding, devoid of vegetation. The highest, known as Tiger Hill, disappears into the clouds. Dras is a lonely town where the local people hunch in cheap woollens against the cold even in summer. It is an improbable place for a war between nuclear-armed powers. Yet it was here in the mountains above Dras that India and Pakistan fought their most intense battles in their first war since the nuclear tests.

* * *

The Kargil War had its origins in a history that long predated the nuclear tests. The area around Dras and Kargil had been contested by

India and Pakistan in their first war over Jammu and Kashmir in 1947–1948. The ceasefire line that then divided the state ran roughly west to east, ending beyond Kargil at map grid reference NJ9842. In the 1949 Karachi Agreement, India and Pakistan stated that from point NJ9842, the ceasefire line should continue "thence north to the glaciers". There appeared to be no need to demarcate the area beyond—an uninhabitable expanse of high mountains, snowfields and glaciers. After the 1971 war the ceasefire line was mapped in greater detail by India and Pakistan and renamed the Line of Control. It ran for 740 kms (460 miles) from the international border, but stopped at the same point as before. In the late 1970s, however, India sparked off a struggle for control of the glaciated area beyond. The biggest of the glaciers there is the 76-km long (47-mile-long) Siachen glacier, which lies at the point where territory held by India, Pakistan and China meet. In 1978, India sent a military mountaineering expedition to explore Siachen. It claimed it was responding to Pakistan's issuance of travel permits to foreign mountaineering expeditions to Siachen and accused it of "cartographic aggression" after the glacier was shown on international maps as Pakistani-held territory. In Pakistan's defence, access to Siachen was easier from the Pakistani side, reachable from Baltistan across passes that led over a mountain spur known as the Saltoro Ridge and down into the glacier. Pakistan was already authorising foreign mountaineers to travel through its territory to reach the nearby K2, the world's second highest mountain, and it was reasonable enough to extend that permission to Siachen.[1]

After India sent its expedition to Siachen in 1978, returning every summer thereafter, Pakistan dispatched its own men to find out what was going on, and by 1984 both countries were secretly preparing to send troops to occupy the passes in the Saltoro. India got there first, taking the risk of sending soldiers on April 13 before the winter had lifted, beating Pakistan which had planned to deploy its own men in May. Pakistan hastily sent troops up to drive the Indians out, only to discover it is nearly impossible to evict an enemy who occupies a higher position in such high mountains. Once initiated, the conflict on the world's highest battlefield proved impossible to stop. Both countries expanded their positions, seeking to occupy whichever high points they could reach first. India had originally planned to deploy troops only in the summer—nobody had ever spent the winter in Siachen.[2] But as

Pakistan sent its men into near-suicidal uphill assaults against the Indian posts, India was forced to dig in. Men fought in brutal conditions above 18,000 feet, a height where the air is so thin that even walking can be an effort. Far more died from the effects of altitude and terrain, were buried by avalanches, disappeared into a crevasse, or succumbed to altitude sickness than in combat. A fresh escalation came in 1987 when Pakistani troops occupied a mountain peak overlooking the Bilafond-la, the main pass leading from Baltistan into the glacier, threatening Indian supply lines. Against all odds, India captured the post after an operation that involved scaling ice-walls by stealth followed by hand-to-hand fighting with grenades and bayonets at 21,000 feet. On top of the original occupation of Siachen in 1984, the loss of the Pakistani post in 1987 became an added humiliation that dug deeply into the psyche of the Pakistan Army. A Pakistani counter-attack on other Indian posts later that year largely failed.

By the late 1980s, both countries had reached a stalemate, with India clinging onto higher positions, but encumbered with longer supply lines. Soldiers on both sides said that "not one inch of land" could be ceded to the other. Attempts at resolving the conflict through talks stumbled on India's insistence that the territory it had won on the battlefield should be recorded in a peace agreement. It was then that senior officers in the Pakistan Army began to debate the possibility of attacking Indian supply lines to Siachen lower down. "The Indians have been stupid in coming into this area; we have been sentimental idiots in trying to grab the remaining peaks and thereafter throw them out," a senior Pakistani commander wrote in his personal diaries in 1989. Pakistan, he said, should fall back and leave the Indian troops alone in the mountains. It should then use artillery fire to disrupt Indian supply lines. Among the places he identified as vulnerable was the Srinagar-Leh road, at the point where it passed through Dras and Kargil.[3] The plan was shelved. But as India would discover in 1999, it was never fully abandoned.

In late late 1998–early 1999,[4] Pakistan Army chief General Pervez Musharraf and a small group of his closest commanders agreed on a plan to send troops across the LoC to set up new posts along a line that ran roughly from the Zoji-la to Point NJ9842. They hoped to mirror the Indian operation in Siachen, moving by stealth in the winter when they were less likely to be noticed and then claiming their new positions as a *fait accompli.* The new posts would give Pakistani troops a vantage point from which to direct artillery fire on the Srinagar-Leh road, impeding the main supply route to Siachen, while strengthening Pakistani positions all along the LoC. By then the fighting on Siachen had sprawled outwards as both armies tried to outflank the other, expanding to the point that it overlapped with the eastern end of the LoC near point NJ9842. After the Kargil War started, Pakistan would face Indian rage and international opprobrium for crossing the LoC. At a purely tactical level, however, its case was not quite as flimsy as commonly assumed. By 1999, the eastern end of the LoC near point NJ9842 was already fraying due to the expansion of fighting in Siachen. According to an account of the Kargil War by former Indian Army chief General V.P. Malik, two "significant" violations of the LoC had taken place in the 1980s. One was by Pakistan near Kargil. The other was by India near point NJ9842 to prevent Pakistan from outflanking its defences in Siachen. These were accompanied by a series of minor violations. [5] Separately, the integrity of the LoC had been challenged by artillery fire. Believing Pakistan was using covering fire to help militants infiltrating into Kashmir, India responded with its own artillery fire, leading to a tit-for-tat confrontation that then gathered its own momentum. By the mid-1990s, the two countries were fighting near-daily artillery duels across the LoC with regular casualties on both sides. But Pakistan's breach of the LoC in the Kargil War was qualitatively different from anything that had happened before. When the Indians began the Siachen War in 1984, they had gone into undemarcated territory, while the Pakistani troops were crossing the mutually agreed LoC. The quantum of difference was not as great as believed in India or internationally. But like so many decisions made by the Pakistan Army, a grain of truth in a partially legitimate grievance—in this case over Indian actions in Siachen—was expanded into a position of such certainty that it was blind to everything else. Unlike the Indian operation in 1984, Pakistan was initiating a conflict between two declared nuclear-armed states, right in the middle of peace talks. The story of the Kargil War— Pakistan's biggest defeat by India since 1971—is one that goes to the heart of why it lost the Great South Asian War.

* * *

Since Pakistan has never had an honest reckoning with itself over the Kargil War, it is impossible to know for sure exactly what Musharraf and his commanders were thinking when they initiated the operation. In his ghost-written memoirs Musharraf claimed rather implausibly that it was merely meant to plug gaps in Pakistani defences in anticipation of an Indian offensive.[6] That assertion was also made in an army-authorised account of the Kargil War by journalist-turned-analyst Shireen Mazari.[7] There is no evidence India was planning an offensive at the time. Musharraf also claimed somewhat more plausibly that "Kargil was not a one-off operation, but the latest in a series of moves and countermoves at a tactical level by India and Pakistan" in the mountains towards the end of the LoC.[8] But not only did Pakistan fail to recognise the significance of the nuclear tests in determining the way Kargil would be perceived internationally, its operation was far more ambitious than the Indian occupation of the passes above Siachen had been. Pakistan also contradicted its own argument that its Kargil operation was merely tactical by tacking on the aim of using it to give a fillip to the flagging insurgency in Kashmir. Contrary to a widespread perception, however, that Pakistan deliberately relied on its status as a nuclear-armed power to launch the Kargil operation without fear of retaliation, it seems more likely that it simply did not think it through. Having planned the operation well before Prime Minister Vajpayee travelled to Lahore in February, Musharraf also failed to anticipate how it would be seen both internationally and in India as an attempt to sabotage peace talks. Instead he focused on extracting revenge for Siachen, a conflict few outside of South Asia had even heard of, while governments in world capitals were transfixed by the fear of nuclear war. Pakistan's calculations also highlighted its chronic inability correctly to assess and predict Indian actions. It assumed, wrongly, that India would negotiate more flexibly under pressure and that "Hindu" troops would not have the courage to fight. This ideological myopia was institutional in the Pakistan Army and predated the nuclear tests. In the 1965 war, President Ayub Khan had declared that, "Hindu morale would not stand for more than a couple of hard blows delivered at the right time and place," only to be caught by surprise when the Indian Army advanced on Lahore.[9] Musharraf made the same mistake in the Kargil War.

* * *

In late January and early February 1999, small detachments of Pakistani troops began moving a short distance across the LoC, according to an Indian official report produced after the war.[10] The bulk of the Pakistani forces, initially held back to avoid detection, joined them in late April, and they moved further forward.[11] As was typical of these heights, the scale of the deployment was limited, and supplies had to be carried in on foot by mules and porters. Most of the men sent forward were from the Northern Light Infantry (NLI), a paramilitary force made up of men from Baltistan who adapted more easily to altitude than troops from the plains. They built *"sanghars"*, shelters of loose rock, to protect themselves from the elements and hide from Indian surveillance helicopters. By the time India realised in May what had happened, Pakistan had set up more than 130 posts along a stretch of mountains running around 85 miles (136 km)[12] from west to east, of which the most important sector was above Dras. At least 1,500 to 2,000 Pakistani troops, along with a large number of porters, had crossed the LoC and their posts were up to 5 miles (8 km) deep.[13] The Pakistani troops had taken advantage of wide gaps between the Indian positions to slip in unnoticed at a time when heavy winter snow made patrolling difficult. In these mountains, the armies of India and Pakistan do not aim to form an unbroken line of defence. Rather they set up posts in high positions from which to survey the surrounding territory. The Pakistani success in moving forward undetected would later lead to a widespread misconception that Indian troops had vacated their posts during the winter. That had been the practice in the past, but according to then Indian Army chief General V. P. Malik, the Indian military had maintained most of their posts through the winter of 1998–1999.[14] India was simply too complacent. Poor intelligence and its expectation of peace after the nuclear tests had lulled it into a false sense of security. Its troops patrolled only the tracks and ravines that would allow Pakistan to send sizeable numbers of combat troops through the mountains, and that too only halfway to the LoC, even as the Pakistanis took considerable personal risks to creep forward in the more remote, higher reaches.[15] When India did start to pick up reports of intruders in early May it assumed, partly because the Northern Light Infantry troops were wearing black *salwar kameez*, it was dealing with mujahideen who would be cleared out in two to three weeks. Such was the lack of alarm that Indian Army chief Malik left for a pre-scheduled visit to Poland and the Czech Republic on May 10. Even after an Indian patrol was captured by Pakistani troops on May 14, Delhi failed to appreciate the extent of the intrusion and its initial military response was over-confident. Indian troops without high-altitude equipment and clothing and lacking time for proper acclimatisation were ordered up into the mountains to drive out the intruders. They were easily repelled after taking heavy casualties.

For a brief period, the Kargil plan appeared to be going well for Pakistan. Pakistani troops had dug into nearly impregnable posts, were well-armed with AK 47s, machine-guns, mortars, anti-aircraft guns and Stinger surface-to-air missiles, and were supported from behind by Pakistani artillery. For Indian troops, the early weeks of what it called Operation Vijay, or "Victory", were brutal. Poorly equipped and poorly acclimatised troops, with no time for reconnaissance, had to scale mountains whose steep flanks were almost devoid of cover. They could move only at night. During the day, the Indian attackers were pinned down by artillery fire with only some scattered boulders for cover. There they would remain, thirsty, hungry and soaking wet from snow and sweat until nightfall when supplies of ammunition and food were brought up and casualties evacuated.[16] For the first couple of weeks, they had no close air support as the air force turned down appeals from the army to provide attack helicopters to back up ground troops.[17] Pakistan appeared to be hoping that as long as its troops held on until the following winter, when fighting would grind to a halt, it would be able to make a permanent change to the LoC while forcing India to the negotiating table to extract concessions on Kashmir. From their vantage points above Dras, Pakistani troops also directed artillery fire from the Pakistani side of the LoC onto the road below. In public, Pakistan insisted only *mujahideen* had crossed the LoC, increasing the confusion of the early weeks.

The initial success of the Kargil operation won the support of Prime Minister Sharif, who only a few months earlier had warmly welcomed Vajpayee to Pakistan. Sharif has denied knowing about the plans when he met Vajpayee at the end of February. According to then Foreign Minister Sartaj Aziz, Musharraf briefed Sharif in March on plans to step up activity around Kargil. Aziz, who attended the meeting, said in his memoirs that Musharraf made no mention of Pakistani troops crossing the LoC. Instead, he spoke of giving Stinger missiles to militants in the Kargil sector to raise the pressure on India in the ongoing peace talks and force it to recognise the urgency of resolving the Kashmir dispute. "We know the Indians," Aziz quoted Musharraf as saying. "They will negotiate seriously only under maximum pressure."[18] At a tense follow-up briefing held by Musharraf and his generals for the government on May 17, by which point the full extent of the operation had become clearer, the description was more explicit. "How have you succeeded in moving so many personnel and supplies without being detected?" Aziz quoted Prime Minister Sharif as asking. The reply came from Lieutenant-General Aziz Khan, the Chief of General Staff and a close Musharraf associate. "Sir, it has been a brilliant tactical operation and the credit goes to our men and officers for carrying out their tasks under such difficult conditions," he said. Sharif followed up with another question. "But India will naturally react strongly and try to reoccupy these posts. Can we hold on to them?" he asked. "Absolutely!" was the reply. "Even eight or ten persons occupying a position on such a commanding height cannot be dislodged by an entire company, without suffering an unacceptable level of casualties." The generals claimed that Pakistani forces had gone across an "unmarked" part of the LoC, an assertion that was patently untrue. But the reassurance, according to Foreign Minister Aziz, helped allay the civilian government's doubts about the operation. "Will this road eventually lead to Srinagar?" Sharif asked. The response came from several participants speaking at once: "*Inshallah*". At any rate, according to Foreign Minister Aziz, Sharif definitely accorded "ex-post facto approval". "Regaining a slice of Indian-occupied Kashmir is something no prime minister of Pakistan can object to in public," he recalled in his memoirs.[19] The official Indian report into Kargil concluded that "it is reasonable to assume that Nawaz Sharif was at least aware of the broad thrust of the Kargil plan when he so warmly welcomed the Indian Prime Minister in Lahore." However, it added witheringly that Sharif might not have been up to understanding exactly what was going on. "Those who know Nawaz Sharif personally believe that he has a limited attention span and is impatient with detail," it said.[20]

If the Kargil plan seemed like "a brilliant tactical operation", it was a strategic disaster. Having assumed, just as it did in 1965, that India would not dare hit back hard, Pakistan had no back-up plan when Delhi escalated the war. On April 17, Prime Minister Vajpayee's government had lost a vote of confidence after thirteen months in office. The government stayed on in a caretaker capacity, but the Bharatiya Janata Party (BJP) was now fighting a national election. Having been so badly wrong-footed at Lahore, it had all the more need to prove its credentials on national security. When India did escalate the war, Pakistan had made no diplomatic preparations to explain its stance or to ease international fears about a possible nuclear exchange. As news of the war began to filter into Islamabad in the middle of May, some began to suspect it might go badly wrong for Pakistan. There seemed little doubt it would be seen as the aggressor, discrediting Pakistan and its position on Kashmir. One retired ambassador said that when he heard about the Kargil War, he went to see Foreign Minister Aziz. "We have lost Kashmir," he told him.[21] By then, there was no going back.

* * *

Although it was late May by the time India managed to muster a coherent response, when it did so, every branch of government and society pulled together. India could be slow to react to events, but its muddled, sluggish and fractured democracy had a remarkable ability to unite the country when necessary. The army and the air force buried their differences under government orders. Diplomats made India's case abroad while the media rallied public opinion at home. In as much as wars are won or lost on the home front, India had a big advantage over Pakistan, whose internal divisions had been exacerbated by years of on-off military rule. The Indian government adopted a twin approach that it would deploy to devastating effect. It would maintain a policy of restraint by ordering Indian forces to stay on India's side of the LoC, thereby reinforcing its argument that it was a victim of Pakistani aggression. At the same time it would hold out the threat of a military offensive across the LoC or international border, frightening the international community into forcing Pakistan to pull back.

For the first time since the 1971 war, the Indian government ordered air strikes to drive out the Pakistanis. These began on May 26. Since the pilots were ordered to stay on the Indian side of the LoC, the air sorties were perilously difficult. The pilots were forced to fly in a narrow corridor, in high mountains, with poor visibility of what was happening on the ground. On May 27, a MiG-27 developed engine trouble and crashed on the other side of the LoC. The pilot bailed out and was taken prisoner. His squadron leader, flying over to see where he had come down in an accompanying MiG-21 fighter, was shot down by a Stinger missile and killed. The next day, a Mi-17 helicopter was also shot down. The crew of four died. After that, helicopters were withdrawn from combat duties, and though the airstrikes continued, Indian fighters were careful to fly high enough to avoid Pakistani missiles. The airstrikes, however, served their purpose. Within the conflict zone, Indian aircraft were soon pummelling Pakistan's overstretched supply lines. Internationally, they added to alarm about a widening conflict that might turn nuclear. At the same time, the Indian Army was mobilised for a wider war. According to Indian Army Chief Malik, Indian troops all along the LoC and international border were given orders to switch to a state of readiness that would put India in a position to launch an offensive anywhere at six days' notice.[22] India also sent naval ships to the Arabian Sea to signal its willingness to take on Pakistan on all fronts. As these preparations were made, India rushed fresh troops and artillery into the Kargil region.

India's armed response was accompanied by a media and diplomatic offensive. Kargil was India's first television war. Correspondents in bullet-proof vests reported live from Dras and Kargil, bringing to millions nationwide news of the coffins coming back from the mountains. With the war beamed right into their living rooms, the Indian public mourned the losses of its soldiers in a way it had never done before. Young officers suffered a high number of casualties given their determination to lead from the front. The public grieved all the more to see men with such bright futures felled by what they saw as Pakistani perfidy. By now, in the words of Foreign Minister Jaswant Singh, the media was "almost a player in the contest".[23] The Indian government held regular briefings in Delhi to win the support of the media and get its point across to the country and the international community. Indian Army headquarters set up an Information and Psychological Warfare Cell run by a major-general with direct access to the army chief. By and large the Indian media reported from the road, because it was too dangerous and difficult to go higher up. But that meant the media coverage would be heavy in heroism and tragedy, while ignoring the more squalid horrors of the actual fighting up in the mountains. The media, the Indian official report on the war noted approvingly, "moulds national and international opinion and can be a potent force multiplier".[24] The harnessing of the media in the Kargil War would have long-term effects that were not always in India's interests. Any government that subsequently wanted to engage in subtle diplomacy with Pakistan would find itself called out by a media baying for conflict. In the short run, however, the media megaphone worked to India's advantage. Meanwhile, Indian ambassadors briefed foreign governments to win backing for the Indian view. Pakistan had started this war and in crossing the LoC breached its international agreements. Whatever mitigation Pakistan might claim—India had, after all, started the Siachen war in 1984—was lost in the noise.

Unprepared for the ferocity of the Indian response, Pakistan was caught short militarily, politically and diplomatically. The secrecy of the Kargil plan meant that not enough people had been consulted in advance to point out the weaknesses of its assumptions. Musharraf, by his own admission, had kept many of his own senior officers in the dark. At the May briefing given by Musharraf, a former army officer turned Minister of Kashmir Affairs, Major-General Majid Malik, had questioned the Kargil plans, according to Foreign Minister Aziz.[25] From a purely military perspective they made little sense—in Kargil, Pakistan had longer supply lines across more difficult terrain than India, which had access through the Srinagar-Leh road. Without fresh ammunition and supplies of food, the Pakistani troops would not be able to hold out indefinitely. The Indian official report reached a similar conclusion. "A number of former Army Chiefs of Staff and Director Generals of Military Operations were near unanimous in their opinion that a military intrusion on the scale attempted was totally unsustainable because of the lack of supportive infrastructure and was militarily irrational."[26]

Pakistan was also unlucky with the weather. An unusually mild winter meant that the Zoji-la, the pass between Kashmir and Ladakh, opened earlier than usual. That made it easier for India to bring in reinforcements and heavy artillery.[27] Pakistan still held the upper hand militarily. But that did not mean it could hold out until the following winter. And unlike India, it did not have the international community on its side. Since the foreign ministry had not been told in advance of the Kargil plans, Pakistan's ambassadors struggled to explain what was going on. Even Pakistan's hyper-nationalist media was confused. Journalists were not allowed near the war zone on the Pakistani side and, adding to the confusion, they continued to be told the operation had been carried out by the mujahideen rather than regular Pakistani troops.

Pakistan compounded its problems with nuclear braggadocio. Though it may not have initiated the conflict with its nuclear weapons in mind, it now turned to them to deter Indian retaliation and draw international attention to Kashmir. At the end of May, Foreign Secretary Shamsad Ahmad, the top civil servant in the foreign office and a man close to the security establishment, said Pakistan was willing to use "any weapon in our arsenal to defend our territorial integrity."[28] Prime Minister Sharif marked the May 28 anniversary of Pakistan's nuclear tests by saying that Pakistanis ''are confident for the first time in their history that in the eventuality of an armed attack they will be able to meet it on equal terms."[29] Most independent analysts have subsequently concluded that Pakistan's nuclear weapons were not fully operational by the time of the Kargil War,[30] an assertion also made by Musharraf[31] and echoed by Indian Army chief Malik.[32] Instead, what probably happened was that Pakistan dispersed its nuclear-capable missiles out of storage sites for defensive purposes. At the time, this was then misinterpreted in US intelligence reports as preparation for deployment.[33] The Pakistani rhetoric, however, combined with these intelligence reports, was enough to alarm the United States and other countries. The Pakistani bluster worked against it. There would now be even more pressure on Pakistan to withdraw troops to its side of the LoC.

The nuclear bluff was followed by an attempt by Pakistan to secure concessions diplomatically. Again it overreached. Foreign Minister Aziz was dispatched to Delhi in June to negotiate an end to the war. At a military briefing before he left, he was told he should offer talks but make no concessions on the military or ground situation. He should not even accept a ceasefire since that would make it easier for Indian Army vehicles to move on the Dras-Kargil road. Foreign Secretary Shamshad Ahmad also insisted there was no question of a Pakistani withdrawal, according to Aziz's account of the briefing. When asked about the risk of a wider war, Shamshad Ahmad "discounted that prospect because of our nuclear capacity," Aziz said. It was a view shared by some of the more hawkish members of Sharif's government. "We should stand firm, neither panic, nor apologise," Aziz quoted the Minister of Religious Affairs, Raja Zafarul Haq, as telling a cabinet meeting. "We are a nuclear power. It will not therefore be easy for India to take the risk of a full-scale war." Musharraf made one more demand of the foreign minister—he must continue to insist that the Pakistan Army was not involved and that the only intruders across the LoC were mujahideen. Pakistan, according to the negotiating position outlined to Aziz in his various meetings, could then offer to persuade the mujahideen to withdraw in return for a reasonable deadline given by India for resolving the Kashmir dispute.[34] On June 12, Aziz flew to Delhi with his hands tied behind his back.

His mission failed before it even started. A day before he landed, India released transcripts of intercepted conversations held in May between Musharraf, while he was on a visit to China, and his Chief of General Staff (CGS), Lt-Gen Mohammad Aziz Khan.[35] In the first conversation, on May 26, Aziz Khan told Musharraf that Pakistan would say Indian air strikes were hitting the Pakistani side of the LoC. That would give the impression it was Pakistan, rather than India, that was under attack. The two men also congratulated each other about their assumed success in bringing international attention to Kashmir, a long-standing Pakistani aim. "Today, for the last two hours, the BBC has been continuously reporting on the air strikes by India. Keep using this—let them keep dropping bombs," the CGS said. "As far as internationalisation is concerned, this is the fastest this has happened." The CGS also reassured Musharraf that Sharif was on board with the operation. In the second conversation on May 29, the CGS said he had told Sartaj Aziz to keep the door to talks open but give no commitment on the ground situation. The Director Generals of Military Operations (DGMOs) of the respective armies would then hold a "comprehensive deliberation" on the demarcation of the LoC. The comments in the transcripts were the clearest Pakistan would ever come to enunciating its objectives in the Kargil War. "Patently, what it wanted was to sit on the heights of Kargil, somehow hustle India into a ceasefire, which implicitly would be an acceptance of the intrusion, and to thereafter negotiate the LoC all over again," Foreign Minister Jaswant Singh complained later.[36] At a

news conference on June 11, Singh said the information in the transcripts "raises doubts about the brief that Minister Aziz carries and at
whose dictates he is actually working." There was more. Three days
earlier, Pakistan had handed over the bodies of six Indian soldiers who
had been taken prisoner in Kargil. An Indian post-mortem, Singh told
the press, "confirms that the soldiers were tortured and then shot at
close quarters."[37]

Singh went to the airport to meet Aziz feeling betrayed and angry
with Pakistan for so abusing the spirit of Lahore. When Aziz proposed
that the two countries agree a ceasefire, reopen the whole question of
the LoC and decide on a timeframe, his suggestions "sounded so irrelevant that I could scarcely hide my impatience", Singh recalled. All that
was left for the Pakistani foreign minister was to pay a brief courtesy
call to an "extremely emotional" Vajpayee, who with a choked voice
reproached Pakistan for starting a conflict at a time he had travelled to
Lahore with sincere hopes of lasting peace.[38]

* * *

By the second week of June, Indian troops had yet to win a single victory. The Indian Army was starved of funds for modernisation and
lacked equipment. "We shall fight with whatever we have," Indian Army
chief Malik told a briefing in June when asked about the severe shortages.[39] And what the Indian Army had was men. In a war fought in the
shadow of nuclear weapons, they flung themselves into frontal assaults
reminiscent of the Great War of 1914–1918. Since the Indian government was wary of escalating the conflict into a wider war, it insisted the
military did not cross the LoC. That meant the army could not attack
the Pakistani posts and their supply lines from the rear. Instead, Indian
troops had to struggle up the mountains towards the Pakistani posts
under a withering artillery onslaught. Civilians controlled the war and
let the military take the brunt. Since the Indian air force and artillery
were operating in close proximity to Indian troops, some would have
been killed too by friendly fire. In contrast to the romanticised image
of men plunging heroically into battle, some 70 to 80 per cent of the
casualties on both sides were due to long-range artillery fire, according
to one estimate.[40]

But the Pakistani troops were suffering badly too. They were running out of supplies and pummelled by Indian airstrikes and artillery.

In the Tololing sector, named after a mountain ridge above Dras, India deployed more than one hundred artillery pieces, mortars and rocket launchers to attack the Pakistani posts.[41] Since these dominated the road, the Indian Army had decided to give them priority. On June 13, Indian troops managed to overrun Tololing Top after a massive artillery barrage followed by five days of hand-to-hand fighting.[42] Men who in many cases spoke the same language and came from the same type of background killed each other intimately with guns, grenades and commando knives. Tololing Top was the first significant post to fall. It would require another week to complete the victory by taking an adjoining high position, Point 5140, less than two miles from Tololing Top.[43] India needed to move quickly since by September the Zoji-la would close and it would no longer be able to bring in reinforcements. Despite the capture of Tololing Top, pressure continued to build for an Indian attack across the LoC or international border.

On June 16, Indian National Security Adviser Brajesh Mishra told his American counterpart Sandy Berger that the government might have to let the army cross the border with Pakistan any day.[44] International anxiety about the war screeched up a gear. President Bill Clinton "worried, of course, that the Kargil War could go nuclear," according to Bruce Riedel, then his adviser on South Asia.[45] On June 18, Indian Army Chief Malik told his military commanders to "be prepared for escalation—sudden or gradual—along the LoC or the international border".[46] The escalation was averted when Indian troops captured Point 5140 on June 20 and gained enough of a foothold to start clearing out other posts. They also achieved another near simultaneous victory in a more remote sector further along the LoC.[47] Afterwards, Musharraf and his supporters would claim that Pakistan won the war militarily and lost it diplomatically. In reality, the military and diplomatic tides turned against Pakistan in tandem.

On the same day that saw the capture of Point 5140, the Group of Eight industrialised nations issued a statement calling for full respect of the LoC. President Clinton also authorised US officials to tell the media Washington had no doubt the intruders were Pakistani regulars and not mujahideen. "Pakistan is the instigator here," the *Washington Post* quoted a senior administration official as saying.[48] For the first time in a Pakistan-India conflict, the United States was publicly siding with

India. General Anthony Zinni, commander of the US Central Command, visited Islamabad on June 24–25 to persuade Pakistan to withdraw its troops. According to Zinni's account of the talks, Pakistan recognised the need to defuse the crisis but needed a face-saving formula. He offered a meeting between Sharif and Clinton, ending the isolation imposed on Pakistan over its nuclear tests.[49] Delhi, ever brittle about outside inference in the region, played down the American involvement, while quietly taking advantage of it. After Zinni's talks in Islamabad, Deputy Assistant Secretary of State Gibson Lanpher, who had accompanied him to Pakistan, went to Delhi to brief the Indian government on the discussions.[50]

Before taking up the American offer, Sharif turned for help to Pakistan's long-standing ally, China. He arrived in Beijing on June 28. But China delivered to Sharif a message that sounded remarkably similar to the one given by the Americans—Pakistan must pull back its troops. It turned out Beijing was in regular contact with Washington to make sure the Chinese and American positions were aligned.[51] China even went as far as issuing a public statement calling for India and Pakistan "to respect the Line of Control in Kashmir and resume negotiations at an early date in accordance with the spirit of the Lahore declaration."[52] Sharif telephoned Clinton and asked for a meeting. It was set for July 4, US Independence Day. Shortly before that meeting, India won another military victory, securing a toehold on Tiger Hill, the mountain visible from Dras. Pakistan's military position was weakening rapidly. According to Foreign Minister Aziz, Musharraf met Sharif at the airport just before he left for Washington and "was much quieter than he was in earlier meetings." Aziz, who was accompanying Sharif to Washington, said Musharraf generally agreed with the prime minister's objectives in Washington: Pakistan should try to obtain the best possible deal but be ready to withdraw.[53]

Clinton met Sharif at Blair House, the official guesthouse of the American presidency. Clinton's approach to the meeting was heavily influenced by the US intelligence suggesting, probably wrongly, that Pakistan was preparing its nuclear forces for deployment. Clinton told Sharif that if he would announce the immediate withdrawal of all Pakistani forces, the United States would support resumption of peace talks between India and Pakistan and urge India to allow the withdrawal to proceed. If not, America would denounce Pakistan for starting a war that could end in nuclear disaster. On top of that, Clinton would blame Pakistan for assisting Osama bin Laden and other terrorists.[54] Sharif was, in the words of his foreign minister, "baffled" by Clinton's strong opening language on the threat of nuclear war. He asked Clinton to persuade India to be more flexible and for help in addressing the Kashmir dispute.[55] Clinton, however, was already fully aware of quite how far India would be ready to compromise. He had kept Vajpayee briefed on US discussions with Pakistan, at one stage inviting him to join the meeting in Washington. Vajpayee had declined the invitation— a three-way summit with India and Pakistan submitting to American mediation would have been anathema to Delhi. But even as the Blair House talks were underway, US National Security Adviser Sandy Berger relayed its progress by phone to his Indian counterpart Brajesh Mishra, going as far—according to an Indian account—as to discuss the wording of the joint US-Pakistan statement to be issued at its conclusion.[56] By the time Sharif and Clinton emerged from their meeting, Pakistan had promised to withdraw. The only concession Sharif extracted was that Clinton pledged to take "a personal interest" in talks between India and Pakistan, including over Kashmir, once the sanctity of the LoC had been restored.

Pakistan was unable even to secure a formal ceasefire to allow its troops to withdraw in safety. The armies of India and Pakistan agreed an informal sector-by-sector ceasefire that quickly broke down. Fighting continued until July 26 when India officially declared the LoC was restored. By the time the war was over, India had lost 473 men and 1,060 were wounded. Among the wounded, just over half had splinter and shell wounds, highlighting the powerful role played by artillery. Twenty-one per cent had gunshot wounds and the remainder had burns, fractures and frostbite, reflecting the multiple risks of operating in the high mountains.[57] Pakistan, still clinging to the fiction that only mujahideen were involved, never gave exact casualty numbers. Indian estimates allege that more than 700 Pakistanis were killed.[58] Other assessments suggest that somewhere between 400 and 500 Pakistani troops died.[59] For all its bravado, Pakistan had failed to secure even one inch of land.

* * *

Less than a year after declaring itself a nuclear-armed power, Pakistan had been humiliated diplomatically and militarily. Far from improving the prospects for a settlement in Kashmir, the war had prompted the outside world to uphold the status quo by affirming the sanctity of the LoC. Clinton's promise to take "a personal interest" in Kashmir offered the only glimmer of hope. That too would be squandered in the years ahead. The opportunity for peace with India created by Vajpayee's visit to Lahore had been lost. So too was any possibility of a settlement of the Siachen war. After Kargil the Indian Army would resist any suggestion of a withdrawal from the world's highest battlefield for fear Pakistani troops would take over its vacated positions. Pakistan also gained a reputation internationally as an unstable country ready to use nuclear blackmail to back up a reckless land-grab. India would go on to win recognition of its status as a nuclear-armed power, its reputation enhanced by its restraint in Kargil.

Rather than confront the miscalculations that had led to the war, Pakistan retreated into obfuscation, domestic recriminations and the familiar cloak of victimhood. It continued to cling to the fiction that the intruders in Kargil had been mujahideen, sparing the military from any real examination. "It is true," Prime Minister Sharif said on national television on July 12, "that the mujahideen were present on several Kargil heights but it was part of their long freedom struggle... Once the mujahideen had succeeded in drawing world attention to Kashmir, it is understandable that they would wish to disengage."[60] Not satisfied with Sharif's attempt to cover up for an ill-conceived war which he had initiated, Musharraf began to blame him for agreeing to pull back Pakistani troops without extracting concessions from India. Army sympathisers in the media were tapped to run criticism of the withdrawal. One described it as "a unilateral strip-tease".[61] Sharif's meeting with Clinton, originally conceived as a face-saver, was rewritten as a panicked dash to Washington. "Had the Kargil tactical operation been allowed to sustain itself for a few more weeks (till the end of August 1999) most military analysts I spoke to felt it would have led to a Pakistan-India dialogue—if Sharif had not dashed to Washington and given in to US pressure," said Mazari in her authorised account.[62] The withdrawal was also portrayed as a betrayal by America. After the September 11 attacks brought the United States into Afghanistan, it became standard fare in Pakistan to blame the US-led war for all its problems. But that readiness to blame Washington for Pakistan's own actions had taken hold long before the first American soldier set foot in Afghanistan. As the army retrieved its position domestically and deflected the blame for the Kargil War onto the civilian government and a collusion between Washington and Delhi, Pakistan became a prisoner of its own propaganda. Defeat at Kargil gave jihadi groups one more reason to stoke up outrage against the United States and India, using this as a powerful recruiting tool. Yet in an early warning of the duality that would see Pakistan both supporting jihadis while being attacked by them, Islamist militant groups blamed the Pakistani state for the withdrawal. No longer willing to trust the Pakistan Army to deliver on Kashmir, more and more would go their own way, a process accelerated after September 11, 2001.

In India, distrust of Pakistan was sharpened. That Pakistan had invited Vajpayee to Lahore with its preparations for Kargil in full swing seemed particularly treacherous. The initial promise that the nuclear tests might usher a new era of peace between India and Pakistan had been broken. Kargil had demonstrated it was possible to have a limited war under a nuclear umbrella and the Indian military slowly began to adjust to the new era. Delhi, however, now had solid grounds for better relations with Washington. In the years ahead the relationship between India and the United States underwent a transformation that often left Pakistan out in the cold. Domestically, the BJP claimed Kargil as a huge victory, carefully avoiding charges that the crisis had developed on its watch and had been resolved by US intervention. It went on to win national elections, though it received a slightly smaller share of the popular vote than in the previous election.[63] Contrary to a popular Pakistani view, war with Pakistan was not an easy vote-winner with an Indian electorate more interested in domestic economic concerns.

The big impact domestically was in Pakistan. Strains between Musharraf and Sharif, although widely rumoured, were papered over initially—the two even went together on a short pilgrimage to Mecca in an apparent sign of unity. But relations between them were irredeemably soured. "It was clear that it had now sunk to the level of a blood feud, and only one would survive," the late Benazir Bhutto recalled.[64] Senior officers began to plan to take action should the prime minister try to sack Musharraf.[65] On October 12 1999, Sharif made his move, announcing the appointment of a new army chief while Musharraf was flying back from Sri Lanka. At first Pakistani authorities refused to let Musharraf's plane land, potentially forcing it to divert to India since it was too short of fuel to go anywhere else. "No one below the prime minister could give such a drastic order. Sacking an army chief is one thing, but hijacking his plane and sending it to India is… diabolical," Musharraf complained later.[66] Troops loyal to Musharraf then seized control of Karachi airport and his flight was allowed to land. The army secured television and radio stations in Islamabad, moved troops close to government buildings and arrested Sharif. The whole thing was over quickly and without bloodshed. Sharif, a prime minister who had been elected with a huge mandate just two years earlier, was led off in chains while Pakistanis distributed sweets in the street to celebrate the coup. A day after Musharraf's coup, Vajpayee, the victor of Kargil, was sworn in as prime minister for the third time.

3

THE GENERAL AND THE POET

FROM THE KARGIL WAR TO THE AGRA SUMMIT

In July 2001, President Musharraf flew to Delhi, the city of his birth, for peace talks with Prime Minister Vajpayee. The summit was to be held in Agra, home to the Taj Mahal, the Mughal monument to love. After the acrimony of the Kargil War and the hijacking of the Indian Airlines flight from Kathmandu to Kandahar later that year, it was meant to offer a fresh start. It would be the highest-level meeting between India and Pakistan since Vajpayee went to Lahore in February 1999. Though no one knew it at the time, it was also the last chance for peace before the September 11 attacks on the United States. The talks not only failed, but poisoned relations further. Vajpayee, regarding the invitation to visit India as an act of generosity, was hoping to lay the foundation for a long-term peace process. Musharraf was a man in a hurry, looking to overturn the status quo in Kashmir in a diplomatic version of Kargil, and return to Pakistan a hero. The talks brought together two men who were as different in personality as their countries were in ideology. A general and a poet.

* * *

Musharraf was a boy of four born into a middle-class family in Delhi when departing British colonial rulers divided the subcontinent into

India and Pakistan in 1947. His family were among the better-off North Indian Muslims known as "Mohajirs", who had formed the bedrock of the Pakistan movement, and did well from Partition. Musharraf's father was posted to Turkey as superintendent of the accounts department in the Pakistan embassy, and Musharraf later claimed his seven years living there as a boy gave him a lifelong admiration for the modernising zeal of Mustafa Kemal, or Ataturk, the father of the Turks. By the time Musharraf joined the army, starting out at the Pakistan Military Academy in 1961, he was already rather different from the others. It was not only that he was a Mohajir in an army led by Punjabi and Pashtun officers, or that he had spent his boyhood in Turkey. He also stood out for bravado bordering on arrogance. In his memoirs he boasted about going absent without leave on the eve of war with India in 1965 to visit his home in Karachi. Only the urgent need for him to serve in the subsequent fighting prevented him from being court-martialled.[1] After the war, he joined the Special Services Group (SSG), Pakistan's elite commandos, where he said—with characteristic lack of self-awareness—that he was seen by his seniors as "an exceptional leader, but also as a bluntly outspoken, ill-disciplined officer." He managed to rise through the ranks while losing none of his over-confidence. When he missed out on a promotion to which he felt entitled in 1997, he complained that the man who was appointed was chosen only because he had better social connections. "I was more of a commoner—a soldier's man at that—who was not at all into such social links and manoeuvring."[2] By the time Prime Minister Sharif was considering appointing him army chief in 1998, confidential army reports suggested that Musharraf, who was then third-in-line for promotion, was not fit for the post. Even the Inter-Services Intelligence (ISI) agency had recorded its doubts about him saying he was not suitable to become army chief since he was "quick in taking action and could be easily roused...Takes action without deep thought."[3] Sharif ignored those warnings and named him army chief in October 1998 precisely because he was an outsider, assuming he would not be able to rally fellow officers in a coup. Within a year Musharraf had lived up to his reputation for impetuosity by initiating the Kargil War and overthrowing Sharif in the October 1999 coup. By 2001, Musharraf was ready for an equally sudden dash for victory—he would make peace with India, settle Kashmir and confirm his position domestically.

In contrast to the abrasive general, Vajpayee was known for his inscrutable silences and ability to govern by consensus. He had inherited from his grandfather a love of Hindi and Sanskrit literature, and from his father, a respected poet in the city of Gwalior, a passion for poetry.[4] Older than Musharraf—Vajpayee was born in 1924 and became a member of parliament in 1957—he was a great orator who worked his way through the parliamentary system to become foreign minister in the late 1970s and prime minister by the 1990s. Yet though Vajpayee came to be seen in later life as a great statesman, he was a complex man, often seeking refuge in ambivalence. Vajpayee himself captured that ambivalence when writing about how his love of poetry sat ill with the requirements of politics. "Politics brooks no compromise with the freedom and the integrity of the creative voice," he wrote in the introduction to the English translation of his *21 Poems*. "Politics, on the other hand, often bows to the compulsion of circumstances and the common denominator of consensus."[5] He was by no means universally liked in India, largely because of his association with the Rashtriya Swayamsevak Sangh (RSS), a right-wing group that uses social and political activism to seek to turn the country into a "Hindu nation". Vajpayee's ambivalence had allowed him to present himself as a moderate even while he rose in the ranks of the Bharatiya Janata Party (BJP), the political party born out of the RSS. He was often seen as part of a tandem with the hardline Lal Krishna Advani, who became his home minister. By the time Vajpayee met Musharraf he had been sworn in three times as prime minister, surviving the rough-and-tumble of Indian politics to preside over a thirteen-day government, a thirteen-month government and, finally, a more stable one elected in 1999. He had ordered the nuclear tests, turned peacemaker in Lahore, and overseen the war in Kargil. He was also the first Indian leader fully to realise the potential for improved relations with the United States, ending the Cold War estrangement of the two democracies. As early as 1998, barely four months after the nuclear tests, Vajpayee had declared in a speech to the Asia Society in New York that India and the United States were "natural allies".[6] His government's cultivation of better relations with the United States had been rewarded with American backing during the Kargil War, and he now felt comfortable enough to invite Musharraf to India.

* * *

The groundwork for Agra was laid in March 2000, when President Bill Clinton visited South Asia. His trip showed how far the American pendulum was swinging towards India and away from its old Cold War ally, Pakistan. Clinton spent five days in India and—marking US displeasure at Musharraf's coup—visited Pakistan for only four or five hours. It was the first official visit by a US president in more than two decades and the people of India clamoured to meet Clinton wherever he went. "India is mesmerised by Clinton," the columnist and novelist Shobhaa De told the *New York Times*. "He's cast a spell. Even the sanest of people have lost their reason." When he addressed parliament, members gave him a standing ovation and jumped on chairs and clambered over benches for an opportunity to shake his hand.[7] He toured the Taj Mahal with his daughter Chelsea; admired the rising high-tech industry in the city of Hyderabad and visited villages where he was showered with flowers. He found time to meet with the parents and young widow of Rupin Katyal, who had been murdered on Indian Airlines Flight IC-814. In his address to parliament, he cited approvingly Vajpayee's words that India and the United States were "natural allies".[8] Out of the public eye, Clinton quietly urged India to hold talks with Pakistan, including over Kashmir, which he had labelled "the most dangerous place in the world".[9] In Pakistan—where in contrast to his rapturous welcome in Delhi, Clinton arrived to empty streets closed over security concerns—he pressed Musharraf to improve relations with India, restore democracy and convince the Taliban to force Osama bin Laden to leave Afghanistan.[10]

In meetings following up Clinton's visit, US diplomats continued to encourage India and Pakistan to talk. The US president's unequivocal backing of India during the Kargil War had opened doors in Delhi that had previously been closed to the United States. But progress on talks had been prevented by Musharraf's coup. Washington was now picking up the threads of Clinton's promise to take "a personal interest" in Kashmir, hoping to prevent a repeat of the Kargil crisis. At the time, although worries about al-Qaeda in Afghanistan had become nagging and insistent, these could not trump US concern about nuclear war. During a visit to Pakistan, US Under Secretary Tom Pickering told Musharraf that Kashmir was the issue "most likely to produce a catastrophe in the near term", according to a declassified cable from the US embassy in Islamabad. "Pickering said he wanted to stress once again the point President Clinton had made during his visit. There was no military solution to the Kashmir problem. The only way to move the issue toward resolution was through dialogue."[11] India had taken steps to lower tensions within Kashmir by releasing separatist leaders from detention, and the United States prodded Pakistan to reciprocate by reducing firing along the Line of Control and militant infiltration into Kashmir. It promised that if Pakistan acted it would press India for a return to dialogue. Notably, according to the declassified cable, Pickering told Musharraf that India had expressed a willingness to resume peace talks. The United States would be prepared to use its bilateral contacts with both countries to help move the process forward. "We would not be at the table, but perhaps 'standing by the door' or 'in the waiting room'," Pickering told Musharraf. The Indians, he said, were amenable to this.[12]

In November 2000, Vajpayee announced that Indian security forces would cease offensive operations against militants in Kashmir, starting on November 26.[13] In a message to his countrymen at the start of 2001, called his "musings from Kumarakom" after the name of the place in Kerala where he was spending his winter holiday, Vajpayee talked of seeking a lasting solution to the Kashmir problem. "Towards this end, we are prepared to recommence talks with Pakistan at any level, including the highest level, provided Islamabad gives sufficient proof of its preparedness to create a conducive atmosphere for a meaningful dialogue."[14]

Soon after that, in January 2001, a 7.7 magnitude earthquake hit western India, not far from where the solid lands of Gujarat state sink into the salt marshes leading into southern Pakistan. Some 20,000 people were killed. The political impact of the earthquake within India would be long lasting, bringing to the fore a new political player in the BJP. Narendra Modi was appointed to replace the BJP chief minister of Gujarat, who stood accused of failing to deal properly with the disaster. In the short-term, the earthquake provided a fleeting opportunity for warmth between the leaders of India and Pakistan. Pakistan sent emergency aid and Musharraf telephoned Vajpayee to offer sympathy. It was the first time the two men had spoken.

In May 2001, Vajpayee announced that he was inviting Musharraf to talks in India.[15] It was a bold move by the poet prime minister, whose last peace initiative had been rewarded with the Kargil War. The invitation would bring Musharraf out of isolation and raise his standing after his coup. It was made even as Pakistan continued to allow militant groups to flourish. Just over a year earlier, Masood Azhar—released during the Indian Airlines hijacking—had announced the creation of a new group, the Jaish-e-Mohammad. It had become one of the most active insurgent outfits in Kashmir, ramping up the violence with the introduction of suicide bombing. In April 2000, fourteen-year-old Afaaq Ahmad from Srinagar blew himself up outside the Indian Army headquarters in the city. In December that year, twenty-four-year-old British Muslim Mohammad Bilal from Birmingham carried out a near-identical attack in the same area. He was Britain's first suicide bomber.[16] In offering peace talks in the face of such violence, Vajpayee was taking a big political risk. The Indian Army, which unlike in Pakistan was kept at a safe distance from politics and diplomacy, was particularly disappointed to see the gains its soldiers had won in Kargil thrown away. It "was not the right thing to do," V. P. Malik, Indian Army Chief during the Kargil War, said in his memoirs. "Many senior officers from the armed forces, and almost all those who had lost their kith and kin in the Kargil War, were surprised and upset."[17]

Musharraf, however, misread the nature of the offer made by Vajpayee. As was so often the case with the generals in the Pakistan Army, he had become convinced by his own propaganda. By then, the official narrative about the Kargil War in Pakistan was that it had been forced to pull back its troops only because of the weakness of its civilian politicians and American perfidy. It may well have been beyond the bounds of Musharraf's imagination to recognise that India had won the Kargil War and Vajpayee's invitation was therefore intended as an act of generosity. He approached the summit with the same impatience and ideological myopia that had blinded him to the risks in Kargil. Convinced of the rightness of its position on Kashmir, the Pakistan Army had no interest in a slow-moving peace process with India of the kind that Vajpayee and Sharif had agreed on at Lahore. The Pakistani military suspected that any attempt to mend India-Pakistan relations slowly through confidence-building measures would favour the status quo, leaving India in control of most of the former princely state of Jammu and Kashmir. It thus sought to sweep away old peace deals, among them the 1972 Simla Agreement and the 1999 Lahore Declaration and start anew. In Kargil, Musharraf had tried and failed to redefine the terms of talks between Pakistan and India. He would now aim to achieve diplomatically at Agra what he had been unable to win militarily at Kargil.

India, however, viewed the talks as an opportunity to return to the spirit of Lahore, not to sweep it away altogether. In that it had support from the Americans. Given that Musharraf had initiated the Kargil War, it was a chance to wipe the slate clean, an opportunity that was his to lose. Instead, he appeared to believe he could achieve with his own personal diplomacy concessions that neither war nor talks had been able to extract before. He claimed to have high hopes of Vajpayee, calling him "the only moderate...surrounded by hawks".[18] In June, he had himself sworn in as president—replacing the title of chief executive that he had used since the coup—apparently to enhance his credibility ahead of his meeting with Vajpayee. "Musharraf may believe that by becoming president before the summit he can get more from the Indians by reassuring them that he will be able to follow through on long-term commitments. As president he may also gain more domestic latitude to explore possible compromises on Kashmir with New Delhi," a US State Department intelligence brief noted.[19] He remained head of the army.

On July 14, 2001, Musharraf flew to Delhi for a visit that was to include a ceremonial welcome in the capital followed by summit talks in Agra. On his way home after what he expected to be successful talks, he was to visit the shrine of a Sufi saint at Ajmer Sharif in Rajasthan. The schedule would be a mix of sentimentality and hard-nosed power—the kind that typically generated a great deal of irrational exuberance in India and Pakistan. But as might have been predicted from the outset, a breakthrough was simply out of the question.

* * *

From the moment he stepped off the plane in a white *sherwani*, accompanied by his wife Sehba, Musharraf was followed everywhere by television cameras. The Indian government quite literally rolled out the red carpet for him, providing all the pomp and ceremony of a state visit against the backdrop of the imperial capital buildings built by the

British. Musharraf paid tribute to Mahatma Mohandas Gandhi at the memorial marking the spot of his 1948 cremation and travelled into the heart of Old Delhi to visit the place of his birth, a grand old *haveli* arranged around a central courtyard that had belonged to his great-grandfather.[20] By the time Musharraf visited the Nehrvali Haveli, the old Muslim quarter where he was born had become a run-down, congested ghetto. Many of the Muslim elite who occupied a part of the city once known for its elegance, culture, poetry and learning had left at Partition. Eight families had moved into Musharraf's ancestral home, and a massive clean-up before his arrival had failed to dent an overriding impression of squalor and overcrowding.[21] Any disappointment he might have felt was quickly covered over by the packed schedule of the official welcome. As the monsoon rains swept over Delhi, he was treated to a state banquet at Rashtrapati Bhavan, the official home of the president of India, built by the British as a residence for the viceroy. President K.R. Narayanan called him "one of Delhi's most distinguished sons" and urged India and Pakistan to build on the spirit of peace agreed upon in Lahore.[22]

Out of the public eye, however, deep divisions were emerging. Indian Home Minister Advani, whose family had fled Pakistan at Partition, challenged Musharraf as soon as the two men met by asking him to sign an extradition treaty with India. Even before this was signed, Advani said, Musharraf should hand over Dawood Ibrahim, a gangster who was the main suspect in 1993 bombings in Mumbai, and who had taken shelter in Pakistan. It was an abrupt demand to make at such an introductory stage of the talks. As recounted in Advani's memoirs published in 2008, "Musharraf's face suddenly turned red and unfriendly. ... 'Now, Mr Advani, that is small tactics,' he remarked."[23] Musharraf in turn irritated his hosts by holding a meeting with political separatist leaders from Indian Kashmir—a gesture that suggested he intended to act as their representative in his talks with India. "A disappointed Vajpayee let it pass, but the seeds of a potentially bitter summit were sown," Indian strategic affairs analyst C. Raja Mohan wrote later.[24]

The delegations from the two countries then moved to Agra for their formal summit. As had happened in Delhi, the Indian government spared no effort to impress its guest during his stay in Agra. Musharraf and his wife were put up in the Amarvilas, a new hotel inspired by

Moghul architecture, where all rooms offered a view of the Taj Mahal. The choice of such a spectacular setting was classic Vajpayee showmanship. In offering access to the Taj Mahal, the Indian prime minister appeared to be acknowledging the loss felt by many Pakistanis who believed they had left some of the finest buildings of their Muslim Mughal inheritance behind at Partition. Musharraf, in his memoirs, duly recorded the "perfect symmetry and ethereal beauty" of the Taj Mahal and posed in front of it for photos with his wife.[25]

On the first day of the formal summit, July 15, both countries rehearsed their opening positions. Pakistan wanted progress on Kashmir while India insisted on an end to violence by Pakistan's Islamist militant proxies. Musharraf had hoped to be able to cut through all obstacles by holding direct talks with Vajpayee and reaching a one-on-one agreement with him. As a military ruler, he had apparently little concept of an elected prime minister who governed by consensus. Vajpayee had taken his senior ministers with him to Agra to advise on negotiations. A draft of a joint statement discussed between Foreign Minister Jaswant Singh and his Pakistani counterpart was reviewed at an informal meeting of the Indian Cabinet Committee on Security convened by Vajpayee on the evening of July 15. It was rejected, according to Advani, because it failed to mention cross-border terrorism, or Simla and Lahore. "Musharraf seemed allergic to these pacts, as they were associated with his political rivals. He probably wanted to signal to his people back home that he wanted to start Indo-Pak engagement on a clean slate, all on his own terms and bearing his exclusive imprint... Our rejection of the draft was communicated to the Pakistani side," Advani wrote in his memoirs.[26] The summit then quickly became one of reasserting positions. Briefing the press that evening, Indian Information and Broadcasting Minister Sushma Swaraj said the two sides were discussing terrorism and nuclear confidence-building measures but angered Pakistan by making no mention of Kashmir.[27]

Musharraf retaliated at a breakfast meeting the following morning with Indian newspaper editors, launching into a tirade about how Kashmir was the main issue confronting India and Pakistan. He suggested Pakistan's honour and dignity were at stake if he were to return home without addressing it. "So if India expects that I should ignore Kashmir then I better buy the Nehr vali Haveli back and stay there," he said. He stressed the importance of the United Nations resolutions calling for a plebiscite. Making matters worse in Indian eyes, Musharraf then tried to draw a parallel between the intrusion at Kargil and Indian support for Bengali separatists in 1971. He insisted Pakistan was not involved in stoking the Kashmiri "freedom struggle", yet also warned India that bloodshed would not stop unless the dispute were settled.[28] One of the editors who had a tape of the breakfast meeting then arranged to have it broadcast on television. To Indian ears, Musharraf, the architect of Kargil, was using the platform provided by the peace talks to threaten more violence. He had also gone behind Vajpayee's back, taking advantage of what was seen in India as a huge leap of faith by the Indian prime minister in inviting him, to broadcast his views on television. "Thus, we in the Indian delegation had the extraordinary spectacle of watching the Pakistani President articulate his rather combative views on Kashmir and cross-border terrorism, even as he was, at the very time, holding closed door talks with the Indian prime minister," Advani complained.[29]

For a short while, the two sides kept going, propelled by the momentum of the summit. Foreign Minister Singh met his counterpart in the morning of July 16 to work further on the joint statement. But Musharraf's televised meeting with Indian editors made negotiations over the draft even harder. "This was getting to be too heavy a load for any conference to carry," Singh wrote later. "General Musharraf seemed not to understand the debilitating impact Kargil had had on the scene and also did not grasp the essence of what Prime Minister Vajpayee had offered—a new beginning; instead he began playing to the stands." Musharraf, Singh noted, was a man more accustomed to military manoeuvres than diplomacy.[30] In an attempt to break the deadlock, he and Pakistan Foreign Minister Abdul Sattar worked with pencil and paper on a joint statement. Abdul Sattar went to consult Musharraf and returned with a few changes. As far as India was concerned, they still had some way to go to agree precise wording.[31]

By this point, Musharraf was becoming increasingly impatient. He wanted to leave that evening or the following morning for Pakistan via Ajmer Sharif. In his version of events, the joint statement was ready to be released; as a military ruler only he needed to approve it. "This declaration contained a condemnation of terrorism and recognition that the dispute over Kashmir needed resolution in order to improve bilateral relations," he said. "The draft, I thought, was very well worded, balanced and acceptable to both of us." A signing ceremony was scheduled for the afternoon in the hotel where Vajpayee was staying and where the talks were held. "Preparations in the hotel were complete, down to the table and two chairs where we would sit for the signing ceremony. The hotel staff and all the delegates were truly exuberant," Musharraf recalled. Musharraf returned to his own hotel to change into his *shalwar kameez* for the signing ceremony. But after barely an hour, he was told the Indians had still not accepted the draft. When he asked why, he was informed that the cabinet had rejected it. "Which cabinet?'" he asked. "There is no cabinet in Agra." Musharraf was convinced the agreement had been torpedoed by Advani. According to Musharraf, the two foreign ministers then went back for another two or three hours of intense negotiations over the wording of a joint statement. Pakistani diplomats returned with a new draft, which he approved. "I thought it carried the essence of what we wanted, except that now the language was different. They returned to the other hotel to make fair copies of the draft. I assured my wife, saying that the 'Agra declaration' would hit the headlines the next day."[32] But when the Indian foreign minister went to show the draft to Vajpayee and his cabinet colleagues, the collective view was that there was not enough emphasis on terrorism. They also baulked at an absence of references to Simla and Lahore.[33]

Musharraf was about to leave for the signing ceremony when he was told that the Indians had rejected the draft.[34] He also discovered he would not be allowed to talk to the media before his departure. After his breakfast meeting, India would not let him use Indian territory again to promote the Pakistani line. The summit was turning into a debacle. Musharraf decided to make one last personal appeal to Vajpayee. "I met Prime Minister Vajpayee at about eleven o'clock that night in an extremely sombre mood. I told him bluntly that there seemed to be someone above the two of us who had the power to overrule us," said Musharraf, in an apparent reference to Advani. "I also said that today both of us had been humiliated. He just sat there, speechless. I left abruptly, after thanking him in a brisk manner."[35] Afterwards when Foreign Minister Singh asked Vajpayee what had happened, he said he had listened and the general had talked. "This is an art at which Atal Bihari Vajpayee, so often and so disconcertingly to those unfamiliar to him, specialises."[36]

With the failure of the Agra summit, Musharraf lost the only gain achieved through the deaths of hundreds of Pakistani soldiers in the Kargil War—Clinton's promise to take a personal interest in Kashmir. It would be nearly three years before Pakistan and India resumed peace talks and by then Vajpayee was on his way out of office. In his impatience at Agra, Musharraf missed an opportunity to embark on a serious peace process with an Indian prime minister who, because of his backing by the Hindu right, had the political capital to deliver concessions. After arriving in India in such style, Musharraf left Agra with his wife in the dead of night, his departing car caught by the flashbulbs of the press pack. All that remained of the glitzy ceremonies and the hours of talks was a photo of Musharraf, casually dressed in a white short-sleeved shirt and trousers, sitting alone with his wife Sehba in front of the Taj Mahal.

4

THE ASSASSINS FROM AFAR

PAKISTAN AND AFGHANISTAN: STRATEGIC BLINDNESS AND STRATEGIC DEPTH

Three months before the Agra summit foundered over Musharraf's insistence on the centrality of Kashmir, Ahmad Shah Massoud had spoken at the European Parliament and delivered a stark warning. His message was directed at US President George W. Bush. "If peace is not restored to Afghanistan, if he does not help the Afghan people, there is no doubt the problems of Afghanistan will affect the United States and many other countries."[1] Massoud, whose Northern Alliance represented the last real resistance to the Taliban, wanted the world to wake up to the threat not from the dispute over Kashmir, but from Afghanistan. By then the jihadi enterprise that had begun with the insurgency against the Soviet occupation had spun out of control. Foreign fighters fed like parasites on the civil war that followed the Soviet withdrawal, growing bigger and more extreme. They survived thanks to the shelter provided by the Pakistan-backed Taliban. Massoud, on his first foreign trip to the West, appealed for greater pressure on Pakistan to end support for the Taliban and force the foreign jihadis to leave. "Behind the whole situation in Afghanistan, in all those extremist groups, there is the regime in Pakistan," he said.[2]

While Massoud was in Europe, France's leading investigating magistrate in charge of counter-terrorism was visiting the United States and also trying to warn the Americans about the jihadi threat. France had faced a string of attacks in the mid-1990s and was one of the first countries to recognise the dangers of a new type of terrorism birthed in Afghanistan and spreading across the world. French investigating magistrate Jean-Louis Bruguière came away from his trip frustrated. Barring a few officials, the Americans had yet to grasp fully the dangers of an Afghan-based nihilistic jihadi movement with adherents around the world. "At the time the Americans had a weak understanding of the threat from radical Islamism," Bruguière recalled. "But in France we were very worried."[3]

India was worried too, seared by the humiliation of the Kathmandu to Kandahar hijacking at the end of 1999. Along with Russia and Iran, it quietly provided help to Massoud's Northern Alliance. There was little more it could do unless Pakistan could be forced to change course.

In the eyes of the Pakistani military, however, Afghanistan was a mere adjunct in its confrontation with India. It would provide "strategic depth" in a war, theoretically giving the Pakistan Army room for manoeuvre in the event of an Indian attack. It was also useful as a base for training Islamist militants to fight India in Kashmir. Pakistan dismissed the international jihadis as either an unfortunate by-product of Taliban rule, or occasional ally. Yet just as it had done in Kargil, it overreached. It parried US-led demands to force the Taliban to expel Osama bin Laden. It failed to change course even when it became clear that it had lost control of many of the foreign jihadis in Afghanistan. The Inter-Services Intelligence (ISI) did not have the range to monitor their growing global networks. By continuing to play with fire, Pakistan would lose Afghanistan as surely as Kargil had lost it Kashmir.

On September 9, 2001, Massoud became a victim of the same jihadis he had warned about at the European Parliament. The assassins sent to kill him were arranged through the same networks that so worried Bruguière and were linked to cells operating in France and Belgium. They travelled through Pakistan into Afghanistan. Massoud was rushed, wounded, to an Indian-run hospital, but died on the way. Two days later, Afghanistan became the launch-pad for one of the most disruptive acts of terrorism in history.

* * *

Afghanistan has always played a role in South Asia that is disproportionate to its size. Before European colonial rulers arrived by sea, invaders came from the north-west. Central Asian ruler Babur used his base in Kabul to launch an invasion of India in the sixteenth century and establish the Mughal Empire. By the eighteenth century, with the Mughal Empire going into decline, another invasion from Afghanistan paved the way for British rule. The Afghan king, Ahmad Shah Durrani, led a huge army into northern India to challenge the rising power of the Hindu Maratha confederacy. In 1761, he defeated the Marathas on the plains north of Delhi in The Third Battle of Panipat, so weakening Indian forces that there would be no united military opposition to the recently arrived British traders from the East India Company.

Afghanistan's outsized historical role was obscured by the British, who deliberately relegated it to the sidelines of their empire. After two disastrous invasions in the nineteenth century to keep Tsarist Russia at bay, Britain decided it was better to manage Afghanistan at arm's length. Afghan rulers were browbeaten and bribed into accepting British tutelage on foreign policy, turning Afghanistan into a buffer state against Russia. An 1893 treaty between Britain and Afghanistan defined their spheres of influence on either side of an ill-defined border called the Durand Line. Afghanistan's inhabitants were deemed too wild to be managed. The British relegation of Afghanistan and its people to the shadows endured in Pakistan. With the country dazzled by its hopes of winning control of the Kashmir Valley, Pakistan's own disastrous policies in Afghanistan and their impact on Afghans themselves went unexamined.

As with so many of Pakistan's policies, its tortured approach to Afghanistan—in which it both encouraged instability there while also becoming a victim of it—had deep roots, going right back to its creation as a state. Pakistan in 1947 inherited from the British a colonial suspicion of Afghanistan but none of their clout. Afghanistan refused to recognise the border negotiated by the British, and initially even rejected Pakistan's very existence. It voted against its admission to the United Nations and demanded a new Pashtunistan to include the Pashtun populations of Afghanistan and Pakistan. Though Afghanistan was too weak to oppose the creation of Pakistan, it continued to dream of extending its territory as far as the Indus river. Pashtuns were the largest ethnic group in Afghanistan, though probably not a majority. An even larger number of Pashtuns lived on lands that became part of Pakistan. Historically, the Pashtuns living on either side of the border considered themselves one and the same people—indeed the identification of Afghanistan with the Pashtun was such that the words "Afghan" and "Pashtun" were treated as synonyms. On Pakistan's side of the Durand Line, one of the most popular Pashtun leaders, Abdul Ghaffar Khan—who became known as the Frontier Gandhi for leading non-violent opposition to British rule—had opposed Partition and was close to the Indian National Congress. When a referendum was held in the North West Frontier on accession to Pakistan, Ghaffar Khan and his supporters boycotted it, and the region was absorbed into the newly created Muslim state. Ghaffar Khan was jailed as a traitor; Pashtuns reconciled themselves to being part of the Pakistani state, and some went on to occupy senior positions in the army and bureaucracy. But the suspicion that Pashtuns might be disloyal to Pakistan lingered. Ghaffar Khan left orders that he be buried in the Afghan city of Jalalabad on his death in a symbol of Pashtun unity. Afghanistan also hosted exiles opposed to the Pakistani state, including Baloch and Pashtuns, aggravating Pakistan, which complained they were being used to destabilise it.

Faced with what it perceived to be the twin threats of Afghan irredentism and domestic dissent, Pakistan supported Islamists in Afghanistan to undermine ethnic Pashtun nationalism. When Afghan Islamist leaders fled to Pakistan in the turmoil that followed the overthrow of the Afghan king in 1973, they found an eager welcome. Pakistan had even more reason to back Islamist militants after a Communist government seized power in Kabul in 1978, followed a year later by the Soviet invasion of Afghanistan. The militants would be used not only to counter Pashtun nationalism, but also to fight a jihad against the Soviet Union, which was then close to India.

Pakistan found allies in the United States and Saudi Arabia, and to a lesser extent China, all keen to roll back the power of the Soviet Union. With their huge financial firepower, the United States and Saudi Arabia industrialised the jihad. They also provided space to General Muhammad Zia ul-Haq, who had seized power in a military coup in 1977, to run a campaign of Islamicisation inside Pakistan. Afterwards

Pakistan would complain it had been used by the United States against the Soviet Union. But Pakistan had backed Islamists in Afghanistan long before the Soviet invasion. It was Pakistan that decided to privilege the Islamist character of the anti-Soviet insurgency over Afghan nationalism. Zia demanded that Pakistan have sole authority over how the jihad should be run and used its control over US and Saudi-funded weapons to manipulate the mujahideen. The United States, believing the religious zeal of the Islamist militants made them natural opponents of the "godless" Russian communists, went along with the Pakistani approach with a naivety it would come to regret.

As the Soviet Union became bogged down in an unwinnable war, Pakistan worked to prevent the emergence of a united Afghan resistance that might threaten its interests, encouraging divisions between Afghan insurgent leaders based in the Pakistani city of Peshawar. Ultimately this meant there would be no united front to take over after the Soviet withdrawal, condemning Afghanistan to decades of instability. "Pakistan used the Afghans as tools in their hands, and if there was something successful in Afghanistan, they destroyed it," said Mustafa Hamid, one of the first Arabs to join the jihad in Afghanistan, in a book he co-authored with Australian academic Leah Farrall.[4] The anti-Soviet jihad also encouraged an influx of Arab volunteers, who brought with them the grievances of the Arab world—from their resentment at repressive regimes at home to the humiliation of Israel's military victories in the Middle East. The Palestinian scholar Abdullah Azzam, who ran the Peshawar-based Maktab al-Khidamat, or Services Bureau, to welcome Arab recruits, provided an intellectual framework for transnational jihad. Pakistan's decision to encourage an Islamist resistance that was deliberately untethered from Afghan politics created a heady environment in which religious extremism could flourish. Among the foreign fighters were hardliners from the Salafi sect, the fundamentalist school of Sunni Islam that dominates in Saudi Arabia. The presence of hardline Salafi factions added to a virulent strain of Sunni sectarianism officially encouraged within Pakistan to counter any rise in Shi'ite power following Iran's 1979 Islamic Revolution.

When the Russians withdrew in 1989, they left behind a government led by President Mohammad Najibullah, a leftist who began to stress the Islamic character of his administration to win support across the country. Had Pakistan been willing to compromise with Najibullah, himself a Pashtun, stability might yet have returned to Afghanistan. But Pakistan, which liked to portray itself as a champion of Pashtun interests in Afghanistan, wanted the right kind of Pashtun, an Islamist rather than a nationalist. In yet another example of strategic blindness and overreach, it pushed the mujahideen to keep fighting so that it could force on Afghanistan an Islamist government of its choice. In 1989, Pakistan's Inter-Services Intelligence (ISI) prodded the mujahideen into trying to seize the city of Jalalabad in 1989. They failed and Najibullah's government hung on until 1992, even surviving the collapse of the Soviet Union, before giving way as Russian funding and supplies dried up.

Kabul was occupied by Ahmad Shah Massoud, who unlike the Peshawar-based insurgent leaders, had chosen a base inside Afghanistan during the anti-Soviet jihad, fighting the Russians from his ancestral home in the Panjshir Valley to the north. Najibullah took refuge in the United Nations compound in Kabul. A new government was set up with Massoud as defence minister and Burhanuddin Rabbani, a fellow Tajik and resistance leader, as president. Pakistan continued to push for a Pashtun Islamist regime in Kabul led by its then favourite, Gulbuddin Hekmatyar. Massoud proved unable to overcome Afghan factionalism to rally government supporters. In the bitter fighting that followed, including the destruction of much of Kabul, Pakistan backed Hekmatyar while India, Iran and Russia supported Rabbani and Massoud.[5]

It was in the ungoverned spaces opened up by the civil war that foreign jihadi groups in Afghanistan mutated into a form that would come to dominate the early decades of the twenty-first century. Azzam was assassinated in Peshawar in 1989, leaving a new generation of Arab fighters—many of whom arrived after the Soviet withdrawal—without a strong, older, leader. These were rebels with no occupying forces to fight, buoyed up with their belief that Islamist militants had brought down the Soviet Union. Cut off from their own countries and the needs of ordinary people, many coalesced into groups whose primary interest was violence. The Arab volunteers often despised the Sufi and Hanafi Islam followed by ordinary Afghans. Such was their dislocation from society that they found it easy to break free of Muslim religious traditions and adopt the *takfiri* ideology that thrives on declaring other Muslims apostates. They could get away with it because there were enough private financiers in the Gulf ready to fund them. "The jihad project has become privatised," wrote Hamid. "Jihad is no longer an activity carried out by the *ummah*; it is jihad led by the rich." Groups like al-Qaeda became akin to security contracting companies; they had no ties to the land or the local people, or respect for their elders. "Many Arabs thought the mission of jihad was martyrdom and to go to paradise, not to defend the land or even to win," said Hamid.[6] Among the Arabs caught up in the new extreme form of *takfiri* jihad in Afghanistan was the Jordanian Abu Musab al-Zarqawi, who would go on to found in Iraq the ruthless sectarian group that became the Islamic State.

In what would prove to be a catastrophic error of judgment for Pakistan, the ISI continued to believe it could manipulate the Islamist militants for its own purposes. It redirected some militants to the separatist insurgency that had erupted in Kashmir in the late 1980s, while allowing Arab jihadis to travel through Pakistan to Afghanistan. Belatedly, the United States began to put pressure on Pakistan, threatening in 1992 to include it on a US list of state sponsors of terrorism. That would have triggered severe sanctions and shut down support from the International Monetary Fund and World Bank. According to former Pakistan ambassador Husain Haqqani, who was working for Prime Minister Sharif at the time, Pakistan decided the United States was bluffing. "We have been covering our tracks so far and will cover them even better in the future," he quotes the ISI chief, Lieutenant-General Javed Nasir, as saying during a meeting with the prime minister, army chief and senior officials.[7] It was a turning point for the ISI and its management of Islamist proxies. Forced to ensure operational deniability, it loosened its links down the chain of command, losing in the process some of its control over the different militant groups.

At the same time, the jihad was expanding well beyond Afghanistan as the collapse of the Soviet Union created space for new conflicts from Bosnia to Chechnya to Algeria in which Islamists played a prominent role. The revolutionary political Islam that had found its strongest form in the 1979 revolution in Shi'ite Iran was now spreading through the Sunni world too. Iraq's invasion of Kuwait in 1990 and subsequent stationing of US troops in Saudi Arabia added to the ferment in the Muslim world. Pinioned by its focus on India, Pakistan failed to adapt to the globalisation of jihad. The ISI could not possibly keep track of the multiple fronts that were opening up.

One of these fronts, in Algeria, would set in motion the events that claimed the life of the man currently in charge in Kabul, Ahmad Shah Massoud. Algerians had been heavily involved in the jihad in Afghanistan. After a civil war erupted in Algeria in 1991–1992, they became one end of a multi-strand network that led back and forth from there to training camps in Afghanistan. These networks caught up along the way French and Belgian youth of North African descent, or looped through London to connect with young men radicalised by the Bosnian conflict. The Algerian civil war provided an early warning of the violence that would dominate the early years of the twenty-first century. On Christmas Eve 1994, gunmen from the Armed Islamic Group (GIA) hijacked an Air France plane due to fly from Algiers to Paris. It was diverted to the southern French city of Marseille and stormed by French commandos. Later, French police uncovered evidence suggesting the hijackers planned to crash the plane into the Eiffel Tower, a precursor to the September 11 attacks. A new form of terrorism was emerging, said former French investigating magistrate Bruguière, quite unlike that seen for example from some Palestinian groups with political aims and a clear command structure. "There was a change of scale, a change of landscape, a change of systems. After 1994–1995, like some viruses, all the groups were spreading. All the groups were scattered, very polymorphous, and even mutant," he said. "In fact the features of these groups look more like criminals than terrorists."[8] In France, they operated through diffuse networks in the North African diaspora, linked through men who happened to attend the same mosque, live in the same suburb, or to have met somewhere by chance. These networks helped new recruits travel to Afghanistan or were used to buy weapons, often from former Eastern Bloc countries, to be sent to Algeria. They provided false identity papers and raised money from petty crime. They found adherents among thieves, drug dealers and disaffected Muslims, some of whom would be sent to camps in Afghanistan for indoctrination and military training. In 1995, they attacked France directly, a bomb ripping through the underground station at St Michel in the heart of Paris. Eight people died and more than 150 were wounded. The attack was followed by eight more bombings or attempted bombings, although none were deadly. Many years later, men from similarly dispersed cells in France and Belgium, linked this time to the Islamic State (ISIS), would demonstrate how far the jihad had spun beyond its roots in Afghanistan when they attacked Paris and Brussels in November 2015 and March 2016 respectively.

The jihad was expanding far beyond anything the ISI had intended. Nonetheless, Pakistan continued to view Islamist militants as useful assets. By now, India had begun to get a measure of the insurgency in Kashmir, agreeing a ceasefire in 1994 with the original Kashmiri separatist group, the Jammu and Kashmir Liberation Front (JKLF). New fighters, trained by the ISI in Afghanistan, were sent by Pakistan to replace them.

In Afghanistan, the ISI tried to assert control by supporting the Afghan Taliban, men who came from rural areas around Kandahar. Their reputation for being incorruptible and readiness to restore order won them some initial popularity among Afghans tired of civil war. With Pakistani military aid and backing, the Taliban seized power in Kabul in 1996.[9] One of their first acts was to haul former president Najibullah out of the UN compound where he had taken refuge. They tortured him, dragged him through the streets and hanged him. Many Afghans believe he was killed on the orders of the ISI.[10] He is still revered as a hero by many Pashtuns. Massoud retreated to the Panjshir without giving battle, and then fought the Taliban from there. Pakistan recognised the Taliban soon after—the orders to do so, according to then Foreign Minister Sartaj Aziz, came directly to the foreign ministry from the head of the ISI.[11] Saudi Arabia and the United Arab Emirates followed suit. The rest of the world continued to recognise the Rabbani government.

The Taliban proved awkward allies, neither commanding enough support among Afghans to be dependable, nor dependent enough on Pakistan to be ordered around. Inside Afghanistan they were disliked by both urban Afghans and non-Pashtuns. They had grown up as refugees from the Soviet occupation in Pakistani Deobandi madrasas and their rural conservatism and hardline version of Sunni Islam imported from Pakistan sat uncomfortably among Afghans who, while religious, wore their faith rather more lightly. Though their leader Mullah Omar tried to assert his authority by declaring himself Amir ul-Momineen (Leader of the Faithful), the Taliban were incapable of building a sound political base. Their vulnerability to military attack by Massoud's forces left them dependent on battle-hardened foreign fighters, among them those sent by bin Laden, who also provided funding. Like previous rulers of Afghanistan, they refused to recognise the Durand Line. Mullah Omar in turn struggled to assert his authority over Arab jihadis whose presence in Afghanistan predated Taliban rule. Reluctant to turf out guests who had fought the Soviets and reliant on some of their fighters, the Taliban thought the presence of Arabs gave them religious legitimacy.

Afterwards, many Pakistanis would remember the period of Taliban rule in Afghanistan as a time of peace that had been interrupted by the US-led invasion after the September 11 attacks. It was typical of Pakistan's ideological blindness, short-termism and dismissal of the interests of ordinary Afghans that it believed the combustible mix of harsh Taliban rule, foreign jihadis and a resentful population could ever be stable. As the Pakistani leftist Eqbal Ahmad said of the Taliban after paying a visit to Afghanistan where music was banned, they had suppressed "an inheritance of a gentler past, an Islam not rigid like the one projected by contemporary Islamists." Then he quotes an old man in Jalalabad as saying, "They have grown in darkness, amidst death. They are angry and ignorant, and hate all things that bring joy and peace in life."[12]

Massoud represented the last serious resistance to the Taliban, acting as military commander of the Northern Alliance, a loose grouping of Afghan opposition fighters. He was a man who had already lived many lives, an ethnic Tajik from the Panjshir raised amongst the elite in Kabul. At college he had sided with the Islamists and fled to Pakistan in 1975, later returning to the Panjshir to fight the Red Army. During the fighting that erupted between different mujahideen factions after 1992, he had proved as ruthless as his Pakistan-backed rivals. Tens of thousands died or fled Kabul as Massoud and his opponents bombarded the city. But as he retreated once again towards the Panjshir in 1996, he sloughed off the brutal reputation he had acquired in Kabul, returning to the role of resistance hero. Photographs captured him standing against a setting sun, wearing fatigues and his trademark *pakol*, the Afghan flat woollen cap. The "Lion of Panjshir" was handsome enough too to become the perfect subject for hagiographies by foreign journalists who would collect their visas from a Northern Alliance office in neighbouring Tajikistan and fly in by helicopter to interview him.[13]

Massoud's Northern Alliance won support from Russia, Iran and India, all with different reasons for wanting to drive back the Taliban.

Even during the Soviet occupation, India had kept its options open by establishing links to the Afghan insurgents, mainly through prominent Afghan exiles in Europe and North America. Among those with whom India had built contacts was Massoud.[14] In 1997, its external intelligence agency, the Research and Analysis Wing (R&AW), negotiated with Tajikistan the right to set up a base at Farkhor on the Afghan border to help Massoud. It was India's first and only foreign base, used to send supplies to the Northern Alliance and service their Soviet-era helicopters. India also set up a field hospital at Farkhor to treat the Northern Alliance wounded.[15] However, India's actions there were rarely discussed in Delhi. Its support for Massoud and the Northern Alliance was an intelligence operation that was never opened up to parliamentary or public scrutiny.

By now the influence of the Arab jihadis was bleeding into Pakistan, finding a receptive audience among those nurtured by the ISI and complicating its task further in keeping them under control. Pakistani Islamist political and religious leaders warned the government not to become party to any American plans to capture or kill bin Laden.[16] Some of those who had taken Pakistan's support to fight in Kashmir were also turning against it, accusing it of using the Kashmir cause to thwart pressure for change at home. "Pakistan harbours many thousands of mujahideen as well as 'would be' ones…hence she must somehow contain this problem, but not by duress for fear of an uprising in her own territory," British jihadi Dhiren Barot wrote in a book about his experiences of fighting in Kashmir published in 1999. "Thus … we have been witnessing Islamabad offering and indeed seriously encouraging these young Muslim males to venture into the Occupied Territories (Indian Kashmir). At the same time as diverting the national threat in their own home front, the Pakistani authorities receive the services of these mostly sincere but unsuspecting young men free of charge."[17]

Some of the smarter and more farsighted Pakistani diplomats recognised the dangers brewing in Afghanistan and tried to end the fighting between the Taliban and the Northern Alliance—a move that might have made it easier to convince Mullah Omar to order the Arab foreign fighters to leave. The men sent to help the Taliban by bin Laden were amongst the best fighters, and Mullah Omar could not do without them as long as enmity with the Northern Alliance prevailed. "Somehow the Northern Alliance were too rigid and the Taliban were too rigid," said one former Pakistani diplomat who recalled flying by helicopter to visit Massoud and being struck by the sight of crate-loads of Iranian weapons marked "Death to America".[18] Some diplomats also tried to persuade the Taliban to agree a compromise on bin Laden, for example by handing him over to the Organisation of Islamic Cooperation (OIC). But the Taliban position hardened as they were shunned internationally over their ruthless imposition of a severe form of sharia and harsh treatment of women. Diplomats who had dealings with the Taliban describe an unworldly self-righteousness that made it impossible for them to grasp the threat of international terrorism. Desperate to have God on their side, they were convinced they were struggling to take over all of Afghanistan only because they were not pure enough.

Meanwhile, the Arab jihadi groups in Afghanistan—of which al-Qaeda was only one—were becoming more ambitious as they competed with each other for recruits and funding. One group based at the Khalden training camp—which ran separately from al-Qaeda—was involved in a bomb attack on the World Trade Center in New York in 1993.[19] In 1998, a young Algerian who had fled to Canada—part of an international network France was then trying to unravel—spent several months at Khalden. Ahmed Ressam was arrested in December 1999 and admitted plotting to blow up Los Angeles International Airport at the turn of the millennium.[20]

From his own camp, bin Laden renewed a call first made in 1996, declaring in February 1998 a "Jihad against Jews and Crusaders" and urging Muslims to kill Americans and their allies, both civilian and military, wherever they could.[21] On August 7, 1998, simultaneous truck bombings linked to al-Qaeda killed more than 200 people at the US embassies in Nairobi and Dar el Salaam, the vast majority of them local citizens. President Clinton retaliated by ordering cruise missile strikes on training camps the CIA had connected to bin Laden. They missed bin Laden, but US investigations established that one camp he had been expected to visit on the Pakistan-Afghan border had been built by Pakistani contractors and funded and hosted by the ISI. Since the camp was also linked to al-Qaeda, "then serious questions are raised by the early relationship between bin Laden and Pakistan's ISI," a US Defence Intelligence Agency assessment said.[22]

Yet still the ISI refused to change course, continuing to back the Taliban and allowing Arab, European and other volunteers to travel through Pakistan to reach jihadi training camps in Afghanistan. The civilian government led by Prime Minister Sharif was left helplessly fielding calls from those angered by its policies. A day after the embassy bombings, the Taliban captured the northern Afghan town of Mazar-e-Sharif from the Northern Alliance. In doing so they overran the Iranian consulate, killing nine Iranian nationals. "The negative side of the Taliban was now bulging rapidly," Pakistan Foreign Minister Sartaj Aziz recalled in his memoirs. "They were unable to pacify non-Pashtun areas of Afghanistan and were overly dependent on foreign fighters. The United States was firing cruise missiles at Afghanistan through Pakistani airspace, and Iran had moved thousands of troops to the Afghan border." Aziz added his voice to those urging the Taliban to persuade al-Qaeda to leave. "The response was always vague and non-committal."[23]

Soon afterwards, Aziz was called to a meeting with Prince Turki al-Faisal, Saudi Arabia's intelligence chief. Prince Turki had just visited Mullah Omar in Kandahar to remind him of an earlier pledge to force bin Laden to leave. Mullah Omar denied ever having made the promise and Prince Turki was enraged by the obduracy and rudeness of the Taliban leader, according to Aziz. He told the Pakistanis that Saudi Arabia would withdraw its envoy from Kabul and stop any further support for the Taliban. When Prince Turki left, Prime Minister Sharif continued the meeting to discuss with his ministers and the head of the ISI what to do. "We must review our entire relationship with the Taliban regime," Aziz quotes Sharif as saying. The prime minister asked Aziz to draw up a paper in consultation with the ISI on Pakistan's future relationship with the Taliban, and present it within two weeks. "The very next morning, Major General Parvez Masud, in-charge of the Afghan desk in ISI, appeared in my office without any appointment," Aziz recalled. His demand was one that Aziz said filled him with anguish. "Please persuade the prime minister to defer his decision to review Pakistan's relationship with the Taliban regime for some time," the major-general said. "After a long time we see the prospect of having a peaceful and friendly neighbour in Afghanistan, because the Taliban are expanding their influence. All other alternatives will be worse."[24]

The United States turned up the pressure. President Clinton tried to convince Sharif to use Pakistan's control over imports into Afghanistan to force the Taliban to expel bin Laden. According to the official report of the US commission set up to investigate the September 11 attacks, Sharif responded by suggesting Pakistani special forces might instead try to capture bin Laden themselves. Nothing happened.[25] Then came General Musharraf's October coup, followed by the December hijacking of the Indian Airlines flight. With the hijacking and release of Masood Azhar, the Pakistani security establishment was aligning itself closer to the jihadis even as the threat from them increased. British jihadi Dhiren Barot called the hijacking "a great landmark in the Kashmir jihad, one that resounded internationally". Its success, he said, showed how "it is activities such as these that often stand a great chance of reshaping world politics."[26]

In December 2000, the UN Security Council passed a resolution that put an embargo on arms supplies to the Taliban. The aim was to hit the Taliban in their battle against the Northern Alliance and to criminalise those who supplied them with arms and military advisers, as Pakistan had been doing. The resolution had no impact on Mullah Omar's willingness to expel bin Laden, or on Pakistani arms supplies to the Taliban.[27] The United States offered rewards to Afghan tribes as well as Massoud to capture bin Laden.[28] But it veered away from giving direct support to the Northern Alliance and embarking on an outright confrontation with Pakistan.

By the time the Clinton administration was preparing to leave office in late 2000, it was too late. Plans for the September 11 attacks were underway. So too were the arrangements for Massoud's death.[29] Given the character and pace of policy decisions made by President Clinton and Bush, "we do not believe they fully understood just how many people al-Qaeda might kill, and how soon it might do it," the US inquiry into the September 11 attacks concluded.[30]

* * *

In the spring of 2001, the Taliban dynamited the giant cliff-carved statues of the Bamyan Buddhas to show their contempt for idols, defying worldwide appeals to spare them. Massoud, on his first visit to the West, flew to Paris to appeal for support against the Taliban. Massoud was an obvious hero for the French, a man educated at a French lycée in Kabul and with a penchant for poetry, who reportedly admired

Victor Hugo and Charles de Gaulle.[31] After meeting the foreign minister in Paris, he addressed members of the European Parliament in the French city of Strasbourg. The Taliban, "would not even last a year" without Pakistan's support, he said.[32] "I am sure that if there were no interference by Pakistan and its soldiers, and along with that, none of bin Laden's foreign fighters, there would be no need for our forces; our own people would put an end to the Taliban."[33] He then went on to Brussels, home of NATO. "He did not ask for military aid," Belgian Foreign Minister Louis Michel said after meeting Massoud. "Above all he asked for pressure on the government of Pakistan. He paid particular attention to that and he was very insistent on the subject."[34]

While Massoud was in Europe, French investigating magistrate Bruguière was visiting the United States, where he had gone to testify at the trial of Ahmed Ressam, the Algerian who had plotted to bomb Los Angeles International Airport.[35] Ressam was convicted a day after Massoud made his appeal to the European Parliament.[36] But Bruguière's own testimony was disallowed, with Ressam's defence lawyer insisting French concerns about "a radical Islamist fundamentalist movement" were overblown.[37] In talks during that trip with US officials, Bruguière ran into the same scepticism. For years Americans had dismissed attacks on France as an Algerian response to French colonialism, blinding them to the new risk of transnational jihad. The United States realised too late that Ressam had known one of the intended hijackers in the September 11 attacks from Afghan training camps. Zacarias Moussaoui, a Frenchman of Moroccan origin, was arrested in the United States shortly before September 11 for breaking immigration laws. He had begun flight lessons to learn how to take off and land a Boeing 747.[38] "The US government took the threat seriously but not in the sense of mustering anything like the kind of effort that would be gathered to confront an enemy of the first, second or even third rank," the US official report into the September 11 attacks said.[39]

By then France was unravelling yet another network linked to men smuggling stolen passports they believed were being used for travel to Afghanistan.[40] The trail led to an al-Qaeda cell of Tunisians based in Brussels as well as to a group of North Africans living in France who sent recruits from Europe to Afghanistan via sympathisers in London. They were linked to a cell at the Omar mosque in Paris of the Salafist

Group for Preaching and Combat (GSPC), an insurgent group that would eventually go on to merge with al-Qaeda.[41] Three men from the network were arrested and eventually convicted in 2005.[42] But two more slipped the net and made it out to Afghanistan where they lived in an Arab camp near Jalalabad. One was a former student and occasional journalist named Dahmane Abd al-Sattar, who belonged to the cell of Tunisians living in Belgium. He, along with a man named Bouari el-Ouaer, were destined to carry out a task that al-Qaeda had deemed necessary to ingratiate itself with its Taliban hosts. They were to assassinate Massoud.

Al-Qaeda worked on its plans to kill Massoud "for a long time—maybe one year", according to Mustafa Hamid.[43] Al-Qaeda's connections in London helped the two men arrange cover as journalists.[44] At the time, much to France's irritation, British authorities were relatively lax about cracking down on Islamist networks in Britain. A man running an Islamic centre in London, the Islamic Observation Centre, provided a letter of introduction saying that the two men were volunteers for his organisation.[45] "The whole thing was organised from London," said Bruguière.[46]

Amrullah Saleh, an aide to Massoud who went on to head Afghanistan's NDS intelligence agency after 2001, said he believed the ISI helped them with visas and contacts within the Taliban. The Pakistanis, he said, knew the likelihood that Arabs posing as journalists might be working for al-Qaeda—they had been warned of this by their own ambassador to Kabul. "I am confident that the ISI knew the plan but didn't know the details," Saleh said.[47] Whether or not the ISI had advance knowledge of the plot, Pakistan had an interest in seeing the Taliban's main opponent killed. It was the same witting or unwitting "alliance of objectives" between al-Qaeda and Pakistani intelligence that had lurked behind the 1999 hijacking. Before the men left Jalalabad for training at a camp set up for the martyrs of al-Qaeda, Malika el-Aroud, Dahmane's wife and a Belgian-Moroccan, travelled to Afghanistan to join her husband. According to French police she brought with her equipment useful for building a bomb.[48] On her return to Europe, she was tried and acquitted of involvement in the plot to kill Massoud for lack of evidence. She went on to recruit French and Belgian volunteers for al-Qaeda and was convicted by a Belgian court in 2010.[49]

By mid-2001, the United States was enjoying its last full summer of peace under newly-installed President Bush, a man who had so little interest in foreign affairs that he had been unable to name the leaders of India or Pakistan when asked to do so during his campaign.[50] Pakistan and India held their failed summit in Agra. On his return home, Musharraf was hailed as a hero for standing up to India and stressing the centrality of Kashmir.[51] Few in Pakistan looked westward to Afghanistan, where Egyptian militant Ayman al-Zawahri was integrating his own band of followers into the Saudi-born bin Laden's al-Qaeda. The Bush administration pressed the Taliban to turn bin Laden "over to a country where he could face justice" and warned them that they would be held responsible for any al-Qaeda attack on US interests.[52] The Taliban refused, naively assuming by some accounts, that al-Qaeda would not so abuse their hospitality as to launch an attack that would bring American vengeance to Afghanistan.[53]

By then, the preparations for the September 11 attack were in place as were the plans for killing Massoud. American intelligence was picking up increasingly loud chatter that a major terrorist attack was imminent—as CIA director George Tenet told the US inquiry, "the system was blinking red". But the relatively new administration was still not sure what action to take. It refused to back Massoud overtly against the Taliban, believing it first must find some Pashtun allies to balance his Tajik-dominated Northern Alliance. Nor was it ready to confront Pakistan and break diplomatic relations. Militarily, it focused on a new mechanism for killing bin Laden: it had already developed surveillance drones and was now looking for a way to arm them.[54]

The United States piled more pressure onto Pakistan, with US Assistant Secretary of State Christina Rocca visiting Islamabad in early August to seek progress, among other issues, on persuading the Taliban to expel bin Laden. A briefing prepared for Rocca by the US embassy in Islamabad warned of likely Pakistani resistance, born out of what it called its "debilitating confrontation with India fuelled by its obsessive focus on Kashmir". A declassified cable summarising the anticipated Pakistani arguments is remarkable in highlighting the consistency of Pakistan's position, one that endured for years after the September 11 attacks. Pakistan would insist, the cable said, that it needed "a friendly government in Kabul". Pakistanis would argue that bin Laden was a burden to everyone, but should not control American policy on Afghanistan. Instead, Pakistan would argue, the best way to protect US interests, would be to engage the Taliban rather than isolate them. The briefing advised Rocca to provide reassurance of continued American commitment and interest in Pakistan to assuage Pakistani worries about the emerging warmth in the US relationship with India.[55]

In early August, Massoud gave one of his last interviews. He accused Pakistan of following a divide and rule strategy to keep Afghanistan permanently weakened. Not only was it favouring Islamist Pashtuns to suppress ethnic nationalism, it also avoided giving support to educated Pashtuns who might challenge Pakistan. The uneducated Taliban, steeped in Islamist fundamentalism and internationally isolated, were more useful clients. The Taliban's choice to describe Afghanistan as "an Emirate", he said, suited Pakistan since it defined it as a place ruled by a powerful, authoritarian emir who could more easily be managed, than one democratically representing the Afghan people. The old emirs of Afghanistan, he noted, far from being independent, were dependent on British aid and support. Pakistan similarly saw the Taliban as a dependent client. "In this way, they endeavour to subordinate Afghanistan culturally, politically and economically to Pakistan."[56] That same month, the two assassins arrived on the pretext of seeking an interview. But their access to Massoud was repeatedly delayed as he busied himself with countering a new Taliban offensive. Many would subsequently believe the timing of Massoud's assassination had been carefully planned to happen just before the September 11 attacks. But both were subject to too many delays and unpredictable interruptions to have been coordinated. "The timing was a coincidence," said a former senior Indian official with close knowledge of Afghanistan.[57] The two assassins had to wait for three or four weeks before Massoud was free.

On September 8 Massoud worked through the night, poring over maps to help one of his commanders beat back the Taliban offensive.[58] Then he spent a few hours with Masood Khalili, the Northern Alliance's ambassador to India who was visiting. They recited a poem by the fourteenth-century Persian Sufi poet Hafiz.[59] After a brief sleep Massoud agreed to give an interview to the two assassins on September 9. They had a TV camera, but no one thought to inspect it. The two journalists were ushered into a room where Massoud sat alongside

Khalili. They chatted while Ouaer, the cameraman, set up his tripod with the lens aimed at Massoud's chest. When Ouaer switched on the camera, it exploded, and Ouaer detonated other explosives strapped around his waist. When Khalili came to, he noticed the smell. Everything was smouldering. Ouaer's body, half-cut in two by his suicide belt, had been flung to the end of the room. Dahmane had escaped, but as he ran away he was killed by Massoud's bodyguards.[60] Massoud was horribly wounded but still alive. His men rushed him to a helicopter for the short flight to the Indian field hospital in Tajikistan, but he died on the way. His men tried at first to keep his death a secret to prevent his supporters becoming so demoralised that their positions would be overrun by the Taliban. But rumours began to leak out. Indian, Russian and Iranian intelligence already knew. Two days after Massoud's assassins struck, the whole world would discover how far the jihad in Afghanistan had spun out of control.

5

"SOMEBODY'S GOING TO PAY"

FROM THE SEPTEMBER 11 ATTACKS TO THE END OF 2001

General Musharraf was inspecting work at the gardens of the mausoleum of the country's founder, Mohammad Ali Jinnah, in Karachi when American Airlines Flight 11 crashed into the North Tower of the World Trade Center. Initial reports given to him by his military secretary suggested only a small plane had been involved. By his own account, he assumed it was an accident, but retained a nagging worry. The World Trade Center had been bombed in 1993, killing six people. The bomber, Ramzi Yousef, had fled to Pakistan before being arrested by Pakistani security services. Musharraf went on to a meeting with his Karachi Corps Commander. He was interrupted only after United Airlines Flight 175 hit the South Tower. As he watched the catastrophe unfold on CNN, he was already thinking about how Pakistan would manage the backlash. The United States would react "like a wounded bear", he recounted in his memoirs. "If the perpetrator turned out to be al-Qaeda, then that wounded bear would come charging straight towards us."[1]

In India, National Security Adviser Brajesh Mishra was holding talks with his Israeli counterpart that day on a bilateral counter-terrorism agreement. Uzi Dayan had slipped without fanfare into Delhi. The Indian-Israeli relationship was not yet so warm that they proclaimed it too publicly. Dayan left the talks to visit the US embassy, smoothing the way in what was becoming a rising convergence of interests between the United States, India and Israel in the face of Islamist militant violence. "I wanted the Americans to know I am in Delhi. I wanted the Indians to know I am kind of coordinating with the Americans," he said.[2] It was while he was visiting US ambassador Robert Blackwill that the Twin Towers were hit. He later returned to talks with Mishra where they watched events in New York and Washington on an old television. They were meeting in Hyderabad House, once designed as a palace for the Nizam of Hyderabad and now used by the government for meetings with visiting dignitaries. Its equipment had never been properly modernised. Though it was a near cloudless day in the eastern United States, the picture seen by two of the most powerful men in Israel and India was shaky and grainy.[3]

In New York, thousands of civilians had been inside the 110-storey Twin Towers when the planes hit. Hundreds were killed when American Airlines Flight 11 ploughed into the upper portion of the North Tower, exploding into a huge fireball that left those on higher floors trapped and unable to escape. More died when United Airlines Flight 175 crashed into the South Tower seventeen minutes later. The South Tower collapsed, killing all those inside along with others in the concourse below. Those still trapped in the North Tower survived for another twenty-nine minutes, making desperate phone calls begging for help. Then the North Tower collapsed. Another hijacked plane, American Airlines Flight 77, ploughed into the Pentagon. A fourth, United Airlines Flight 93, crashed in an empty field in Pennsylvania after passengers tried to overpower the hijackers.[4] A total of 2,977 people were killed in the deadliest act of terrorism in history.

President Bush was sitting in a classroom during a visit to a school in Florida when an aide told him about the second plane crashing into the South Tower. He carried on reading to the children, hoping to convey an impression of calm.[5] Bush heard about the plane crashing into the Pentagon while being driven from the school to the airport. He boarded Air Force One and called Vice President Dick Cheney. "Sounds like we have a minor war going on here," Bush told Cheney, according to notes of the call. "We're at war…somebody's going to pay."[6] That evening, Bush addressed the American people, promising to hunt down those behind the attacks. "We will make no distinction between the terrorists who committed these acts and those who harbour them," he said.[7]

Within days, the United States reversed its swing towards India and turned for help to Pakistan, a country that in Delhi's eyes fitted rather precisely Bush's description of a place that harboured terrorists. It abandoned its commitment to democracy by relying on a military ruler to execute a U-turn in Pakistan's policies on Afghanistan. It turned a blind eye to Pakistan's continued use of proxies against India in return for help against the Taliban and al-Qaeda, a Faustian bargain that angered India all the more. In its rush to respond to the September 11 attacks, the United States embarked on a toxic co-dependency with Pakistan that led to the longest war in its history.

Years later, the world's view of the September 11 attacks and their aftermath would give way to the casual certainties of politics, ideology and nationalism. Some would accuse the United States of unleashing the post 9/11 wars out of vengeance and an imperial desire to reorder the world. Others insisted it should have tried harder to convince the Taliban to expel bin Laden before starting the war in Afghanistan, or said its decision to turn to Pakistan as its main ally doomed the entire enterprise from the beginning. Since Pakistan was the cause of the jihadi problem in the region, it could not also be the solution. Another version claims the United States might have succeeded in Afghanistan had it not diverted its attention almost immediately to Iraq. Those arguments will run and run, becoming more simplistic over the years as younger generations forget the enormity of the fear and grief many Americans felt that day.

As far as India and Pakistan were concerned, however, what was remarkable was how little changed. Pakistan made just enough concessions to dodge the American wounded bear while continuing with its old policies of supporting Islamist militant proxies. It missed a historic opportunity to change course. Though it would subsequently blame the US-led war in Afghanistan for its problems, the tide had begun to turn against Pakistan long before the September 11 attacks. The jihad had spun out of control. The 1991 collapse of the Soviet Union had prompted new international realignments, displacing Pakistan's old Cold War assumptions. With its economic liberalisation and warming ties with the United States, it was India that caught the tide. Though not immediately obvious in 2001, India was on course to win the Great South Asian War even as Pakistan clung to its failed and outdated policies.

* * *

In the immediate aftermath of the September 11 attacks, India assumed the United States had finally woken up to the threat of terrorism from Pakistan. Breaking with its politics of non-alignment that prohibited foreign troops on Indian soil, it offered the Americans the use of its military bases.[8] Prime Minister Vajpayee wrote to Bush to say that, "we stand ready to cooperate with you in the investigations into this crime and to strengthen our partnership in leading international efforts to ensure that terrorism never succeeds again." Foreign Minister Jaswant Singh said Delhi was ready to provide logistical help or act as a staging ground for a US military strike.[9] The Indian Cabinet Committee on Security agreed "to offer all cooperation and facilities for any US military operation".[10] Although the Americans would still have to go through Pakistan to reach Afghanistan overland, even with the use of Indian military bases, it nonetheless served as an important rhetorical marker. The "natural allies", as President Clinton had called them, were India and the United States.

In the short-term, Pakistan turned itself into what, effectively, was an unnatural ally for Washington. Bush's inner circle decided the United States should spell out to Pakistan and Afghanistan that they must take immediate action against all terrorist groups. They agreed that anyone supporting al-Qaeda would be punished, and concluded that if Pakistan decided not to help, it too would be at risk.[11] In his memoirs, Musharraf said Deputy Secretary of State Richard Armitage summoned Lieutenant-General Mahmud Ahmed, the Director-General of the Inter-Services Intelligence (ISI), who happened to be visiting Washington, and told him if Pakistan did not cooperate, "then we should be prepared to be bombed back to the Stone Age."[12] US versions do not mention that particular threat, but are equally clear that the situation was "black and white, not grey" and that Pakistan was "either with us or not with us".[13] The US accounts, contained in declassified cables, say both Musharraf and Mahmud were unhesitating in their promise of unqualified support. For good measure, said one cable, Mahmud insisted that "Pakistan has always seen such matters in black-

and-white. It has in the past been accused of 'being in bed' with those threatening US interests. He wanted to dispel that misperception."[14]

Afterwards, Pakistanis would complain that Musharraf had succumbed too easily to American pressure. At the time, however, such was the shock over the September 11 attacks that few would have dared do otherwise. On September 13, the United States gave Pakistan a checklist of the cooperation they expected. It called on it to stop al-Qaeda at the Afghan border, intercept arms shipments through Pakistan and end all logistical support for bin Laden. It insisted that Pakistan provide "blanket overflight and landing rights" and territorial access to US and allied military intelligence for operations against the perpetrators of terrorism, including the use of Pakistan's ports and air bases. It also called for intelligence-sharing and for Pakistan to not only publicly condemn the September 11 attacks but to "curb all domestic expressions of support" for terrorism. Finally Pakistan was to cut off all supplies of fuel and recruits to the Taliban, stand ready to break ties with the Taliban should they continue to harbour bin Laden and al-Qaeda, and help the United States destroy bin Laden and his network.[15]

Musharraf decided Pakistan had no choice but to cooperate. He accepted all the US demands except blanket overflights and the full use of Pakistan's air bases. Instead he offered a narrow flight corridor, along with two air bases—Shamsi in Balochistan, and Jacobabad in Sindh.[16] Shamsi would later be used for US drone attacks in Pakistan's tribal areas. On September 14, Musharraf convened the army's Corps Commanders and convinced them Pakistan should agree to help the United States if it wanted to influence the American reaction to the September 11 attacks. "The impact of 9/11 was so overwhelming that the question of denying support to the US appeared foolhardy, regardless of the perceived importance of the Taliban regime to Pakistan's interests," Kurshid Kasuri, who would become Musharraf's foreign minister in the later years of his rule, said of that time. "Pakistan hoped to convince the Taliban to extradite Osama and avert the oncoming disaster but that was not to be."[17]

Musharraf began bargaining almost straight away, his objectives geared towards retaining Pakistan's old policy stances on India and Kashmir rather than helping his country adapt to the changing regional and global environment. He insisted India must have no role in the

Afghan war nor in the government that would follow the Taliban, according to Bruce Riedel, then on the National Security Council at the White House. Musharraf also said that while Pakistan would arrest al-Qaeda fighters who fled from Afghanistan, Pakistani citizens—including Punjab-based groups like Lashkar-e-Taiba—would be off-limits in counter-terrorism.[18] In his memoirs, Musharraf said one of the main reasons he had decided to cooperate with the United States was that he could not take the risk of driving it towards India. "What would happen then?" he asked. "India would gain a golden opportunity with regard to Kashmir. The Indians might be tempted to undertake a limited offensive there; or, more likely, they would work with the US and the UN to turn the present situation into a permanent status quo." Refusal might also jeopardise Pakistan's nuclear weapons. "We did not want to lose or damage the military parity that we had achieved with India by becoming a nuclear weapons state." It was, in his mind, "no secret that the United States has never been comfortable with a Muslim country acquiring nuclear weapons" and the Americans would have taken the opportunity to launch an invasion to destroy them.[19] On top of all that, cooperating would bring Pakistan relief from sanctions. It was fatally flawed reasoning. Pakistan would still lose Kashmir, but not until thousands of its own citizens had been killed in a failed "good Taliban, bad Taliban" policy that sought to preserve some militants for use against India while attacking others. Since the different militant groups had links; some would end up working together against the Pakistani state. Those who retained favour with the Pakistani state ensured that the ideological milieu in which they flourished grew stronger.

On September 19, 2001, Musharraf addressed the nation, telling the people that Pakistan faced its most difficult challenge since 1971. His speech followed a formula that would become familiar over the years: he invoked the presumed Indian threat to justify his decisions. Were Pakistan to refuse US demands, he said, the country's very survival could be put at risk and its "critical concerns" harmed. "And, when I talk about critical concerns, I mean that our nuclear strength and our Kashmir cause may be harmed," he said. India, he added, had offered its military bases, facilities and logistics support to the United States. "They want the United States to side with them and to declare Pakistan a terrorist state." Then, using language that should have spelled out the difficulties the United States would face in Afghanistan in the years ahead, he asserted Pakistan's right to dictate the composition of the government in Kabul. "India does not have any border with Afghanistan. It has no connections with Afghanistan... In my view, they want a change in Afghanistan and the establishment of an anti-Pakistan government there," he said. "If you look at their television, you will find that an anti-Pakistan propaganda is being carried out all the time—morning, afternoon, or evening. I only want to tell them in English: 'Lay off'."[20]

At the time, Musharraf was still popular and many Pakistanis were inclined to trust him. His self-deprecating sense of humour and ability to speak extemporaneously helped him to come across as witty and relaxed. Those not implacably opposed to army rule—and critics of the military were then a minority amongst the upper and middle classes who wielded political power—found him charming. He reassured the public, easing their foreboding about the fall-out on Pakistan from the September 11 attacks, even as others quietly muttered that these had been an inside operation to defame Islam and find an excuse to attack Muslim countries.

Musharraf also convinced the United States that he was an essential bulwark against the Islamist-inspired instability he claimed would sweep Pakistan were he not in power. Western diplomats, influenced by a pro-military urban elite, appear to have largely gone along with this argument. They mistook the whisky-drinking social liberalism exemplified by Musharraf and the urban elite for pro-Western political liberalism. "If President Musharraf is ousted in the wake of popular unrest, he almost certainly will be replaced by senior, more Islamic-leaning officers from Pakistan's military," a declassified State Department cable said. The anti-terrorism cooperation promised by Musharraf would be withdrawn, said the cable, headlined "Pakistan: The Look of a Post-Musharraf State—Speculative Scenario." Extremist religious parties would make a bid for power, Pakistan could become a safe haven for terrorists, and confrontation with India over Kashmir would become more likely, it said.[21] The analysis of Musharraf's position was badly awry. It would be Musharraf who encouraged religious parties to bolster his own domestic position and undermine more secular political parties. As much a product of his institution as anyone else, he would also continue the military's long-standing policies of backing Islamist militants to counter India.

But the United States was in a hurry. The September 11 attacks had such a profound impact on Americans that retaliation was inevitable. Given the overwhelming firepower of the United States, it was also inevitable that this retaliation would be military. "The power of the American military is impressive," said Lee Hamilton, a former Democrat Congressman and vice-chairman of the 9/11 Commission set up to investigate the attacks. "What is missing is the economic, political, propaganda aspects," he said. "We certainly overreacted, and we still are."[22] Whatever doubts Washington harboured about allying with a military ruler in Pakistan were ignored. The Americans had been absent from the region for too long and did not have the intelligence assets of their own to handle Afghanistan. The one Afghan leader who commanded respect and opposed the Taliban, Ahmad Shah Massoud, was dead. And so Washington franchised part of its battle against al-Qaeda to Musharraf and the ISI while counting on Pakistan to turn against the Afghan Taliban. In making an ally of Pakistan, the United States gave it leverage over American policies in Afghanistan, locking both into a war in which they were on opposite sides.

* * *

India watched with a mixture of despair and cynicism. No one in India suspected Pakistan of involvement in the September 11 attacks— Pakistan had no interest in allowing an attack that brought American military might charging into the region. "For once they are innocent," said a former senior Indian official involved in policy discussions at the time.[23] But in the Indian view Pakistan had created the permissive environment that allowed al-Qaeda to flourish. Out of naivety, expediency and reliance on old contacts between the CIA and the ISI, the United States had let India down. "They feared that if we were made the ally we would ask too much as a *quid pro quo*. Pakistan was available and payable," the former Indian official said. "Musharraf played with a low hand and the Americans went in only for themselves, looking to what served their interests best. Pakistan was considered more manageable."[24]

India had less reason to worry than it imagined. Historical trends were moving in its direction. On the economic front, Pakistan's GDP per capita was still higher than India's in 2001,[25] and it was about to benefit from a fresh influx of US aid. But India's economic reforms of the early 1990s had put it on an upward trajectory that would eventually allow it to overtake Pakistan. On the international front, the collapse of the Soviet Union with its attendant diplomatic and arms support had forced India to look more widely for friends. Its resulting warming ties with the United States would prove far more enduring than Pakistan's temporary alliance with Washington. Economic liberalisation had also required India to become more pragmatic about its foreign policies as it opened up to outside markets and sought energy supplies for its growing economy. As it built relations with Middle East oil suppliers it discovered it was possible to do this without maintaining its traditional hostility to Israel. Once a champion of the Palestinian cause, India gave full diplomatic recognition to Israel in 1992 and went on to strengthen Israeli-Indian links, as underlined by Dayan's visit on the day of the September 11 attacks.

While India had become more pragmatic and outward-looking, Pakistan had become more ideological and isolated. Pakistan had misread the collapse of the Soviet Union as having been caused by the anti-Soviet jihad in Afghanistan and evidence of the benefits of Islamist proxies. Unable to see beyond its immediate neighbourhood, it disregarded the many other causes of the collapse—the Soviet Union had been rotting from within for decades for reasons quite independent of Afghanistan. Pakistan's backing for the Taliban and Pakistan-based groups fighting in Kashmir through the 1990s had also deepened its well of support for Islamist militancy. It increasingly presented itself as a champion of Muslims worldwide, defining the defence of everyone from Kashmiris to Palestinians as a matter of national interest. Saddam Hussein, whose 1990 invasion of Kuwait had been defeated by a US-led coalition, was seen as a hero. Islamist groups sold posters of Saddam in schools, where he was pictured on a prayer mat with war imagery in the background. Though much of this support for Muslim causes worldwide was largely rhetorical, it had the effect of radicalising the domestic population while winning Pakistan few friends outside. Even Pakistan's closest ally, China, distrusted Islamist ideology, fearing its spread to the Muslim Uighur population in its Xinjiang province. Pragmatically focused on growing its economy, China also had no patience for a conflict with India caused by Pakistani adventurism, as shown by its refusal to back Pakistan in the Kargil War.

Most challenging of all for Pakistan, Musharraf had agreed to an alliance with the United States that ran against the grain of the worldview of the Pakistani public—one, ironically enough, shaped by the Islamic nationalism of the Pakistani military. A strong current of anti-Americanism had always run through Pakistan. In 1979, for example, protesters attacked and burned down the US embassy in Islamabad. But it had been given freer rein after the collapse of the Soviet Union and loss of American interest. Pakistan became more explicitly anti-Israel, freed of the constraints of circumspection required by its Cold War alliance with the United States. The popular response to the September 11 attacks showed how deeply its anti-American anti-Israeli stance had been woven into society. While authorities publicly condemned the attacks, and many Pakistanis were deeply shocked, there are many stories of people who were privately pleased to see America brought low. Islamist parties said the attacks were part of an Israeli-US-Indian plot to defame Pakistan and the Taliban. The Urdu-language media repeated the anti-Semitic conspiracy theory that no Jews had been killed in the Twin Towers since Israel had warned them not to go to work that day.[26] Hamid Gul, a former head of the Inter-Services Intelligence (ISI) agency, told *Newsweek* that the September 11 attacks were an Israeli-engineered coup against the government of the United States to force it into being more subservient to Israeli interests.[27] These anti-American, anti-Israeli stances gave Pakistan an ideological worldview that was dangerously close to that of al-Qaeda. This was all the more perilous for Pakistan given the alliance of objectives between the Pakistani security establishment and Islamist militants. Given that many Islamist militants did not recognise the sovereignty of individual nations, it made the Pakistani state particularly vulnerable to corrosion from within.

Over time, the historical trends that were turning against Pakistan and in favour of India would reassert themselves. The immediate aftermath of the September 11 attacks was nonetheless a bruising time for India. Thousands of lives too would be lost across the region before the knot tied between the United States and Pakistan after September 11 was loosened.

* * *

In the official Pakistani versions of events that followed, Pakistan tried hard to convince Taliban leader Mullah Omar to hand over bin Laden to avert war in Afghanistan. "We told him that his country would be devastated, but he did not understand. He really believed that American forces could be defeated," Musharraf said. "In this he was misled first by Osama bin Laden himself, but also by other misguided religious thinkers, even in Pakistan."[28] Various accounts, however, suggest that Pakistan followed different lines in public and private, with some ISI officials trying to convince the Taliban to hold out.[29] ISI chief General Mahmud Ahmed travelled twice to Kandahar to talk to Mullah Omar. By some accounts, instead of convincing him to hand over bin Laden, he advised him to pull back into the mountains and wage a guerrilla insurgency, as had happened during the Soviet occupation.[30] Pakistan also tried to reassure the Taliban of its support even while telling the United States it would turn against them. According to then Taliban ambassador to Islamabad Abdul Salam Zaeef, Pakistan promised to protect the Taliban in the event of an American invasion. In his memoirs, Zaeef said the ISI chief told him in one of their meetings: "We want to assure you that you will not be alone in this jihad against America. We will be with you."[31] Musharraf subsequently sacked General Mahmud, leaving open the possibility that the ISI chief was acting alone. Either way, whether through incompetence or duplicity, Pakistan failed to come up with a solution that might have prevented a war on its doorstep. It also allowed thousands of Pakistani volunteers to head to Afghanistan to defend it against an expected American invasion.

While the ISI chief allegedly promised support to the Taliban, Musharraf was subtly rewriting Pakistan's Afghan policies in talks with the Americans. He claimed that in supporting the Taliban, Pakistan had backed ethnic Pashtuns in the interests of stability in Afghanistan. Decades of Pakistan encouraging Islamists to suppress ethnic Pashtun nationalism were forgotten, as was its preference for less educated Pashtuns over those like Najibullah, the former Pashtun president of Afghanistan murdered by the Taliban in 1996. In a meeting on October 2 with US ambassador Wendy Chamberlin, Musharraf said Pakistan needed a friendly Pashtun-led government in Afghanistan, according to a declassified US account of the meeting. He said Pashtuns made up the majority of the Afghan population—they formed the biggest ethnic group, but probably not an overall majority—and warned against the possibility of a takeover by the India-backed Northern Alliance. He also said Pakistan had no choice but to support the Taliban, but now preferred a different descriptive term for them. "We should refer to the Pashtun majority," the cable said. [32] While there was an element of truth in the need for strong Pashtun political representation in Afghanistan—one that the Americans subsequently ignored—the equation of ethnic Pashtuns with the Taliban was profoundly misleading. Yet it was a myth that would endure for years, allowing Pakistan to portray the insurgency in Afghanistan as a Pashtun ethnic rebellion against the dominance of non-Pashtuns in the US-backed government installed after the Taliban were overthrown.

Pakistan's befuddling public and private rhetoric was matched by confusion inside Afghanistan. Many in the Taliban leadership failed to grasp the extent of American military firepower. Even bin Laden reportedly underestimated the likely strength of the American reaction, instead expecting a small contingent of US troops that he and his followers would fend off from the Tora Bora cave complex in eastern Afghanistan. [33] Those in the Taliban who did understand what was coming tried and failed to persuade Mullah Omar to expel bin Laden in order to save Afghanistan. [34] The Taliban leader parried them by asking for proof of bin Laden's involvement in the September 11 attacks. [35] One retired Pakistani diplomat said he had met a senior figure in the Taliban and tried to convince him they were going to be mauled. He talked about American airpower. "We have been your friends, do something," he told him. The response was a powerful farewell embrace and the words, "I know you are right, but we are helpless." [36]

The American bombing began on October 7, 2001. A day later, Musharraf sacked General Mahmud. He pulled most Pakistani military advisers out of Afghanistan and cut off supplies to the Taliban. The Taliban collapsed and retreated towards Pakistan, where they would eventually regroup. By then, India was already confronting the aftermath of the agreement made by Musharraf with the United States that had allowed him to leave Pakistan's anti-India militant groups intact as it turned against the Taliban and al-Qaeda.

* * *

Six days before the US bombing of Afghanistan began, a suicide car bomber and three gunmen had attacked the state parliament in Srinagar, Kashmir, killing thirty-eight people in the blast and gun-battle that followed. It was the worst single attack by militants in Kashmir.[37] It was only by chance that senior members of the state parliament had not been killed—they had left the building moments before. The attack was initially claimed by Jaish-e Mohammad—the group set up by Masood Azhar—but it backed away from that claim after the United States condemned the attack.[38] In the immediate aftermath of the World Trade Center and Pentagon attacks, Pakistan could not be seen to be allowing Pakistani militant groups to attack civilians.

The Indian government was now even more aggrieved. The United States had failed to take Indian concerns about Pakistan-based anti-India militants seriously after the September 11 attacks and now it was paying the price. A list released by the United States of groups on which sanctions would be imposed excluded all but one militant outfit active in Kashmir. The only one it named, Harkat-ul-Mujahideen, was defunct. Lashkar-e-Taiba and Jaish-e-Mohammed, the two main Pakistani militant groups operating in Kashmir, were left untouched and resumed operations within two weeks of the September 11 attacks.[39] In a letter to Bush, Vajpayee reminded him that, "India joined wholeheartedly with the United States" in its aim of defeating terrorism. "With you we condemned any nation that continues to harbour or support terrorism," he said. Yet now the Pakistan-based Jaish-e-Mohammed had claimed responsibility for the attack in Srinagar and named a Pakistani national based in Pakistan as one of the suicide bombers. "Pakistan must understand that there is a limit to the patience of the people of India."[40]

Secretary of State Colin Powell visited India and Pakistan later that month but only aggravated Delhi further by stressing the importance of resolving the Kashmir dispute.[41] The Bush administration also made it clear that while it regarded those who had attacked the United States as terrorists, the attacks in Kashmir were the result of a political dispute and not, as Indian insisted, cross-border terrorism. Moreover, priority was to be given to operations in Afghanistan. "I think it is very important that India and Pakistan stand down during our activities in Afghanistan and, for that matter, forever," Bush had said.[42]

Western diplomats played down the dangers of an outbreak of out-right hostilities between India and Pakistan and insisted there could be no distractions from the campaign in Afghanistan. "There is an under-standing in Delhi about the need to work with Pakistan to put an end to Afghan-based terrorism. India has as much interest in that happening as other countries," said a senior western diplomat in Delhi. "Let's go back to the focus. Don't try to do too much. The focus of the interna-tional community has to be on the government in Afghanistan."[43] The United States and its allies believed—wrongly, as it turned out—that Pakistan would in any case be forced to drop its use of Islamist militant proxies because of the sheer weight of international pressure to crack down on terrorism across the board. For the first time, the UN Security Council had imposed mandatory obligations on all UN mem-bers to cut off terrorist financing and end safe havens for terrorists. Those who funded them, who laundered their money, or covered their tracks were to be considered as guilty as the men who committed acts of terrorism. Pakistan just needed time to roll up the different militant groups on its territory.

Further evidence of the United States indulging Pakistan was yet to come. In November, India began to pick up reports of a massive Pakistani airlift from the town of Kunduz in northern Afghanistan, in part thanks to communications intercepts collected by its base in Tajikistan and in part from its contacts in the Northern Alliance.[44] By then the Taliban had retreated in their thousands to Kunduz, their last stronghold in northern Afghanistan. Along with them were al-Qaeda fighters, Pakistan Army officers and intelligence advisers and Pakistani volunteers who had been fighting in support of the Taliban. Northern Alliance troops, supported by US Special Forces, had the town under siege. Foreign reporters in Afghanistan began to run stories on the airlift, based on their own contacts with the Northern Alliance, saying it was designed to avoid a massacre of non-Afghan fighters as the Taliban prepared to surrender in the town. *The New York Times* reported that the air rescues were being carried out by Pakistan Air Force planes.[45] India confronted the Americans privately about these reports, only to be told that the runway at Kunduz was not in good enough shape and that no airlift was possible. Subsequent published accounts, however, suggest that for 10 to 15 days in the second half of November, one or two Pakistani military flights per day airlifted some 2,000 people, as well as weapons and communications systems.[46] The American investigative journalist Seymour Hersh cited unnamed US officials as saying the United States believed it was worth it to spare Musharraf the humiliation of losing thousands of his own men and possibly being thrown out of power. The Americans had also hoped that by allowing Pakistan to bring out some Taliban leaders it might be easier to stitch together a postwar settlement including elements of the Taliban. Once under way, the airlift became chaotic. "Everyone brought their friends with them," Hersh quoted an American defence adviser as saying.[47]

The US decision to turn to Pakistan after September 11, the Srinagar bombing, and now the Kunduz airlift convinced the Indian government that it was on its own. Prodded by the strategic community in Delhi, the mood in India turned increasingly belligerent. Senior officials feared that the Srinagar bombing might be the first in a series of attacks. With the Americans busy in Afghanistan and dependent on Pakistan, said one retired senior official, the Pakistani security establishment seemed to believe it had an opportunity to hit India without facing international retribution.[48] The swift American retaliation in Afghanistan for the September 11 attacks had also revived questions in Delhi about India's reluctance to take similar action against Pakistan. Perhaps, some argued, India should follow the US example. The trigger came on December 13, when five men stormed the Indian parliament in Delhi, pitching India and Pakistan into their biggest crisis since the Kargil War.

6

THE ATTACK ON THE INDIAN PARLIAMENT

THE TRIAL OF AFZAL GURU

In a country that complains about the crime, corruption and bickering of many of its politicians, the Indian parliament building has retained the reverence that its occupants have lost. It is a massive, domed circular building on a base of red sandstone, standing to one side and slightly obscured from view in the grandiose imperial capital designed by Edwin Lutyens for the British. The first floor is ringed with an open verandah, colonnaded with 27-feet high pillars. Because of its girth, the building seems rather squat, the delicately tiered upper floors sitting awkwardly on the elephantine base. But inside, with its high ceilings and long corridors, it exudes power and privilege. Here is the heart of the world's biggest democracy, the place where Prime Minister Jawaharlal Nehru promised on the eve of independence in 1947 that India had met its "tryst with destiny". Children lining up in uniform on a school tour would be told to stand straight by their teachers before being ushered inside.

The building is surrounded by watered lawns, enclosed in turn by a sandstone wall with iron gates to allow traffic to enter. Until 2001, journalists and bureaucrats with parliamentary passes for their cars used the road that ran through the compound as a short-cut. They would enter through a gate on Sansad Chowk, or Parliament Square, into a tree-lined avenue that followed the curve of the parliament building on their right, past the heavy entrance portico used by ministers and other VIPs and drive straight on out the other side. It was through this gate on Sansad Chowk that five gunmen drove into the parliament compound on December 13, 2001.[1]

They arrived at about 1130 am in a white Ambassador car—the 1950s-style four-door saloon used by government ministers and their entourages—fitted with what looked like a standard VIP red light. Parliament had just adjourned and Prime Minister Vajpayee had left. Given the amount of traffic passing through, the car did not attract suspicion. In any case it had a home ministry pass on the windscreen. No one even noticed what the five men had inside the car: automatic assault rifles, pistols, grenades, electronic detonators, spare ammunition and improvised "tiffin" bombs. In the boot was a more sophisticated bomb made with a large quantity of ammonium nitrate. "The fire power was awesome, enough to engage a battalion, and had the attack succeeded the entire building with all inside would have perished," an Indian court noted during the trial of the men accused of planning the attack.[2] With the exception of Vajpayee, most senior ministers were still inside, along with hundreds of parliamentarians and office staff.

By chance, Vice President Krishan Kant was about to leave the building and his motorcade was waiting for him outside, blocking the way. The driver of the Ambassador veered towards the left, making a security officer suspicious enough to order him to stop. Instead he reversed, hitting the vice-president's car. He was about to drive away again when the security officer and the driver of the vice-president's car ran towards him. The five attackers jumped out of the Ambassador and started a firefight. Unable to obtain the easy access to the building that they had expected, the assault team ran from entrance to entrance trying to find a way in. Security officers inside hastily bolted the doors and herded panicked politicians away from the gunfire. Soon Indian television channels, whose cameramen had been patiently standing outside to record an ordinary day in the winter session of parliament, were broadcasting an increasingly ferocious gun battle live to the nation. Men ran back and forth, shouting above the crack of gunfire; others crouched behind walls and trees. Indian security forces could be seen firing down from the verandah above. Occasionally an Indian policeman ran across an open space and dived for cover. One of Delhi's black crows, usually so self-confident, skittered away from them. "I saw many people firing at the same time. I couldn't make out who was who," said Member of Parliament Kharbala Sain.[3] The gun battle went on for half-an-hour before the attackers were killed. By the time it was over, nine people, including eight security personnel and a gardener were dead along with the five attackers, and sixteen people were wounded.[4]

The attack was seen in India as its 9/11. Though the death toll was relatively small, the symbolism was huge. The parliament, the heart of Indian democracy, had been attacked. The government was convinced the gunmen had intended to wipe out India's top political leadership and that only the swift action of Indian security forces had prevented a national catastrophe. "I can only imagine how horrifying it would have been if the suicide squad… had succeeded in its objective," Home Minister Advani said. "It seems their objective was somehow to get inside Parliament House, fully armed with their AK-47s and grenades, while parliament was in session and all the members of the Indian government, all the members of parliament, including the political leaders of the country, were inside."[5]

India blamed Pakistan, brushing off its denial of involvement. In the sour atmosphere created in the aftermath of the September 11 attacks, Delhi had no interest in giving Pakistan the benefit of the doubt. Vajpayee had already warned the United States that India's patience was running out after the October 1 attack on the state parliament in Srinagar. On December 13, it snapped. "This was not just an attack on the building, it was a warning to the entire nation. We accept the challenge," Vajpayee said in an address to the nation. "We have been fighting terrorism for the past two decades. The fight is in the last stages. It will be a do-or-die battle."[6] After his cabinet met in emergency session, the Indian government hardened its position further. "We will liquidate the terrorists and their sponsors wherever they are, whoever they are," the ministers said in a resolution.[7]

The outside world, which less than three months earlier had registered its horror at the attacks on New York and Washington, hurried to express its outrage. The United States denounced the raid on parliament as a "brutal assault on the heart of Indian democracy" and President Bush called Vajpayee to offer the help of US counterterrorism teams.[8] Musharraf sent a letter to Vajpayee condemning the attack and saying he was "saddened by the loss of life".[9] For India, such expressions of outrage were not enough. It wanted Pakistan to dismantle "the infrastructure of terrorism" on its soil once and for all. It feared the United States was unwilling to lean on Musharraf too hard because it needed his help in Afghanistan. Somehow India needed to bare enough teeth to force Pakistan and the United States to take it seriously, while working within the constraints imposed by the region's nuclear weapons. The day after the attack, the Indian Foreign Ministry summoned Pakistan High Commissioner Ashraf Jehangir Qazi and served formal notice demanding Pakistan stop the activities of the Lashkar-e-Taiba and Jaish-e-Mohammed, the two groups it then suspected of organising the assault, though it later decided only Jaish was involved. It called on Pakistan to detain their leaders and block their financial assets. Foreign Minister Jaswant Singh said Pakistan should fulfil the promises it made after September 11 to stand with the international community in its fight against terrorism.[10]

Pakistan responded by accusing India of deliberately stoking up tension. Military spokesman Major-General Rashid Qureshi suggested India had carried out the attack itself as a propaganda stunt to gain international sympathy. "The attack on parliament is a drama staged by Indian intelligence agencies to defame the freedom struggle in occupied Kashmir," he said.[11] Pakistan put its forces on high alert in expectation of Indian military action. The United States, still convinced Musharraf must not be pressed too hard, hedged its bets. It added the Lashkar-e-Taiba (LeT) to a list of terrorist groups whose assets were to be frozen. But it ignored long-standing Indian complaints that groups like the LeT and Jaish-e-Mohammed flourished only because they had the support of the ISI. "Lashkar-e-Taiba is an extremist group based in Kashmir," Bush said. "LeT is a stateless sponsor of terrorism, and it hopes to destroy relations between Pakistan and India and undermine Pakistan's President Musharraf."[12] Bush's ambivalence could hardly have been calculated to rile India more. Neither the LeT nor Jaish were based in Kashmir; they were Punjab-based groups with roots in the anti-Soviet jihad in Afghanistan. They had been used by the ISI to harden the revolt against India in Kashmir. Far from undermining the Pakistan Army, as Bush suggested in his comments about Musharraf, they were an extension of military power.

THE ATTACK ON THE INDIAN PARLIAMENT

The Indian government ratcheted up its response. It recalled its High Commissioner from Islamabad, suspended air, rail and bus communications with Pakistan and mobilised its army. Truckloads of soldiers could be seen trundling through Delhi heading to the border. Pakistan in turn reinforced its own positions to block any Indian advance and soon both countries had close to a million men mobilised along the border in the biggest troop build-up since the 1971 war. Yet for an attack that brought the two countries to the verge of a war far bigger than the Kargil conflict, the full details of how much Pakistan knew about the assault on parliament have never been established. The truth of what really happened may reside in one man, a former militant from the Kashmir Valley. And he is dead.

* * *

By the time Mohammad Afzal Guru was hanged for involvement in the attack on parliament, his role had become one of the most contested in India's troubled history with Kashmir. The Indian state executed him as a traitor. Human rights activists and his defence lawyers said police tortured him into confessing and planted evidence against him. Some activists suggested he was set up by Indian security forces in Kashmir in a plot so murky that no one dared investigate it. Others believed him to be guilty, but argued that he had not been given a fair trial. Afzal had good reason to be angry about the situation in Kashmir. He had suffered years of harassment and mistreatment by Indian security forces. His story is one from which neither India nor Pakistan emerges well.

Like many young men of his generation, Afzal was swept up in the Kashmir separatist revolt that erupted in the late 1980s. Abandoning his medical studies, he slipped across the Line of Control at the age of twenty to seek military training from Pakistan. By his own account, he became quickly disillusioned on realising Pakistan was exploiting Kashmiris for its own purposes, and surrendered to Indian forces in the Kashmir Valley in 1993.[13] It was a time when the Kashmir insurgency was heading into a particularly dark period. With Pakistan ramping up support and sending in Pakistani fighters, India was turning surrendered militants into informers or counter-insurgents who could be used against their former comrades. The counter-insurgents were ruthless and undisciplined, exploiting their protection by Indian security forces to terrorise the local population. Indian specialist forces set up to fight the insurgency were equally unaccountable: among them were the Special Operations Group (SOG) and Special Task Force (STF). At the same time, both India and Pakistan were trying to infiltrate the various groups ranged against them. No one knew who was working for whom. For an ordinary Kashmiri it became nearly impossible to tell whom to trust between Indian and Pakistani spies, militants, renegades and security forces, and those simply trying to make money from trading information and weapons, or from blackmail and extortion. Surrendered militants like Afzal were expected to spy for the Indian security forces, leaving them at constant risk of being killed by their former comrades. If they refused, they could be picked up and tortured by Indian security forces, or "disappeared". Thousands of young men vanished during the insurgency. Indian authorities claimed they had gone across to Pakistan; many were killed in real or fake encounters, and buried in an unmarked grave.

According to Afzal, he had been keen to settle down, but was picked up and beaten repeatedly by Indian security forces.[14] He had married a Kashmiri woman, Tabassum, in 1996 and they had a son, named Ghalib, after the nineteenth-century poet. Later, Tabassum would tell an Indian reporter that her memories of her husband were of a man who cooked for her, who holding a book in one hand, would read her stories while she sat nearby and he prepared the meal.[15] "Tabassum witnessed both my physical and mental wounds," Afzal told an Indian interviewer. "Many times I returned from the torture camp, unable to stand; all kinds of torture, including electric shock to my penis. We did not have a day of peaceful living. It is the story of many Kashmiri couples. Constant fear is the dominant feeling in all Kashmiri households."[16] Unable to get a government job because he was a surrendered militant, he started a business selling medicines and surgical instruments on commission. He provided bits and pieces of information about militants culled from a local newspaper to keep security forces off his back. But in the summer of 2000, he was picked up by Indian police in the STF on suspicion of hiding weapons, held without charge for more than three weeks and tortured.[17] Among their favoured methods along with electrocution of the penis was to force petrol or chillies into the rectum. He had to hand over his savings and his wife had to sell her gold jewellery to pay enough to get him out. "But now I was a broken person," he said.[18]

It was then, depending on which version you believe, that he either decided to exact revenge, or was set up by one of the many shadowy forces operating in Kashmir. Indian prosecutors said he had agreed to work for the leader of the Jaish-e-Mohammed in Kashmir, who went by the *nom de guerre* Ghazi Baba and was from Bawahalpur in Pakistan. Ghazi Baba was the mastermind behind the attack on parliament. Afzal was introduced to Ghazi Baba, prosecutors said, by a man who went by the name of Tariq. It was Tariq too who asked him to help "Mohammad", the leader of the group who attacked parliament.[19] Afzal admitted to accompanying Mohammad to Delhi and helping him rent an apartment and buy a car. He claimed, however, that he had no knowledge of the plans to attack parliament. Moreover, he said he believed Tariq was working for the Indians in the STF. "Tariq had told me that if I face any problem due to Mohammad he will help me as he knew security forces and STF very well," Afzal later told an Indian court.[20]

Two days after the attack on parliament, Afzal was picked up by police in Kashmir, as was his cousin Shaukat Guru. They were flown to Delhi and formally arrested there. A third man, Syed Abdul Rahman Geelani, a teacher of Arabic at Delhi University and a Kashmiri, was arrested in Delhi. All three came from the same district in Kashmir and police said they had evidence from cellphones retrieved from the bodies of the parliament attackers linking them to the plot. Geelani had also officiated at the wedding ceremony of Shaukat to a Sikh woman in 2000 who converted to Islam and changed her name to Afsan Guru. Pregnant at the time, she too was arrested in Delhi. Before being flown to Delhi, Afzal said he was beaten by police in Srinagar and told that his wife and family would be harmed if he did not cooperate. His younger brother, Hilal Ahmad Guru, was taken into police custody and held for two to three months. It was in Delhi, Afzal said, that he was forced into a confession.[21] Indian police said Afzal led them to the hideouts where the five attackers had stayed. Inside, police found chemicals and other explosives materials and detonators. He also identified the five attackers in the mortuary, and took police to various shops where the gunmen had bought chemicals and other materials for preparing explosives, as well as other articles needed for the attack, including mobile phones, the red light for the Ambassador car, and dried fruits to eat. He and the other three were formally charged on December 19, their separate confessions supposedly implicating each other in the plot.[22]

The next day, police called the media to a press conference where they compelled Afzal to confess on camera—a confession he said was the product of torture and police intimidation. In the footage, Afzal appears calm, confidently answering questions put to him; it does not sound obviously rehearsed. Clean-shaven, bespectacled and wearing a pale brown sleeveless pullover, he speaks in a mix of Hindi and English. He had helped bring the attackers to Delhi and had arranged hideouts for them, he said. Their leader, Mohammad, was a Pakistani national and a Jaish militant sent on the orders of Ghazi Baba, the Jaish commander in Kashmir. The gunmen, he said, had phoned him just before the attack on parliament asking him to find out who was still inside and which ministers were there. They knew the parliament was in session, but wanted more details. They phoned him two more times before going in. "They took all sorts of help from me," he said. "I am the person who brought them here. I am the person who made all the facilities available."

The three men and Shaukat's pregnant wife were sent to Delhi's Tihar Jail until a court ruled on their case. A year later—despite some evidence of discrepancies that cast doubt on the prosecution's claims that it had a solid case against all four—Geelani, Shaukat and Afzal were sentenced to death. Afsan Guru, who had been forced to give birth in prison, was sentenced to five years for concealing knowledge of the conspiracy.[23] It was a difficult time for anyone connected to Kashmir. The conditions the four likely faced, both before and after their convictions, were spelled out in detail by another Kashmiri detained in Delhi months after the parliament attack. Iftikhar Gilani, an affable young man and respected journalist in Delhi, was detained in June 2002 and accused of breaking the Official Secrets Act—a draconian 1923 law inherited from the British. He had to spend seven months in Tihar Jail—the same huge, overcrowded prison complex in Delhi where Afzal, Shaukat, Geelani and Afsan were sent—before he cleared his name. His story is one of a callous state system that rarely released its victims after they were caught up in its machinery, particularly if they were from Kashmir.[24] His house had been searched by Indian police looking into alleged tax irregularities, primarily because he was the son-in-law of a pro-Pakistan Kashmiri separatist leader, Syed Ali Shah Geelani. While searching his house, police found on his computer a document produced by Islamabad's Institute of Strategic Studies giving details of Indian troop deployments in Kashmir. Though the document was publicly available, they charged him with breaking the Official Secrets Act. Police even produced a statement attributed to him admitting to spying for the ISI and leaked false stories to the media about his supposed treachery. When he first arrived in Tihar, he was beaten unconscious as a traitor by jail staff and inmates. When he came to, he was forced to clean a filthy toilet with his blood-soaked shirt and then made to put the shirt on again and wear it for three days. Refused bail, he languished in Tihar Jail while discovering many prisoners inside who said they were victims of questionable police investigations. It was only when the journalist community managed to rally enough support from senior ministers that his case was dropped. He came away painfully aware that anyone caught up in the labyrinthine world of the secret security services, law enforcement and justice would find it extremely hard to get out again.

Afzal, Shaukat, Geelani and Afsan had no such influential friends on the outside. After their conviction, activists from the militant Hindu fundamentalist outfit, the Shiv Sena, were among the first to celebrate the death sentence. Ever suspicious of Indian actions, many Kashmiris came to believe that Afzal Guru and his alleged co-conspirators had been framed. On October 29, 2003, the Delhi High Court acquitted Geelani and Afsan Guru on appeal, casting doubt on the fairness of the original trial. It upheld the conviction of Afzal and Shaukat and confirmed their death sentences.[25] Geelani had by then spent nearly two years in jail for a crime the high court decided he had never committed and for which he had been sentenced to death for. His wife and children had been evicted from their apartment and he would continue to be regarded with suspicion in Delhi even after his acquittal. Afsan Guru was broken by the experience.

It was another two years before Afzal and Shaukat's appeal came up before the Supreme Court, which made its ruling in August 2005. The Supreme Court judgment, which runs to nearly 80,000 words, is remarkably candid in its view of the Indian police. It acknowledges, for example, the "inhuman treatment often meted out by overzealous police officers and the archaic, third degree methods adopted by them during the investigation of the cases." Recognising what it called the "fear and panic, anxiety and despair" of suspects in police custody, it noted that Indian law had built in safeguards to prevent false confessions made to the police being used in court. These safeguards required that suspects see a lawyer while in police custody and then be produced in front of a magistrate to make a statement. They were then meant to be remanded into judicial custody rather than returned to police custody, with the idea that this would make them feel safer about complaining to the magistrate about police abuse. Since these safeguards had not been respected in the case of the parliament attack, it quashed the confessions.[26]

The Supreme Court did, however, argue at length that even with a confession quashed, information gleaned from that confession could still be used as evidence. Thus for example if a man were to say under torture that he had stabbed his neighbour and hidden the knife in the garden, the confession would be quashed, but the knife—if then found by police—could still be used in evidence against him. This was the argument that would doom Afzal. Evidence included witness testimony from landlords and shopkeepers identifying Afzal as the man who had either rented hideouts, bought materials for the attack, including explosives, or been seen with the attackers. This evidence, said the court, showed Afzal was associated with the five attackers in almost everything they did and established his involvement beyond reasonable doubt. Under Indian law anyone party to a crime punishable with death was also liable to the death sentence. The Supreme Court found him guilty of murder and described the attack on parliament as one of the "rarest of rare cases" where death sentence was appropriate. "The incident, which resulted in heavy casualties, had shaken the entire nation and the collective conscience of the society will only be satisfied if the capital punishment is awarded to the offender." It also found him guilty of "waging war" against the state of India. "The planned operations if executed, would have spelt disaster to the whole nation," it said. "A war-like situation lingering for days or weeks would have prevailed." For the crime of waging war on India, it gave him a second death sentence. In Shaukat's case, the Supreme Court ruled that having suppressed his confession, the case against him was substantially weakened. It was no longer possible to conclude beyond reasonable doubt that he was an active member of the plot to attack parliament. The court did however insist that it was reasonable to infer that he had enough knowledge of what was going on to be guilty of concealing a crime. It sentenced him to ten years imprisonment.

Afzal languished on death row for years, submitting and losing an appeal for mercy. He was secretly hanged in Tihar Jail on February 9, 2013. His wife and child were not told in time to allow them to say goodbye. The government refused to hand over his body, burying him instead inside the jail complex.[27] His death failed to dispel persistent doubts about irregularities in the case. Gaps in information about exactly what services he was providing to Indian security forces added to the murkiness. Those gaps could have been due to a need to maintain security, or a desire to cover up for incompetence or negligence, but nonetheless went unexplained. "Once you reject the confession, the least you can do is spare his life," said Sushil Kumar, who defended him at the Supreme Court. "There are so many suspicious aspects of his case which are now buried with him in his grave in Delhi. Those facts will never come out."[28] In public, the people of Kashmir protested in favour of Afzal and declared his innocence. Private opinion in Kashmir was more divided, with some believing he was guilty. It was not unreasonable to think he had snapped after years of harassment by security forces. Guilty or not, after he was hanged by the Indian state, all that mattered in the Valley was that he was a Kashmiri.

* * *

To this day, many questions remain unanswered about the attack on parliament. Musharraf has denied all knowledge of it and convinced many in both the foreign and domestic media at the time that it had taken him by surprise. Pakistani officials argued that Pakistan had no interest in starting a conflict with India at a time when it was trying to cope with the upheaval in Afghanistan. Indian officials offer various explanations for the attack. One former senior diplomat suggested Musharraf might have ordered militant groups to turn up the heat on India after the failure of the Agra summit. Such was the loosening of the chain of command and Pakistan's own need for deniability, this campaign would have been allowed to run its course without the army leadership being consulted. Even after the September 11 attacks, the former diplomat said, "the machinery kept turning".[29] A retired senior government official suggested a more direct connection with the military leadership. With the US involved in Afghanistan, Pakistan might have thought it had a good opportunity to strike India without facing international opprobrium. "The Americans are now busy. Here is our chance. Americans won't say a thing to us. The intention was just to hit India."[30] A third possibility was that Jaish acted independently. At the time, senior al-Qaeda leaders were fleeing Afghanistan, often into safe houses in Pakistan organised by Pakistani militant groups. The attack on parliament would provide a welcome distraction. High-profile attacks which gained maximum publicity were also the bread-and-butter of jihadi groups which used them to gain credibility, funding and recruits. And unlike the Lashkar-e-Taiba, Jaish had more of a tendency to go its own way—the group split after the September 11 attacks, with some turning against the Pakistani state. As one former Indian ambassador said, "Lashkar is more a creature of the army's breeding than the Jaish, which has its own links which may or may not always coincide with the Pakistan Army."[31] Lieutenant-General Javed Ashraf Qazi, a former ISI chief who was a government minister in 2001, has suggested Jaish had acted alone, saying it had been behind the attack on the Indian parliament as well as assassination attempts against Musharraf.[32] According to Arif Jamal, a Pakistani journalist who has written extensively about the Kashmir-focused militant groups, the attack was planned by Jaish and an ISI officer known as Brigadier "Riaz" in meetings held in Pakistani Kashmir. It was unclear if Musharraf had signed off on it.[33]

Whatever the exact details, the parliament attack and subsequent investigation point to two broad conclusions. The first concerns India's actions in Kashmir. Assuming Afzal Guru was guilty as convicted, anti-India resentment in the Kashmir Valley ran high enough for Pakistan to exploit and was in part driven by the harshness of Indian security forces. When Ghazi Baba, the Jaish commander, was killed in a shoot-out in Kashmir in August 2003, huge crowds turned out to mourn him at his funeral.[34] The willingness of many in the Valley to believe Afzal had been set up by Indian security forces also pointed to the lack of accountability of organisations like the STF and the deep distrust with which they were viewed by Kashmiris. This distrust fed off numerous smaller incidents in which the details given by security forces, militants and ordinary people never seemed to match, to the point that all you could say for sure about the insurgency was that almost nothing could be known for sure. Disinformation by Indian intelligence, of the kind that Afzal Guru claimed he had been victim, was widely believed in Kashmir to be used to flush militants out of hiding, sometimes by prodding them into attacks in which they would be caught. Years later, however, Jaish claimed Afzal Guru as one of their own. An attack on an Indian airbase in Pathankot in Indian Punjab in January 2016 was reportedly carried out by Jaish in revenge for Afzal's hanging.[35] Gunmen who attacked the Indian consulate in Mazar-e-Sharif in Afghanistan that same month left behind graffiti saying their intention was to avenge Afzal.[36] Material published by Jaish claimed Afzal had joined it in 1998, having been recruited by Gazi Baba.[37]

The second conclusion, and the one that mattered to Delhi in December 2001, was that the anti-India militant groups still flourishing in Pakistan posed a threat of an attack that could shake India to its foundations. Musharraf might not be responsible for every single act of terrorism against India. There might be different levels of autonomy both within the ISI and within the jihadi infrastructure. But ultimately, despite the shock of the September 11 attacks, Pakistan continued to regard jihadi proxies as a tool of statecraft against India. The attack on parliament, coming so soon after the Jaish assault on the state assembly in Srinagar, was the last straw. After years of anger over Pakistan's use of Islamist proxies, and months of frustration that the September 11 attacks had failed to produce a change, the Indian government ordered the army to the border to try to force it to dismantle its militant groups once and for all.

7

PURSUIT OF VALOUR

THE INDIA-PAKISTAN MILITARY STANDOFF, 2001–2002

In the foggy December of 2001, India dispatched hundreds of thousands of troops to forward positions along the border with Pakistan. By the time the mobilisation was completed, the Indian Army would form an unbroken line that ran from Siachen high up in the Karakoram, down through the mountains on the Line of Control (LoC), and southwest through farmland and desert to the Arabian Sea. As truckloads of soldiers rumbled out of Delhi, the atmosphere was heady. In the public imagination it was time for a war to end all wars. With Pakistan also moving its troops forward, soon close to a million men were deployed along the border. On the LoC, Indian and Pakistani troops exchanged hundreds of rounds of artillery every day. Along the international border, soldiers moving into forward positions believed they would finally be allowed to cross into Pakistan. The mobilisation had been given a name that suggested glorious exploits ahead: Operation Parakram, after the Sanskrit word for valour, *paraakrama*. The outside world looked on aghast at the prospect of another conflict between two nuclear-armed powers, this time on a far bigger scale than the Kargil War. Then the Indian advance stopped. The war to end all wars ground to a halt in the deserts of Rajasthan, Gujarat and Punjab.

The military stand-off continued for ten months. Twice the two countries appeared to be on the brink of war, panicking the United

States and its allies into frantic diplomacy to defuse the crisis. At the height of the crisis, western embassies told their citizens to leave India and Pakistan, so worried were they at the prospect of the world's first nuclear war. And then the troops were pulled back, almost as though nothing had happened. Pakistan publicly claimed victory, believing its nuclear weapons had helped it see off the biggest military threat from India since 1971. India fretted about the futility of its mobilisation. It was only with the benefit of hindsight that it became clear that Pakistan had come out weaker from the confrontation. In 2001–2002, with international backing, India put enough pressure on Pakistan to force it to stop using Kashmir as an outlet for its surplus jihadis. Over time, infiltration slowed to a trickle, making it easier for India to douse the insurgency. Pakistan lost one of the more important pressure valves that it had relied on to prevent jihadis turning on the Pakistani state. Combined with the overthrow of the Taliban and General Musharraf's alliance of convenience with the United States, the new curbs on the eastern front added to pressure inside Pakistan. It would increasingly become a victim of the militants it had nurtured for export to Afghanistan and Kashmir. The confrontation was for India an incomplete victory. Its mobilisation after the attack on parliament was humiliatingly chaotic. Violence against India by Pakistan-based militants would continue afterwards, though less so in Kashmir. But to India's advantage, it had the international diplomatic support that Pakistan lacked and a democratic system that did not allow the Indian Army the war it wanted. Pakistan had a military dictator focused on shoring up his position domestically who was vulnerable to American pressure.

* * *

When the Indian government ordered the mobilisation on December 15, it had yet to decide whether it was to be used for coercive diplomacy or punitive strikes against Pakistan. Foreign Minister Jaswant Singh wrote down the government's aims on a scrap of paper. The plan was "to defeat cross-border infiltration/terrorism without conflict; to contain the national mood of 'teach Pakistan a lesson'; and in the event of war, to destroy and degrade Pakistan's war fighting capabilities."[1] He also talked of strategic restraint, of the need to carry the international community and isolate Pakistan diplomatically.[2] No precise military objectives were articulated. Nor had the Indian Army any say in the decision to mobilise. In a country that had coup-proofed its democracy by relegating the military to a subservient position, the Indian Army had always been kept at arm's length from political decision-making. But once ordered to mobilise, it prepared for war. "The directions were vague enough to be interpreted by the military in many ways," Rear Admiral (Retd) Raja Menon observed in a study of Operation Parakram. "What the politician and bureaucrat do not understand is that militaries cannot simply be mobilised. They have to be mobilised to a certain purpose, and if the politician cannot give the purpose, the military will find their own purpose."[3] All leave was cancelled, soldiers were recalled for active duty, trains brought reserves of ammunition to forward positions and operational plans for an attack across the international border in the desert plains were refined and updated. Everyone below the level of the service chiefs who had direct access to the government believed they were going to war. "Our deployment was based on the premise that the Indian Army was going into Pakistan to sort out the perennial problem of state-sponsored terrorism," recalled General V.K. Singh, who would later go on to become army chief.[4] Unanswered was the question of what war they were meant to fight. The army could cross the LoC to destroy militant training camps, while also seizing pockets of territory to straighten out the ceasefire line and make it easier to defend. In this scenario the mobilisation along the border would deter a Pakistani counterattack. More drastically, India could use its three strike corps to cross the international border into Pakistan. "In the first week of January 2002, expectation about the impending offensive action had reached fever pitch and morale was at an all-time high," recalled Brigadier (retd) Gurmeet Kanwal.[5] But the political go-ahead to launch the offensive never came. "The chiefs so wanted a chance, 'to have a crack' as the military would put it," said Foreign Minister Singh. "I had not only to persuade but also convince them otherwise."[6]

The reasons for the hesitation were political, military and diplomatic. On the political front, Prime Minister Vajpayee was reluctant to take India into a war whose consequences were so unpredictable. "From the very beginning, from the mobilisation, he has been very sceptical about the use of military force," a western ambassador remarked at the time.[7] On the military front, the mobilisation ran into serious practical difficulties. Since Partition, the Indian Army—with 1.1 million men compared to 550,000 in the Pakistan Army—had the advantage in terms of numbers. But it was a lumbering beast. India's vast size meant the army was spread more thinly across the country than in Pakistan, acting as a brake on mobilisation. Its three armoured strike corps, designed to attack deep into Pakistani territory, were based in Central India and took nearly three weeks to manoeuvre into position because of their sheer size.[8] The slowness of the mobilisation gave Pakistan enough time to prepare its defences. Indian military modernisation, moreover, had been held back by bureaucratic and political indifference. Corruption scandals, including allegations of politicians taking bribes to buy Bofors guns from Sweden in the 1980s, had also taken a heavy toll on procurement. Much of the equipment pressed into frontline service, from Vijayanta tanks of 1970s vintage to even older artillery pieces, was barely suited to fighting a modern war. It was only when the Indian Army began to mobilise that its slowness and shortages—of road vehicles for deployment, missiles, ammunition and war stores—became apparent. "The very first few days of Operation Parakram exposed the hollowness of our operational preparedness," said General V.K. Singh, who was then with the XI Corps in Punjab.[9] Having lost the advantage of surprise because of its slow mobilisation, the Indian Army did not have enough superiority in numbers and equipment to guarantee a decisive victory. Nor could it rely on air power to make up for its weakness on the ground. At independence, India had abolished the role of commander-in-chief of all armed forces, replacing it with three weaker, co-equal, service chiefs who each had a tendency to go their own way. Thus though India's air power was superior to that of Pakistan in 2001–2002, the different branches of its armed forces were not integrated enough to consider a ground assault backed by air strikes and close air support.[10] Had India pressed ahead with an attack on Pakistan that January—and in such situations the advantage is with the defender—it risked becoming quickly bogged down. "The slender edge that India had could have led to nothing but a stalemate and...a stalemate between a large and a much smaller country amounts to victory for the smaller country," said Brigadier Kanwal in an analysis of India's military preparedness.[11] Nor did India have the capacity to dig in for a long war where its greater size relative to Pakistan could have eventually triumphed. Thanks to cutbacks, it had run down stocks of ammunition to save money.[12] Even without Pakistan's possession of nuclear weapons to deter an Indian invasion, the balance of power of conventional forces was enough to give pause for thought.

The enforced hesitation gave the United States and its allies time to use diplomacy to prevent a war. The outside world had watched the military build-up with a mixture of horror and frustration. Not only did the mobilisation raise fears about a drift to war that could easily turn nuclear, but Pakistan was moving towards the Indian border some of the troops meant to stop Taliban and al-Qaeda fighters fleeing Afghanistan. More than 70,000 troops were moved away from the Afghan border, according to US officials.[13] Behind the scenes, the United States worked with Britain and other allies to defuse the crisis. They set up regular trips to Delhi and Islamabad by senior officials on the assumption India would be unlikely to invade Pakistan while they were in the region.[14] Among the first to visit in January 2002 was British Prime Minister Tony Blair, who according to his then press secretary Alastair Campbell was seriously worried about the possibility of a nuclear war. The British government, Campbell said in his published diaries, believed Pakistan could use its nuclear weapons and if they did, "they wouldn't be averse to unleashing them on a big scale." Blair returned with a gloomy assessment of the situation, the firm impression that Vajpayee was really upset, and serious concerns about the impact on the Afghan war.[15]

Anxieties about a nuclear exchange were exacerbated by the way India and Pakistan talked about nuclear weapons which, compared to the careful nuclear signalling worked out by the United States and the Soviet Union during the Cold War, appeared remarkably casual. At a news conference at Indian Army headquarters on January 11, Indian Army chief General S. Padmanabhan announced that India was fully prepared for war. Asked about Pakistani nuclear threats, he warned that India had enough to obliterate Pakistan were it to attempt any first use of nuclear weapons. "When you talk of a sufficiency of nuclear weapons, take it from me, we have enough," he said.[16] India at least had promised it would not be the first to use nuclear weapons. Pakistan had made no such pledge. It made it clear it would resort to nuclear weapons if it felt its survival was at stake. Since the country was narrow enough to be cut in half relatively easily by an army strong enough to do so, that "red line" for unleashing nuclear weapons could in theory be hit within less than forty-eight hours. Pakistan was also deliberately ambiguous about its red lines, letting it be known that it was setting its threshold for using nuclear weapons relatively low to deter Indian military action. In December 2001, General Khalid Kidwai, the head of the Strategic Planning Division responsible for Pakistan's nuclear weapons, informally outlined the country's "red lines" to a group of Italian researchers. These included significant losses of territory, destruction of large parts of the army or air force, or efforts at economic strangulation and domestic destabilisation.[17] As new nuclear powers, India and Pakistan had developed none of the safeguards introduced by Washington and Moscow, who established hotlines and maintained frequent high-level contacts to reduce the risk of nuclear war. As the Kargil War had shown, they could drift into outright conflict without either side fully assessing the likely reaction of the other. Compounding the situation was the fact that India and Pakistan believed they understood each other, as they were carved out of the same country. By 2001 they had been separated for fifty-four years.

For all the worries about war, however, the United States and its allies were clear which of the two countries needed to be subjected to the most pressure to defuse the crisis—Pakistan. India's diplomatic overtures to Washington since the late 1990s had served it well. The priority was to convince Musharraf to halt the infiltration of militants across the Line of Control into Kashmir—at the time one of India's biggest concerns. Senior US officials seized on Musharraf's intention to deliver an address to the nation as a major opportunity to reduce tensions between India and Pakistan. Washington provided detailed advice to Musharraf on the content of the speech.[18] Musharraf's television address on January 12 turned out to be a three-way balancing act between reassuring his own countrymen, appeasing India and convincing the Americans of the seriousness of his intent. To the Pakistanis, he promised that "Kashmir runs in our blood" and Pakistan would continue to provide diplomatic and moral support to the people of Kashmir. To the Indians, he said that "no organisations will be allowed to carry out terrorism on the pretext of Kashmir." To the Americans, he said the majority of Pakistanis supported his decision to join the United States to fight terrorism after the September 11 attacks.

India remained sceptical. It saw Musharraf's pledges as a temporary, tactical move to ease the pressure on Pakistan. An apparent crackdown in Pakistan on militants—which included the arrests of hundreds of men who would be released months later—was seen in Delhi as mere window-dressing. Musharraf's speech was enough to stop the drift into war. But the armies remained on the border, the mobilisation on hold rather than retracted.

* * *

India was now in a difficult position. The United States would twist Musharraf's arm only so far. It tried to test the sincerity of his promises by pressing him to hand over to India twenty men wanted for acts of terrorism. Top of the list was Jaish-e-Mohammed leader Masood Azhar.[19] Fourteen of them were Indian citizens who had fled to Pakistan, many living openly in Karachi.[20] US Secretary of State Colin Powell duly stated while visiting the region that he hoped Musharraf would "do what is the appropriate thing to do in the case of each one of those twenty individuals".[21] None were subsequently handed over to India or expelled from Pakistan. At a joint briefing in Delhi with Foreign Minister Singh, Powell also praised Pakistan for "the detention of extremists, over 1,900; the closing of extremist organisations and their offices; and a number of other steps that are encouraging. We have also seen some efforts with respect to controlling activity across the Line of Control."[22]

On the frontline, the army cooled its heels, neither allowed to attack nor to return to peacetime positions. "The logical thing that needed to be done at this stage was to cut our losses and pull back the bulk of the troops..." General V.K. Singh wrote later. "With the army literally sitting on the border, we were now in a face-to-face confrontation; frankly neither side knew what to do next."[23] The Indian Army decided to switch from an offensive posture to a defensive one and ordered its troops to start laying mines to protect their positions. But such were the problems in military procurement that many of the mines were faulty. "A large number of mines had fuses that wouldn't fit and in true

Indian Army style, the men would try and force the fuse in. Mine after mine exploded, killing men in numbers that were shockingly high," said General Singh. Even those mines that had been laid were displaced by sprouting reeds. Regularly triggered by accident, they added to the Indian dead and wounded. Casualties were beginning to overtake the numbers seen in Kargil. "After a while we seemed to be at war with ourselves," General Singh said.[24] The Indian government later admitted the death toll from the mobilisation was nearly 800 men, compared to 473 in the Kargil War. Of those, 176 men were killed by mines, mis-handling ammunition and explosives, and traffic accidents in the period to March 15, 2002.[25] Unlike the heroes of Kargil, their deaths went unnoticed by the media.

Diplomatically, India appeared to have achieved as much as it could with the mobilisation. It had drawn international attention to groups like the Lashkar-e-Taiba and Jaish-e-Mohammad and forced the United States and its allies to increase pressure on Musharraf to curb their activities. But Washington was still reluctant to push Musharraf too hard, unsure how strong his position was within Pakistan. "The December crisis worked for India. There was a tangible shift in position and international support," said one western diplomat at the time. "But Musharraf can't do more without endangering his position. The Indians are playing for more than they can get, because they think they can get what they want."[26] As it turned out, further concessions would in fact be wrung out of Musharraf in May and June when India and Pakistan came to the brink of war for the second time. In the short run, though, both countries had more pressing domestic issues to address.

In Uttar Pradesh, India's most populous state, Vajpayee's Bharatiya Janata Party (BJP) was fighting to retain power in state elections in February 2002. The northern Indian heartland state sent more deputies to the national parliament than any other and political dominance there could help it secure victory in the next India-wide elections. Seeking to draw on an elixir of nationalism, the BJP played up its role as a war-fighting government and suggested that voting against it would be a victory for Pakistan. The state's outgoing BJP Chief Minister, Rajnath Singh, campaigned from a truck painted with pictures of Indian sol-diers, tanks and planes. Confrontation with Pakistan, however, cut little ice with the average voter, more concerned about the condition of the roads, jobs or the price of diesel for irrigation pumps. As summed up by a typical voter in India's rural heartland, "we don't know anything about Pakistan. We are not interested. It is for the big people."[27] After running Uttar Pradesh, the BJP lost badly in the state elections, falling to third place behind two regional parties.

At the end of February, communal violence in the western state of Gujarat, run by a BJP government headed by Chief Minister Narendra Modi, drew all attention away from the India-Pakistan standoff. On February 27, fifty-eight people were killed in a fire on a train packed with Hindu activists as it passed through the Gujarati town of Godhra. Though the cause of the fire remains contested to this day, organisations from the Hindu right blamed arson by Muslims and began a campaign of revenge across the state. At least 1,000 people were killed, most of them Muslims, in the worst communal violence in a decade. Pregnant women were knifed; travellers unlucky enough to be stranded on the roads were burned in their cars. A prominent Congress politician, Ehsan Jafri, spent hours telephoning authorities pleading in vain for help from a mob outside his home before being hacked to death. Ninety-five people, including women, children and the elderly, were killed in a massacre in a poor Muslim quarter in the main city Ahmedabad. After a few days—long enough, said the BJP's critics, to leave time for revenge over Godhra—the Indian Army was called in. Troops had to be pulled back from the border to help restore order. The army imposed curfews in the worst affected towns, while soldiers marched through the streets to curb the violence. Modi, who would later become India's prime minister, was accused of turning a blind eye to the killing or actively encouraging it. A Gujarat court subsequently found no evidence for prosecuting Modi.[28] He would, however, become the main beneficiary of the polarised atmosphere in Gujarat that followed the violence, galvanising the Hindu vote to win state elections that December. The ugly lurch into communal violence in a BJP-run state shook Vajpayee's government and rattled international confidence further in regional stability. Two nuclear-armed countries had close to a million men on the border, while on the Line of Control their armies were firing hundreds of rounds of artillery every day. Meanwhile India was threatening to tear itself apart in communal violence that recalled the darkest days of Partition.

In Pakistan, the problems were no less troubling. Hundreds of Taliban fighters, along with other militants, were fleeing from Afghanistan into Pakistan where they were allowed to regroup. Musharraf downplayed the possibility of jihadis using Pakistan as a new base. In January, he told CNN that bin Laden was most likely dead of kidney disease.[29] Later that month, American journalist Daniel Pearl was lured to his death in Karachi in a kidnapping organised by Omar Sheikh, the British-Pakistani released during the 1999 hijacking. Khaled Sheikh Mohammed, the mastermind behind the September 11 attacks and one of several senior al-Qaeda members then hiding in Karachi, later said he had personally beheaded Pearl.[30] Omar Sheikh surrendered to the ISI, and when US ambassador Wendy Chamberlin pressed for his extradition, Musharraf promised he would be tried quickly in Pakistan and hanged in secret.[31] It was one of many promises that were never fulfilled. Omar Sheikh was held instead in a Pakistani jail, whatever secrets he knew about the links between his mentor Masood Azhar, al-Qaeda and the ISI kept safely away from the prying eyes of western intelligence agencies. Then having promised an early return to democracy after his coup, Musharraf held a referendum in April 2002 allowing him to remain president for another five years. The vote was denounced by his political opponents as rigged.

By May, the troops mobilised five months earlier were sweltering impatiently in the desert. Like the Pakistani troops facing them, Indian soldiers had been trained to fight in the most appalling of conditions in places like Siachen and Kargil. Now they just had to wait for orders from a government that seemed unsure of what to do. Even India's battle tanks were overheating in the intense summer sun. Vajpayee was trapped between the desire of Indian hardliners for military action and his reluctance to start a war.[32] Then came another big attack by gunmen from Pakistan.

* * *

On May 14, three men in army uniform boarded an early morning local bus headed for the city of Jammu, the winter capital of Jammu and Kashmir. As it approached Kaluchak, a lightly guarded compound for the families of soldiers on forward deployment, the men stopped the bus, shot the driver and conductor, and opened fire on the passengers. Then they attacked the compound. Inside, mothers were getting their children up and ready for school. The gunmen ran into the family quarters, firing at the women and children. By the time the three men were killed nearly four hours later, thirty-one people were dead, including eighteen members of army families, and forty-seven were wounded. In the roll call of the dead are the names of young wives in their twenties and their children. Some of the children killed were toddlers two or three years old. The oldest of the army children to be killed was an eighteen-year-old girl, who died with her mother. One man lost his mother and six-year-old daughter. A two-month-old baby died in hospital that night.[33]

The Indian government said all three attackers were Pakistanis from Faisalabad and Gujranwala in Pakistani Punjab who had snuck across the nearby border and deliberately chosen a place where they knew they would find women and children. A claim of responsibility was made by an organisation believed by Indian intelligence to be a front group for Lashkar-e-Taiba.[34] India was now under intense pressure to respond. But it still faced the same limitations as in January. Even if it took the risk of crossing the international border, it could not be guaranteed a quick victory. A more limited offensive across the LoC, restricting the conflict to Kashmir, could easily get bogged down in the thickly forested mountainous terrain. India would then be forced to send more troops to reinforce those at the front, escalating the war. Another option might have been to use air strikes, but to be effective these would have to be against targets deep within Pakistan and nestled among the civilian population—including for example, a large Lashkar-e-Taiba compound at Muridke outside Lahore. Air strikes on militant training camps nearer the LoC would do little more than appease public anger. India knew where many of these camps were. They were, however, small and easily vacated—makeshift tents or huts, or just a few houses in a village. India might kill a few cows or some unlucky civilians. Even that could trigger a broader Pakistani counter-attack. "These camps are not classically like military camps," said an Indian lieutenant-general. "Take six to eight homes on the outskirts (of a village or small town). Put up a poster, ask for volunteers. Free food is provided. Get a mullah or a leader of a spiritual community preaching a distinct aspect of Islam and then introduce them to the weapon and that's a camp."[35] The real problem, in Indian eyes, was the Pakistan Army, without whose help most of these camps would not exist.

A few days later, India expelled Pakistan's High Commissioner, Ashraf Jehangir Qazi, after accusing him of handing over cash to Kashmiri militants. While it seemed relatively unlikely that a top envoy would get involved in handling money himself, the accusation served as a cover to establish parity. India had withdrawn its own High Commissioner to Islamabad after the attack on Parliament. Indian television showed live footage of the High Commissioner beginning the sombre journey home in a convoy of official vehicles that would take him by road from Delhi to Amritsar and across the border at Wagah to Lahore. The dramatic video footage had a quaint feel to it, as though in this severing of high-level diplomatic representation India and Pakistan were copying the symbolic gestures of twentieth-century Europe on the eve of war. A scaled-back presence of junior diplomats would remain in place but without their top envoys. Vajpayee visited the troops on the frontlines and told them the time had come to fight a "decisive battle".[36] Then, inscrutable as ever, he retreated for a five-day break in the mountain resort of Manali. There he reiterated that India's patience was running out, but called on world leaders to put pressure on Pakistan to end cross-border terrorism.[37] In doing so, he left the door ajar for diplomacy. Afterwards Vajpayee's admirers would praise him for "strategic restraint". His critics called him indecisive. No one, in public at least, would admit the possibility that he might be being realistic. The Indian Army was not in a position to deal a decisive blow against Pakistan. Vajpayee's best option was to use angry rhetoric to force the international community to squeeze more concessions from Pakistan.

Musharraf gave another address to the nation on May 27. He accused India of behaving irresponsibly and said Pakistan too was a victim of terrorism—by then it had begun to suffer blowback from militants who had turned against the state. "I had said in my January 12 address that Pakistani soil would not be allowed to be used for terrorism against anybody. I repeat we will not allow this," he said. "We do not want war. But if war is thrust upon us, we would respond with full might, and give a befitting reply."[38]

Musharraf's speech did nothing to ease tensions with India, and the United States and its allies ratcheted up their diplomacy. Washington continued to work with other governments to ensure a steady stream of official visits to the region. The permanent members of the United Nations Security Council managed to work together, with Russia and even China cooperating fully. "The 'dog that did not bark' in all this was China," a report by the Stimson Center quoted a former senior Bush administration as saying. "All we had to do was keep the Chinese informed...we had good relations with the Chinese and, for that matter, the Russians....They did not stick their noses into it except to counsel moderation....They let the US and EU lead [on this]."[39] China could in theory have eased the pressure on Pakistan by threatening to open a second front against India. But there too, diplomacy had served India well. Since the 1990s, India and China, though still rivals, had brought their relationship onto a reasonably even keel, setting aside their border dispute in order to pursue trade and economic growth.

The stream of diplomatic visits to India and Pakistan served to underscore the urgency of the situation, adding to an atmosphere of crisis. British Foreign Secretary Jack Straw told reporters in Delhi at the end of May that "war is not inevitable."[40] His double negative made war seem more rather than less likely. It was not so much that people expected a war. Indians were dismissive of westerners who read too much into emotional South Asian rhetoric. It was more that nobody could see how the armies were meant to be pulled back without either side losing face. Both India and Pakistan flexed their muscles by testing their nuclear capable missiles.

Behind the scenes, though, the pressure was steadily building on Musharraf. The priority, as before, was in stopping infiltration across the Line of Control. Privately, Musharraf promised this would be frozen, according to another western ambassador, while he also undertook to ensure less violence in Kashmir. The language used in Pakistan was becoming much more realistic compared to the days when it insisted it provided only moral and diplomatic support to militants fighting in Kashmir, he said. "Musharraf is no longer trying to pretend that there is no terrorism...supported by Pakistan."[41] Musharraf continued to hedge by pledging to deal first with infiltration and with the militant infrastructure at a later stage. The latter promise was never fulfilled. But the bedrock of Pakistan's Kashmir policy since the start of the insurgency in the late 1980s—arming, funding and training militants who would then slip across the LoC, often under the cover of Pakistani artillery fire, was being slowly chipped away.

India remained sceptical, and as the summer monsoon approached, time began to run out. If India were going to act, it had to do so before the rains came or run the risk of its invasion becoming bogged down in mud. At the end of May, western embassies told their nationals to leave India and Pakistan. Their reasoning, explained in background briefings by ambassadors, was that if war did start, the air space would close and the roads and trains descend into chaos so that it would become impossible to get out. Although western diplomats continued to judge the possibility of war as reasonably low, even the minimal risk of nuclear weapons being used was enough, they said, to justify their travel advisories. Embassy spouses and their children were among the first to leave. As the Indian government fretted about the potential damage of the foreign evacuation to the economy, Indians privately noted that they had seen no evidence of the elite packing their own families off to London, as would have happened if war really were imminent.

Yet the hair-trigger mobilisation was vulnerable to any number of miscalculations, from a local commander acting on his own initiative, to misinterpretation by the other side, all the way up to nuclear war. President Bush decided to dispatch Assistant Secretary of State Richard Armitage and Defense Secretary Donald Rumsfeld to the region. As Armitage prepared to travel to urge restraint in Delhi and to elicit new assurances from Musharraf, he consulted with South Asia hands at the State Department, according to the Stimson Center report on the crisis. "At one such meeting, he asked for a show of hands around the room of who thought there would be a war between India and Pakistan. Almost every hand went up," the report said.[42]

All five permanent members of the UN Security Council, including Russia and China, shared the same anxieties about the risks of a full-scale conflict. At an Asian security summit in Almaty, Kazakhstan, Russian Defence Minister Sergei Ivanov told the Russian media that, "I tend to agree with the Chinese forecast that should this conflict escalate and the two sides use nuclear weapons, 12 million people will be killed and another seven million will die afterwards."[43] Vajpayee had refused to meet Musharraf at the summit, hosted by Russian President Vladimir Putin and attended by India, Pakistan, Russia and China, among others.

He insisted there could be no talks until Musharraf did what he had promised to do in January—end infiltration. The stalemate was summed up by foreign ministry spokeswoman Nirupama Rao: "Pakistan is holding a gun to our head," she said. "We don't want to talk about it. We want them to throw away the gun."[44] A day after the summit, United States, Britain and other western countries upgraded their travel warnings, telling their citizens to leave immediately.[45]

But Vajpayee's long exercise in coercive diplomacy, born out of genius or indecision, was beginning to bite. Bush telephoned Vajpayee and Musharraf. In separate calls, he told Musharraf that Washington expected Pakistan to live up to its commitments to end all support for terrorism and urged Vajpayee to respond with steps to de-escalate the crisis.[46] Arriving in Pakistan on June 6, Armitage's aim was to convince Musharraf permanently to end infiltration into Kashmir. He also presented him with evidence of militant training camps on Pakistani soil.[47] The Americans had come a long way from the early months after the September 11 attacks, when they were ready to turn a blind eye to Kashmir-focused militants. Musharraf promised Armitage that infiltration across the LoC would be stopped for good, according to American accounts of the meeting. In return, Musharraf asked for US help in encouraging substantive talks between India and Pakistan on Kashmir.[48] Armitage met Vajpayee and his inner circle of advisors in Delhi the next day. Western diplomats said Musharraf had given a commitment to the United States to end infiltration, a promise repeated in a phone call between Musharraf and US Secretary of State Colin Powell. Armitage then took the unusual step of announcing in public in Delhi that Musharraf had pledged to stop infiltration once-and-for-all.[49] Defense Secretary Rumsfeld reiterated that commitment in a follow-up visit to the region.[50]

Years later, Musharraf's promise to end infiltration would come to seem like a relatively small concession. The jihadi infrastructure remained intact, leaving India vulnerable to attack. In 2001–2002, however, infiltration into Kashmir was running high and thus a major preoccupation. Any reduction in violence in the Kashmir Valley would also help India politically since the government planned to hold state elections in Jammu and Kashmir later in the year to try to draw Kashmiris into the democratic process. Musharraf's commitment to the Americans was enough to defuse the crisis. Within the week, India announced it was lifting its flight ban on Pakistan. India also said it was ending patrols by its warships in Pakistani waters and was preparing to appoint a new High Commissioner to Pakistan.[51] The Indian Army, however, would remain mobilised on the border to test Musharraf's sincerity and ensure peaceful conditions for the Jammu and Kashmir elections. "A key litmus test for Musharraf is whether he interferes in these elections," said a western diplomat. If the elections were allowed to proceed reasonably peacefully, he said, India would resume talks with Pakistan.[52]

* * *

Afterwards Musharraf was publicly contemptuous of the Indian mobilisation. "The standoff lasted ten months," he wrote in his memoirs. "Then the Indians blinked and quite ignominiously agreed to a mutual withdrawal of forces."[53] He carefully avoided any mention of the concessions he had made to curb infiltration and reduce violence in Kashmir. Though he only partially delivered on his promise, the total number of deaths in Jammu and Kashmir, including civilians, militants and security forces, came down to 3,022 in 2002 from its peak of 4,507 the year before. These numbers continued to fall every year thereafter as infiltration slowed.[54] Vajpayee used the space to hold elections for the state assembly in Jammu and Kashmir in September and October 2002. Peace began to return to the Kashmir Valley. While pretending he had seen off an Indian threat of war, Musharraf had conceded far more than he admitted. Under pressure from the United States and others, he was forced to keep a tight grip on anti-India militants, ultimately intensifying discontent within Pakistan and eroding its own security. Pakistan also effectively handed the Kashmir Valley to India less than a year after it had seen its Taliban allies driven out of Afghanistan. Had Pakistan accepted defeat then and there and begun to disarm militants on its territory, it might have benefited from enough international goodwill to re-emerge as a prosperous, stable country. Instead it decided the setbacks were merely temporary and clung on to its militant proxies for use in both Afghanistan and against India at a future date. It would prove to be a deadly decision both for Pakistan's neighbours, and for Pakistan itself.

Pakistan also misread the role of its nuclear weapons in guaranteeing its security. It came away convinced these had saved it from an Indian invasion. The standoff proved, according to former Foreign Minister Sartaj Aziz, that Pakistan had made the right choice to match India's nuclear tests in 1998. "What would have happened if Pakistan had chosen the alternative path of restraint?" he asked in his memoirs. The answer came in 2001–2002. "The forces remained on the border, ready for offensive action for ten long months, but were finally withdrawn due to the danger of a nuclear retaliation by Pakistan."[55] It went on to expand its nuclear arsenal further, allowing its interpretation of events to reinforce its belief that it was an insecure state that could be protected only by military force, including nuclear weapons and jihadi proxies. While concerns about nuclear weapons certainly influenced Indian thinking, their role was not quite as dominant as Pakistan assumed. The weakness in India's conventional forces and its inability to deal a decisive blow to Pakistan had also made it difficult for it to launch a successful invasion. Operation Parakram should have given the lie to the myth of India's presumed conventional superiority over Pakistan. But it was a myth Pakistan continued to cling to after 2001–2002. It was one that Pakistan was temperamentally incapable of reconsidering.

More importantly, India's most powerful weapon had not been its military power but its diplomacy. Just as in Kargil, India found a relatively sympathetic ear in the United States—though Delhi thought Washington was still not nearly harsh enough on Pakistan. Even China had looked the other way as the United States and its allies arm-twisted Musharraf. Having succeeded with diplomacy, Vajpayee turned his attention to democracy. With the violence of the Kashmir insurgency pushed back, he hoped that free and fair elections would help win over the people where the use of force had failed. Operation Parakram was officially ended on October 16, 2002 after the voting in Jammu and Kashmir was over.

8

IN THE NAME OF THE PEOPLE

A SHORT HISTORY OF THE KASHMIR DISPUTE
FROM 1846 TO STATE ELECTIONS IN 2002

The small group of men in the town of Anantnag in south Kashmir are hunched in the mid-morning October chill like aimless urban youths at a street corner. One man begins a cry of "Azaadi"; his shout taken up by others. It is a word that can carry different meanings in Kashmir— freedom from India, independence, support for Pakistan, release from the humiliation of occupation, an end to violence. Today, in October 2002, it means a rejection of the elections to a new parliament in Jammu and Kashmir. "This election is a fraud. We want freedom," one says. "Azaadi," the cry comes again, and some of the men reluctantly pull their arms out of their woollen *pheran* cloaks to raise a clenched fist in protest. Apart from the protesters, the streets are deserted.[1] South Kashmir has a history of political agitation and violence is expected. When the full-blown insurgency against Indian rule erupted in the late 1980s, Anantnag's geographical location made it a useful way-station. In the forested hills above lay remote villages where militants could hide as they found their way through the mountains of the Pir Panjal range to and from Pakistan. Masood Azhar was arrested on his way to Anantnag in 1994. Nearby is the tourist resort of Pahalgam, where the westerners kidnapped in 1995 began their ill-fated trek.

Over the years of the insurgency, villagers who once came to Anantnag to watch Bollywood movies at its Heaven Cinema visited the town instead to seek information from Indian authorities about missing relatives, or to seek compensation for the dead. They did not even dare refer to the town by its traditional name, Islamabad, for fear of being beaten by Indian security forces.[2]

Behind the small group of protesters, the Islamia Hanfia College is being used as a polling station, with booths set up around an open courtyard. It is nearly empty, boycotted by voters and vulnerable to attack from gunmen seeking to sabotage the elections. We are now into the third round of elections—by spreading voting out over four stages, Indian security forces can move across the state—and today is expected to be the most violent polling day. By the time the day is over, militants will have killed eight people in separate incidents—civilians shot by gunmen who storm a bus; soldiers killed when their vehicle runs over a roadside bomb, a political activist assassinated. General Musharraf's promise to end infiltration into Kashmir has been only partially implemented and militants, both from within Kashmir and without, remain active.

But the trend in violence that spiked in 2001 has been halted. The number of civilian deaths are down on the previous year[3] and will continue to fall in the years ahead, making these elections a turning point of sorts—a time when Pakistan's backing of the insurgency is slowing, and India is seeking means other than the use of force to manage Kashmir. The real significance of these elections is neither the violence, nor a poll boycott, but that they are the fairest ever held in the state. They are an exercise in managed democracy, with Delhi setting the terms in which political parties compete. They nonetheless give the people an opportunity to hold their government to account in an election which is free of the rigging which marred earlier state polls. Beyond Anantnag, people are queuing up to vote, not in huge numbers, but enough to show a longing for a return to a peaceful life. By the time all four stages of voting are over, turnout across the state will average 44 per cent.[4] The people are cowed, weary of violence by all sides, and the insurgency, for now, is broken.

"Azaadi!" The chant resumes from the fringes of the little protest group. The sound is too reedy to be a roar of freedom, the numbers too small to matter. It is a gesture of rebellion against Indian security forces and a sop to militants hiding in the shadows. The aspiration for Azaadi remains, but it has become more plaintive than threatening. This is how the separatist revolt in Kashmir peters out among a bruised people who can barely muster a protest against an Indian-run election. "What do we want?" shouts one man. "Azaadi!" comes the reply. Then they scatter as Indian security forces move towards them.[5]

* * *

Nearly two centuries earlier, British explorers William Moorcroft and George Trebeck passed through Anantnag during a visit to Kashmir in the 1820s. "It was as filthy a place as can well be imagined, and swarmed with beggars, some of whom were idle vagabonds, but the greater number were in real distress," Trebeck wrote.[6] By the time Moorcroft and Trebeck visited, the Kashmir Valley had passed through the hands of a series of foreign rulers. The history of the Valley would afterwards be communalised by Pakistan to paint a picture of Muslim inhabitants oppressed by Hindu rule. But the watershed event in its loss of independence was actually to Muslim Mughal invaders, who celebrated Kashmir as "paradise on earth". After that came decades of exceptionally harsh Afghan rule. This was followed by equally unforgiving rule by the expanding Sikh empire, which conquered the Valley from its base in Lahore in 1819. Visiting soon after, Moorcroft discovered a people living "in the most abject condition; exorbitantly taxed by the Sikh government, and subjected to every kind of extortion and oppression by its officers."[7] The Jama Masjid in Srinagar, a cavernous wooden-columned mosque with space for tens of thousands of worshippers, was shut to prevent Muslims from gathering to plot against Sikh ruler Ranjit Singh. The land was considered his property and the people forced to hand over most of their produce to his government, leaving them facing poverty, hunger and disease. "The Sikhs seem to look upon the Kashmirians as little better than cattle," Moorcroft wrote. "The murder of a native by a Sikh is punished by a fine to the government, of from sixteen to twenty rupees, of which four rupees are paid to the family of the deceased if a Hindu, and two rupees if he was a Mohammedan."[8] In the centuries ahead, that deep-rooted resentment about foreign rule, one coloured by both economic and religious oppression, would never be fully expunged.

It was in the decades after Moorcroft and Trebeck visited that Kashmir became the heart of the kingdom of Jammu and Kashmir. Trade and cultural links between Kashmir and the other mountain states in the western Himalaya, including Ladakh, Gilgit and Baltistan, had informally connected the region for centuries. After their conquest of Kashmir, the Sikhs had an interest in formalising these links. By controlling Ladakh, for example, the Sikhs could secure a monopoly of supplies of the pashm wool that came from there for use in the Kashmiri pashmina shawl trade. Between 1834 and 1842, Gulab Singh, a Sikh ally in the vassal state of Jammu, conquered Baltistan and Ladakh. A Hindu from the Dogra ethnic group, Gulab Singh then switched allegiance to the British, who defeated the Sikh empire in 1846. The British had acquired the Kashmir Valley from the Sikhs, but decided it would be too much trouble to administer it directly, so they sold it to Gulab Singh. Thus the kingdom of Jammu and Kashmir (J&K) was forged, bringing together Kashmir, Baltistan and Ladakh with Gulab Singh's home base of Jammu. Over time, he would expand his kingdom to include Gilgit and other mountainous regions. His younger brother controlled the neighbouring state of Poonch. In the present day, J&K has come to be seen as an artificial state forced by an ambitious ruler on the diverse peoples of the region. Gulab Singh, however, was no different from other rulers fashioning Westphalian "nation-states" in the nineteenth century. Belgium, for example, traces its history as an independent state to 1830, while the consolidation of the different states that make up modern Italy was completed only in the second half of the nineteenth century.

Within the Kashmir Valley, and indeed elsewhere in the kingdom, ordinary people saw little improvement in their living conditions under Dogra rule. In 1929 a visitor made a similar observation to the one made by Moorcroft one hundred years earlier, that the people of Kashmir were "governed like dumb-driven cattle".[9] The absence of basic rights, combined with J&K's ethnic, linguistic and religious diversity, would make it particularly hard for the people to form a coherent political opposition to their autocratic maharajah. When they did rebel, this lack of coherence contributed to a splintering in opinion that continues to bedevil the state to this day. With a Hindu maharajah ruling over a Muslim majority, opposition was partly informed by religion. In

1931, when rumours swept the Kashmir Valley that the Koran had been desecrated by state officials in Jammu, thousands protested in Srinagar. Twenty-two people were killed when police opened fire on demonstrators on July 13, 1931, in what is still known as "Martyrs Day".[10] But religious identity was far from being the sole driver of resistance. In the 1930s, the opposition split into the secular National Conference, more popular in the Kashmir Valley, and the Muslim Conference, which backed the growing movement for the creation of Pakistan. That split would play a major role in determining how J&K would eventually be divided between India and Pakistan. National Conference founder Sheikh Mohammed Abdullah, who was close to the Indian Congress party, was a towering figure in the politics of the Kashmir Valley. Though a Muslim, he was suspicious of the communalism that underpinned the movement for the creation of Pakistan and preferred the secular socialism of India's first prime minister, Jawaharlal Nehru. Abdullah feared—rightly as it turned out—the Pakistani leadership would be taken over by Punjabis who would ride roughshod over the rights of smaller ethnic groups. He also believed that progressives would have little hope in Pakistan, which far more than India, was dominated by feudal interests.[11] In the geographically distant and culturally distinct Poonch and Mirpur regions to the south-west, quite different factors came into play. Poonch was formally incorporated into Jammu and Kashmir only in 1935–1936, and people resented their change of status. Poonch and Mirpur also bordered what became Pakistani Punjab, making their inhabitants particularly pro-Pakistan. Many had enlisted as Punjabi Muslims in the British Indian Army and after World War Two at least 50,000 demobilised men returned to Poonch and Mirpur,[12] swelling the ranks of the opposition with experienced fighters. Poonch was the first part of J&K to launch an armed rebellion against the maharajah in 1947, soon joined by Mirpur.

In the run-up to the dissolution of the Raj, Pakistan assumed a right over the entire princely state of J&K, based on its Muslim majority. The maharajah's subjects were 77 per cent Muslim, 20 per cent Hindu, and three per cent other—mostly Sikhs, along with some Buddhists.[13] India believed it had popular support through the more secular Abdullah, though his mandate from the people was never tested. Under the terms set by the departing British, it was up to the rulers of princely states to determine their futures, and they were strongly advised to accede either to India or Pakistan. As Independence Day passed in August 1947, Maharajah Hari Singh was undecided, and toyed with the idea of retaining independence. As he hesitated, he began to lose control of his kingdom. In Poonch and Mirpur, armed rebellion was fuelled by communal violence spilling over from Punjab in British India. The rebels attracted the interest of Pashtuns in the North West Frontier Province, who were their main suppliers of weapons. Soon Pashtun tribesman jumped into the fray, launching—with some support from Pakistan—an invasion of the Kashmir Valley to try to seize control of the kingdom's political heartland. The Poonch rebels formally declared their independence from the maharajah as the State of Azad Jammu and Kashmir. But their hopes of taking over all of the state were stymied when their Pashtun allies slowed down to rape and plunder on their way to the Kashmiri capital Srinagar. It was then that the panicked maharajah appealed for Indian help and signed the Instrument of Accession.

When Lord Louis Mountbatten, then Governor-General of India, formally accepted the princely state's accession to India, he added a condition that its final status "should be settled by a reference to the people."[14] Nehru, perhaps trusting Sheikh Abdullah to bring a majority in India's favour, echoed those sentiments. The people, however would never be consulted. After India and Pakistan partitioned J&K with their first war in 1947–1948, the people also lost any opportunity to forge a united future for their state. Nor would they gain anything from a UN-proposed referendum letting them decide whether they wanted to join India or Pakistan, given the two powerful countries controlling the state failed to provide the conditions for such a vote. The UN Security Council had called for the full withdrawal of Pakistani forces first, followed by a thinning out of Indian troops.

Afterwards India argued that the entirety of J&K had been legally ceded and blamed Pakistan for starting the conflict. Pakistan believed the maharajah had lost his right to decide, and that the Kashmir Valley had been stolen from it by Indian perfidy. Both based their arguments not only on their respective national positions but on a different understanding of the political impulses within J&K. India's view was informed by Sheikh Abdullah, who it assumed to represent the people of the Kashmir Valley. Nobody can say for sure what they actually thought, since they were never asked. Nehru's initial willingness to back a plebiscite, however, suggests he believed enough of them would rally behind Abdullah's promise of socialism, equality and land reforms to swing the vote for India. Pakistan tended to see the pro-Pakistan sentiments of Poonch and Mirpur as representative of the entire state. It denounced Sheikh Abdullah as a traitor for helping India retain control of the Kashmir Valley. A separate pro-Pakistan rebellion in Gilgit that had broken out in 1947 reinforced this worldview. The different understandings in India and Pakistan of the history of the dispute were consolidated into their public positions. India continued to treat J&K as a one-time unitary state by officially claiming it in its entirety, while suggesting it was ready to compromise by settling for a permanent division down the Line of Control. Pakistan played down the unitary nature of the state by focusing mainly on the Kashmir Valley and assuming the parts of J&K it already held were its to keep. The UN resolutions calling for a plebiscite had treated the princely state as a whole, rather than disaggregated into its constituent parts. The people of J&K were to be asked whether they wanted the state to join India or Pakistan, and independence was not offered as an option.[15] Pakistan, however, pretended the UN resolutions applied only to the people of the Kashmir Valley and suggested they alone had been deprived of the right of self-determination. Its position added another layer of complexity to the dispute, divorcing it from the history of the former princely state.

* * *

Over the years, India and Pakistan intensified their grip on the state, manipulating the politics within the parts they controlled in what became both a territorial and ideological contest between the two of them. It was what Josef Korbel, chairman of the UN Commission on India and Pakistan until 1949, described as "the uncompromising and perhaps uncompromisable struggle of two ways of life".[16] The interests of the people of the state were ignored.

India supported Sheikh Abdullah in reducing the maharajah to a figurehead. It also allowed what had become the Indian state of Jammu and Kashmir to retain the special status accorded to it by the Instrument of Accession, under which India had powers only over foreign affairs, defence and communications. Unlike other Indian states, it was given the right to its own flag and to be run by a prime minister rather than chief minister. The special status was enshrined in Article 370 of the Indian constitution in 1952. But when Abdullah fell out with Delhi in 1953 and began championing the cause of independence, Nehru had him thrown in jail. Resentment simmered but remained inchoate, driven by grievance against Indian rule, occasionally expressed in religious terms, but never reaching a clarity of political purpose. Thousands came out to protest in the Kashmir Valley when a relic believed to be a hair of the Prophet Mohammed's beard disappeared mysteriously from the Hazratbal mosque in Srinagar in 1963. Anti-India sentiment after 1947, however, was never entirely driven by religion—the Kashmir Valley had a pluralist Sufi culture in which Hindus and Muslims lived alongside each other without violence. Nor did anti-India sentiment equate to being pro-Pakistan. When Pakistan tried to trigger a revolt in the Valley in 1965 by infiltrating its own men, it was unable to drum up enough local support and failed.

On the Pakistani side of the divide, Pakistan publicly touted its support for the UN resolutions, while denying political rights to the people of Azad Jammu and Kashmir (AJK) and Gilgit-Baltistan. It refused to incorporate these regions as full provinces of Pakistan, hoping to add control of the Kashmir Valley before doing so, while using their undetermined status as an excuse to dominate them. When elections were eventually held in AJK, candidates were forced to swear allegiance to joining Pakistan.

To assert its authority on its side, India made a succession of deals with Sheikh Abdullah, and later with his son Farooq Abdullah, giving power to their National Conference party in exchange for cooperation with Delhi. Kashmir became 'a constituent unit of the Union of India' and the autonomy promised by Article 370 was gradually watered down. The National Conference came to be seen as Delhi's representative in Kashmir rather than Kashmir's representative in Delhi. Then when an alliance of secular and Islamist parties banded together in the Muslim United Front (MUF) to challenge the party in 1987 state elections, the polls were widely seen as rigged in favour of the National Conference. After that, rumbling discontent slowly gathered steam until it became a full-blown separatist revolt. With no hope of having their grievances addressed through the democratic process, young men crossed the LoC to seek military training from Pakistan. Militants began targeting officials from the state government as early as 1987, followed by bombings in Srinagar the following year. Then in 1989, the daughter of Indian Home Minister Mufti Mohammad Sayeed, himself a Kashmiri, was kidnapped by separatists. The Indian government freed five prisoners in exchange for her release—a concession that emboldened the separatists further. Anti-India sentiment grew, while never becoming fully pro-Pakistan. "In 1989–1990 the first and foremost thing was to get rid of Indian rule. We never knew what was happening in Pakistan," said a former forestry commission official.[17] People shouted for Pakistan or waved Pakistani flags, but *Azaadi* primarily meant freedom from India.

A heavy-handed Indian response by paramilitary forces and the army made matters worse. Intensive cordon and search operations swept hundreds of young men into their net. In January 1990, paramilitary troops opened fire on crowds of protesters in Srinagar killing over 100 people. The state government was dissolved and legislation enacted or amended to give security forces sweeping powers. This included the Armed Forces Special Powers Act (AFSPA), which shielded security forces from prosecution. Summary executions were common, as was the systematic use of torture.[18] Women were raped or became "half-widows" after their husbands disappeared; mothers prayed for dead sons whose bodies they had never seen. Militant groups also turned on the minority Hindu Pandit community, leading to their exodus from the Valley. In the first few months of 1990, over 100,000 Kashmiri Pandits fled. Some 160,000 have left since then.

Pakistan manipulated the insurgency to its own ends. At the start of the unrest, many Kashmiris supported the pro-independence Jammu and Kashmir Liberation Front (JKLF). But while the Inter-Services Intelligence (ISI) had initially agreed to cooperate with the JKLF, it moved quickly to undermine them. When in 1992 thousands of JKLF supporters in Azad Jammu and Kashmir marched to the Line on Control in solidarity with the people on the other side, Pakistani troops opened fire, killing twenty-one people.[19] Within the Valley, Pakistan first tried to break the JKLF by encouraging splinter groups, then decided it wanted a new militant group sponsored by the ISI to serve its interests.

Its favoured group became the Hizb-ul-Mujahideen (HuM), formed through a consolidation of Islamist groups in 1989.[20] The JKLF, the militant group that could most properly be considered to represent *Azaadi*, found itself bearing the brunt of the Indian security crackdown as well as the wrath of the Pakistan-backed HuM, which set out to eliminate its rivals. According to one estimate, the HuM killed some 7,000 people from rival militant groups, possibly shooting, torturing or beating to death more men than were killed by Indian security forces in a campaign started in 1991.[21] The ISI-backed militants benefitted from an influx of Pakistanis who had fought in Afghanistan. Unfettered by family ties, these men were feared more by the people than the "local boys". The Valley faced an escalation in bombings, assassinations, arson, kidnappings and intimidation. The pan-Islamism of the Pakistani-backed groups also infected the more tolerant atmosphere of the Valley; cinemas were attacked and forced to close; some women suffered acid attacks. As with any insurgency, the militants also attracted thugs, criminals and opportunists. Over the years, Pakistani militants too raped Kashmiri women and tortured their prisoners.

In 1994, the JKLF declared a ceasefire. But the violence faced by the civilian population remained as grim as ever. India for its part failed to use the opportunity to open up real political space for Kashmiris. Pakistan continued to pump in men, money and arms to keep the insurgency alive, the leverage thus obtained compelling Delhi to keep some 400,000 troops tied down on the Indian side of Jammu and Kashmir. In doing so, it stoked the dangerous jihadi currents at home that would eventually start to overwhelm it in the twenty-first century. Pakistan, said one former senior Indian official, "should have realised that by 1994–1995 it was getting increasingly evident they won't succeed. They kept throwing good money after bad."[22]

To break the insurgency, India turned to the Ikhwan, militants who had been trained in Pakistan who were bribed or coerced into working for Delhi and given immunity from prosecution. These men provided intelligence, local knowledge and understanding of militant tactics. They countered terror with terror and were hated by Kashmiris. By 1996 India had managed to wrest control of the situation enough to hold state elections that returned the National Conference to power with Farooq Abdullah at its helm. It was pacification rather than democracy. Local boys, having grown up knowing India only through the actions of its security forces, continued to join the insurgency, swelling the ranks of the militants sent by Pakistan. Even by the turn of the century, gunmen from outside Indian Kashmir shot dead by Indian security forces made up only about 30 per cent of those killed.[23] But for a brief period India appeared to be gaining the upper hand.

Pakistan doubled down, using its own groups to harden the insurgency. The Lashkar-e-Taiba specialised in *fedayeen* attacks in which young gunmen would rely on a military-style assault to storm a target before fighting to the death. Between mid-1999 and the end of 2002 at least fifty-five *fedayeen* attacks were targeted at police, paramilitary and army camps and government installations, mainly in the Kashmir Valley.[24] Most were attributed to the Lashkar-e-Taiba. In May 2000, the Jaish-e-Mohammed carried out its first suicide attack in the Valley when it sent a seventeen-year-old high school student to explode a car bomb at the entrance to the headquarters of the Indian Army's 15 Corps. In December that year, it sent a British Pakistani from Manchester in another car bomb against the same target—Britain's first suicide bomber.[25]

As the new century began, the people of the Kashmir Valley were battered and bitter. By 2001, the number of civilians killed was back up to the levels seen at the peak of the insurgency in the mid-1990s, according to figures collated by the Delhi-based South Asia Terrorism Portal. Once fatalities among militants and security forces were added, the death toll in 2001 reached 4,507 people, the highest since the insurgency began, of whom 1,067 were civilians.[26] Indian Army chief General S. Padmanabhan called 2001 an "annus horribilis", with a spike in infiltration and violence. Seventy per cent of the militants killed by Indian security forces were Pakistanis, he said, transforming the insurgency into an outright proxy war.[27] Many of those infiltrating into Kashmir were Punjabi-speakers.[28] Inside the Valley, the region was bristling with soldiers, a constant reminder that daily life could be broken at any moment by a bomb explosion, a grenade or the crack of automatic fire. In Srinagar, Indian troops huddled behind bunkers and sandbags, or stood alone and vulnerable on sentry duty, shivering in the cold. Army jeeps drove through the streets, five men standing on a raised plinth, pointing their machine guns hedgehog-style in different directions. The Jama Masjid, the mosque that was closed to suppress Muslim resistance to Sikh rule when Moorcroft visited, had become a hub of Islamist anti-Indian sentiment. On the outskirts of town, soldiers stopped buses and forced the passengers outside to be searched in a daily humiliating routine. An after-dark curfew emptied the streets in the capital and military convoys dominated country roads... Yet Srinagar had been spared the worst of the violence—it was largely "sanitised" by India to provide a stable administrative base. The villages bore the brunt of cruelties inflicted by all sides. It was in the remote villages that Pakistani militants turned up at the door, young men with guns and satellite phones demanding food and shelter. People knew that to refuse was to die; to agree was to run the risk of being killed by Indian security forces. At least 47,000 died and thousands more disappeared in more than a decade of fighting.

Along with security crackdowns, India continued to manipulate Kashmir's politics. It deliberately sidelined a separatist political leadership formed in 1993 out of twenty-six pro-independence religious, social and political groups, the All Parties Hurriyat Conference, in part because of its links to Pakistan. It used bribes to buy the loyalty of separatist leaders and other prominent players, and pumped in enough money to the Valley to keep Kashmiris dependent while ensuring they could not grow strong enough to break away on their own. As put by Kashmiri politician Sajad Lone, "the Kashmiri whose belly is only half-filled with rice will ask for rice. The Kashmiri full of rice will ask for Azaadi."[29] Since Pakistan also pumped in money to buy loyalty, the more unscrupulous in Kashmir grew rich in the years of the insurgency.

Indian intelligence also worked to bring militant leaders back from Pakistan to woo them into talks. When Pakistan-based Hizb-ul-Mujahideen commander Majid Dar decided that the ISI had nothing to offer except more violence, India helped him return home to Kashmir to begin a dialogue with Delhi, according to former head of R&AW Amarjit Singh Dulat.[30] He surfaced in Kashmir in July 2000 and announced a unilateral ceasefire. Vajpayee's government followed up by announcing its own ceasefire in September. Dar's efforts to get serious talks going would come to nothing. He was shot dead in Kashmir in March 2003, possibly by Hizb-ul-Mujahideen gunmen still loyal to the Pakistan-based leadership, or on the orders of the ISI.

Nonetheless, in Dulat's telling, the return from Pakistan of such a respected Kashmir-born commander as Dar encouraged Vajpayee to believe that a breakthrough on Kashmir might be possible.[31] His defection, Dulat said, "broke the back of indigenous militancy and was to have far-reaching consequences, not least of which was the success of the 2002 elections."[32]

By 2002, the total number of deaths in Jammu and Kashmir, including civilians, militants and security forces, came down to 3,022 from its peak of 4,507 the year before and continued to fall every year thereafter.[33] It was enough to let Vajpayee push ahead with state elections. If Musharraf believed that nuclear weapons had strengthened Pakistan's claim to Kashmir, he was wrong. India intended to improve its standing in Kashmir by widening the ambit of participatory democracy.

* * *

The Indian Election Commission worked for months to prepare for the polls, checking electoral rolls and registering voters. They were to be held using Electronic Voting Machines, making it harder to rig the results by stuffing ballot boxes. Clear instructions were sent down from Delhi that authorities were not to intimidate people into voting, according to J.M. Lyngdoh, then India's highly respected Chief Election Commissioner.[34] The Intelligence Bureau (IB) for its part stepped up its operations to limit the possibility of militants disrupting the polls. It unearthed and crushed militant sleeper cells and cracked down on illicit funds coming into Kashmir through the hawala trade used for informal international financial transfers.[35] As before, the elections would be held within strict limits—candidates would have to promise loyalty to the Indian constitution. But voters were to be given a choice, albeit between two parties approved by Delhi. After the 1996 elections, Farooq Abdullah's National Conference had irked Delhi by passing a resolution in the state assembly demanding full autonomy. In response, the Indian government had allowed—or encouraged, according to some versions—the rise of the rival People's Democratic Party. (PDP), founded in 1998 by Mufti Mohammad Sayeed, the former home minister whose daughter had been kidnapped in 1989. Then in an effort to bring a fresh face to the National Conference, India also convinced Farooq Abdullah to cede the leadership to his son Omar.

Only thirty-two years old, Omar Abdullah came across as more of a rising technocrat than a Valley politician, constantly checking his laptop while giving interviews to journalists where another might have chain-smoked or ordered up lavish quantities of tea and cake. He had been born in England where his father worked as a doctor during one of Sheikh Abdullah's spells in jail. Omar's mother was English and he had spent a brief spell in the corporate sector. Elected to the national parliament in 1998, he became minister of state for external affairs in Vajpayee's government. At the end of 2002 he resigned to focus on the National Conference and the upcoming state elections. He represented both continuity and generational change, and according to Dulat— who had moved from R&AW to the prime minister's office by then— he was Vajpayee's favourite to win.[36] But the People's Democratic Party (PDP) positioned itself as the party that could bring change, and offered its own version of a generational shift by encouraging Mufti Sayeed's elder daughter, Mehbooba Mufti, to play a leading role in the campaign. The PDP promised to bring a "healing touch" by reaching out to political separatists and addressing the suffering of the population. Among the PDP's demands were the repeal of draconian security laws, the release of political detainees and the disbandment of the Special Operations Group (SOG) counter-terrorism police branch.

The elections were an exercise in managed democracy—a long way from the plebiscite the people of Jammu and Kashmir had once been promised. Outside the Valley, however, the election campaign was a reminder of how polarising a plebiscite could be. In Ladakh, the Buddhists who dominated politics in the capital Leh resented the resources and attention lavished on the Kashmir Valley. They were campaigning to sever the links between Kashmir and Ladakh and build closer ties with India. "We have been crying right from 1947," said Tsering Samphel, president of the Ladakh Buddhist Association which was leading the campaign to break away from Kashmir. "We are at the mercy of the Kashmiri Muslims," he added. "We want more integration with India. They want separatism. We are for India. The majority of them are for Pakistan."[37] Yet just as the Buddhists of Leh resented the dominance of Srinagar, Muslims in the Kargil district of Ladakh fretted about being dominated by Leh. Beyond Kargil lay a remote Buddhist enclave that depended on it for communications and supplies. And so it continued into multiple possibilities of Balkanisation. In Jammu, where Hindus made up 60 per cent of the population, some on the Hindu right wanted the state divided into three separate regions, Ladakh, Jammu and Kashmir, with a fourth area to be carved out of the Valley to provide a safe haven for Kashmiri Pandits. Jammu's Muslims, making up about 30 per cent of the population, feared being dominated by Hindus were the state to be split up. They in turn were divided between Kashmiri-speakers and non-Kashmiris. Even within the Valley itself, people were split between those who were pro-independence, those who backed India and those who favoured Pakistan. Under such conditions, even if India had been willing to hold a plebiscite only on its side of the LoC, a referendum would have created as many problems as it solved.

* * *

The road from Srinagar to Anantnag runs through open farmland that turns from the purple and yellow of saffron and mustard crops in the spring to the pale green of ripening rice in the autumn. On the October morning of the state elections, soldiers in sandbagged bunkers guard the entrances to villages that are half-hidden behind the tall poplars that line the road. Locals are out threshing freshly-harvested rice in fields that stretch away for miles; the snow-capped mountains of the Himalaya rising in the distance. By the standards of Indian elections, it is unusually quiet. Very occasionally party political flags can be seen strung out across the road. But it has none of the exuberance of Indian polls, where music blaring out in streets filled with party banners turn them into festivals of noise and colour. Though this is the main road south, there is little traffic beyond the military convoys that hurtle down it at high speed to avoid being hit by an improvised roadside bomb hidden in the dust or in a drainpipe. The army has swept it for landmines early in the morning. But with the elections underway, militants have an added incentive to advertise their presence by attacking security forces. From time to time, Indian soldiers can be seen yelling from the side of the road, exhorting the villagers out threshing rice to go and vote. The villagers tell passing reporters that they had promised to vote, but would not do so. That the soldiers leave them alone is, however, progress by the standards of Kashmir elections. They are not being frogmarched at gunpoint into polling booths. Though there are still some scattered reports of Kashmiris being forced to vote, the relative absence of coercion is the whole point of these elections. Vajpayee has gambled that fair elections will be more effective in winning over Kashmir than decades of political manipulation. In the town of Anantnag only three people have voted at the polling station set up in Islamia Hanfia College by mid-morning. The little band of youths outside shout "Azaadi" and "Allahu Akbar" and then crowd around to insist they want freedom or nothing. "We can lay down our lives for this cause. The cause of freedom. We cannot compromise," says a young man who gives his name to reporters as Mohammed Amir. Yet these youths are not here to sacrifice their lives any more than Indian authorities are there to force them to vote. In other places people are queuing up outside polling stations, chatting cheerfully in the crisp winter sunshine. Voters, among them many women, insist their intention is not to endorse Indian rule, but to choose a candidate who might improve their daily lives and give their families better access to health and education. Many still long for *Azaadi*, but the insurgency has long ago turned sour, and women are among the first to understand it.

By the time all four stages of voting were over, the 44 per cent turnout across the state—or 31 per cent in the Valley[38]—was low enough to show that India had not tried to rig the vote or force people into polling stations. Turnout in 1987 had been a less plausible 75 per cent, while in the 1996 state polls it had been 54 per cent.[39] But it was just high enough for Delhi to claim the election as a success. Assessments offered anecdotally within the Valley suggested it was the fairest held in Jammu and Kashmir. The Delhi-based Institute of Social Sciences think tank concluded that it had been a fair election, but, because of the all-pervading sense of fear due to violence in Kashmir, it could not be called free.[40] The institute's director, George Mathew, said the polls endorsed the importance of the democratic process, but cautioned against "taking this election as a plebiscite".[41] When the results were counted, the National Conference had won the highest number of seats with twenty-eight elected members. But it had lost many more than it had held in the outgoing assembly. Omar Abdullah lost his seat in his own constituency—further evidence that the elections had not been rigged. The elections had achieved something that Pakistan, with its half-century-old resentment of the Abdullah dynasty, had failed to do by force. Delhi, however, continued to manage the outcome. Rather than giving the National Conference time to try to form a coalition government, the national Congress Party allied itself with the PDP—which won sixteen seats—and other smaller parties. PDP leader Mufti Mohammad Sayeed became the new chief minister at the head of a new coalition government. From a citizens' perspective, the rush to form a government in alliance with an Indian national party still allowed for an assumption that their politics were being manipulated by Delhi. The aspiration for *Azaadi* had been subdued but not extinguished. Vajpayee would now need to engage both the people of Kashmir and Pakistan if he were to achieve his hopes of lasting peace.

* * *

With the elections over, India pulled back the troops mobilised on the border since the attack on parliament, though on the LoC the two armies continued to engage in sporadic firing. In April 2003, Vajpayee visited Srinagar and said he wanted to extend "a hand of friendship" to Pakistan.[42] He also promised that Kashmir should be resolved through the three principles of Insaaniyat (humanity), Jamhooriyat (democracy) and Kashmiriyat (the pluralist cultural traditions of Kashmir). His reference to shared humanity was a softening of Delhi's stance that talks could be held only if the people of the Valley acknowledged they were part of India. Musharraf too decided that the time was ripe for peace talks with India, according to his foreign minister, Khurshid Mahmud Kasuri.[43] The United States continued to prod Musharraf to fulfil the commitments he had made during the 2001–2002 standoff. When US Assistant Secretary of State Richard Armitage visited Islamabad in May 2003, he asked Musharraf to end infiltration into Kashmir permanently in exchange for help promoting talks with India, said Kasuri, who attended their meeting. Musharraf, according to his foreign minister, told Armitage he would do so, and in return asked that President Bush put pressure on India to begin serious talks on Kashmir.[44]

Away from the public glare, diplomats representing Vajpayee and Musharraf held discreet talks about how to improve relations. In late summer, the two countries' intelligence agency chiefs met to discuss a ceasefire on the LoC, according to Dulat, the former R&AW chief.

The meeting between then R&AW chief C.D. Sahay and the ISI's Lieutenant-General Ehsan ul-Haq led to a sharp fall in infiltration across the LoC by October 2003.[45] On Nov 26, 2003, India and Pakistan announced they had agreed on a ceasefire that for the first time would include both the LoC and Siachen. As of midnight, the guns fell silent. It was the biggest breakthrough in years. In December 2003, Musharraf said he was willing to set aside the UN Security Council resolutions on Kashmir if this would lead to serious talks with India. It had long been clear that the UN resolutions were defunct, but Pakistan clung to them as a rhetorical and legal device to keep its claim alive. The two countries, Musharraf said, needed to meet half way. "We are for United Nations Security Council Resolutions. However, now we have left that aside."[46]

At the start of January 2004, Vajpayee and Musharraf met on the sidelines of a South Asian regional summit in Islamabad and—unlike their failed talks at Agra—were able to agree on a joint statement. "President Musharraf reassured Prime Minister Vajpayee that he will not permit any territory under Pakistan's control to be used to support terrorism in any manner," the statement said. The two leaders agreed that as of February they would begin a comprehensive dialogue covering all issues, including Kashmir.[47] Then, in contrast to their bitter parting at Agra, they exchanged gifts. Among them was a book of poetry from Vajpayee. Musharraf gave Vajpayee CDs of Pakistani singers and a pair of Pakistani sherwanis with Kashmiri embroidery. Musharraf wished Vajpayee luck in national elections coming up in India in May.[48] The unlikely combination of the general and the poet had given India and Pakistan their best opportunity for peace in decades.

9

THE NOBLE LIE

THE INDIA-PAKISTAN PEACE TALKS (2004–2007)

"We were making fast progress. That I know." Pervez Musharraf, out of power and in exile, is talking about the peace agreement on Kashmir that came tantalizingly close in his final years as leader of Pakistan. It is January 2011 and he is in his London home in an unostentatious apartment block near Edgware Road, the favoured area for Pakistani exiles. "We had found the basic parameters...now we were in the process of drafting an agreement. Obviously there were differences on the wording and the expressions."[1] Former prime minister Manmohan Singh echoed those sentiments when he acknowledged that, "at one time, it appeared that an important breakthrough was in sight".[2] The draft agreement was honed through a series of "non-papers" exchanged between India and Pakistan—a diplomatic convention that means nothing is agreed until everything is agreed. In essence it said that India and Pakistan would give maximum autonomy to the people of all of the former princely state of Jammu and Kashmir while retaining authority over foreign policy, defence and communications on their sides of the Line of Control. There would be no exchange of territory, but both countries promised to work together to make borders irrelevant by encouraging trade, travel and tourism across the LoC. A "joint mechanism" involving the people of J&K along with Indians and Pakistanis

169

would be set up to coordinate areas of mutual interest.[3] "Kashmir is not that easy," said Musharraf. "I don't know whether we could have shown that kind of guts and leadership that we arrived at a conclusion within six months, but we were making fast progress…"[4] He did not hold onto office long enough to find out, and when he was forced out of power, the possibility of a historic agreement between India and Pakistan disappeared.

The story of how close the two countries came to making peace between 2004 and 2007 and why they ultimately failed is also the story of why Pakistan lost the Great South Asian War. The peace deal fell foul of circumstances before it could be finalised—from domestic politics in India to turbulence in Pakistan to international compunctions that went far beyond Kashmir. If India was slow to grab the opportunity for compromise offered by Musharraf, Pakistan dragged its feet in disarming its Islamist militant proxies. But the deal might have survived Musharraf's departure from office had Pakistan not been a prisoner of its ideology. No attempt had been made to prepare the country for compromise. The draft peace agreement depended on the will of a military ruler and Musharraf's successors disowned it. Within the Pakistan Army, the presumed threat from India remained the organising principle. In the broader population, views of India and Kashmir were too ingrained. Without a fundamental change in the way Pakistan defined itself, no peace talks were sustainable.

* * *

One of the many consequences of Pakistan being an "insufficiently imagined" country was that it left people all the freer to define its history according to their politics. Official narratives tried to find roots in the arrival of the first Muslim conqueror in the eighth century and in nineteenth-century Muslim opposition to British colonial rule. But the idea of Pakistan was not even thought of until the 1930s and was very much a product of its times. It was forged by men who lived or were educated in Europe during the 1930s when Europeans were looking for new ways to structure political systems. Whether inspired by communism or fascism, they started to believe in the possibility of an idealised society. Pakistan's national poet and ideological father, Muhammad Iqbal, argued that only the creation of a new country would allow the introduction of a modernised form of sharia to tackle Muslim poverty. He wrote admiringly in the early 1930s of Hitler and Mussolini as examples of what he called the essence of Islamic economics that would "render the growth of large capitals impossible."[5] Even the name Pakistan—the Land of the Pure—came from the early 1930s, at the high point of fascist zeal in the supposed purity and glory of unmixed races. The Cambridge student who coined the name Pakistan in 1933, Choudhary Rahmat Ali, claimed that in the Pakistan movement, "the destiny of the whole of Islam" was at stake. So too was the fate of millions who were "the custodians of the glory of Islam in India", he said in a pamphlet that ended in apocalyptic terms: "The issue is now or never. Either we live or perish forever."[6] The result was that from the outset Pakistan contained within it the seeds of a millenarian ambition to prove Muslim rule superior to Indian "Hindu" rule. This may not have been what Muhammad Ali Jinnah intended—his first speech to the newly created Pakistan in 1947 called for a secular homeland for Muslims.[7] But it was what it became. Having defined itself in opposition to India at the start, the insecurity and need to prove Muslim rule superior became indispensable to Pakistan's identity.

The loss of East Pakistan in the 1971 War amplified both. It was then that Pakistan turned in earnest to a "noble lie"—a term coined by Plato for a myth told by the elite to maintain social cohesion. President Zulfikar Ali Bhutto reinvented his country as a champion of pan-Islamic unity. He hosted a summit of the Organisation of Islamic Cooperation (OIC) in 1974, Lahore's main cricket ground was renamed the Gaddafi Stadium and the city of Lyallpur became Faisalabad after King Faisal of Saudi Arabia. Gambling and alcohol were banned and the revivalist Muslim Ahmadi sect renounced as apostates. General Muhammad Zia-ul-Haq Islamicised Pakistan further while promoting jihad in Afghanistan. Pakistanis became convinced they had a special role as a champion of Muslims worldwide and by the time Musharraf took over in 1999, this worldview was deeply ingrained. "Pakistan Studies"—a compulsory school and university course on the country's history and ideology—declared Muslim causes from Kashmir to Palestine a matter of vital national interest, while perversely insisting that Pakistan, a highly militarised state, stood for peace. Thus a typical Pakistan Studies textbook—in this case one published in 2012 for use at the Islamia College university, Peshawar—defines Pakistan as "a Muslim, ideological, developing and nuclear state" that "is bound to play her role in fostering unity among the Muslims across the world."[8] Geographical frontiers blurred into the ideological frontiers of the Muslim world, steering Pakistan's noble lie perilously close to the thinking of al-Qaeda. Domestic propaganda conflated anti-Hinduism with pan-Islamism and rewrote history to focus only on the Muslims of the subcontinent. A rebellion against British rule in 1857—also known as the Mutiny or First War of Indian Independence—might have succeeded but for the treachery of the Hindus, according to the Pakistan Studies textbook. "Alas! The Hindus on account of their primordial psyche converted this possibility into an impossibility," it says.[9]

The notion of a peaceful country forced into a reluctant imperial role in defence of Muslims outside its territory served Pakistan's security establishment well, allowing it to justify a large and powerful army. It was also self-perpetuating. Pakistan's behaviour—exerting influence through the use of Islamist proxies—led to such difficult relations with India and Afghanistan that it could then reasonably claim to be encircled by hostile neighbours. A strong military in turn was able to manipulate domestic politics, making it impossible for civilian leaders to challenge the ideology. It was exceptionally heavy ballast to be carrying into peace talks. Musharraf, steeped in the institutional thinking of the Pakistan military, did not have the imagination to prepare Pakistan for a compromise on Kashmir. Instead he relied on secret talks whose outcome was then meant to be sprung on a reluctant nation.

* * *

The 2003 ceasefire on the LoC and meeting between Musharraf and Vajpayee in Islamabad in January 2004 paved the way for an intensive series of secret talks on Kashmir between personal envoys of the two men. At the time, Musharraf was at the height of his powers. The resumption of US aid and lifting of sanctions in 2001, combined with economic reforms—including the liberalisation of banking, media and telecoms—created an economic boom in Pakistan. Politically, Musharraf had bolstered his position by the referendum in April 2002 in which Pakistanis voted for him to continue as president for another five years. In October 2002, a national election handed victory to a party engineered by Musharraf to ensure parliamentary loyalty. He sidelined mainstream political parties who were in favour of peace with India while promoting Islamist parties who were guaranteed to resist such a deal. As at Agra, Musharraf assumed he alone could strike a deal, his role as head of the army giving him the space to make concessions that no civilian politician would dare suggest.

Vajpayee appeared to be the ideal counterpart, a man who as the leader of the Bharatiya Janata Party (BJP) could carry the Indian hawks, and with the subtle imagination required to reach a compromise. As the BJP went into national elections in May 2004, the Musharraf government quietly hoped Vajpayee would win. But it was not to be. The elections handed an unexpected victory to the Congress party. Its leader, Sonia Gandhi, the widow of former prime minister Rajiv Gandhi, decided against taking the top job herself to avoid political sniping over her Italian birth. Instead she brought in Manmohan Singh as prime minister and nominal head of the Congress-led United Progressive Alliance (UPA). Singh had been finance minister in 1991 at the time of India's successful economic reforms and was widely respected as a man of integrity and international experience. But he had no political base of his own—he was made prime minister precisely because he would not become a political rival to Gandhi and her son Rahul, the young heir-apparent. The India-Pakistan talks continued. But they would be slower now. Singh could not afford to take the same risks as Vajpayee. Once in opposition, the BJP would also become far more inclined to criticise Congress for talks it had itself initiated while in power.

In September, Singh met Musharraf for the first time on the sidelines of the United Nations General Assembly in New York. In April 2005, a new bus service was launched between Srinagar and Muzzafarabad in Azad Jammu and Kashmir, taking advantage of the LoC ceasefire to allow divided families to meet, some for the first time in decades. That same month, Musharraf made his first visit to India since the failed Agra summit, using a one-day international cricket match between India and Pakistan as an excuse to hold talks with Singh. Their meeting produced a joint statement saying the two leaders had determined that the peace process was now irreversible.[10] While their envoys debated Kashmir in secret "backchannel" talks, the two leaders talked publicly about finding an early solution to the Siachen war. In June, Singh visited the Siachen region and called for it to become a "peace mountain".[11]

It looked promising enough. In both countries, constituencies for peace were growing. Leader of the opposition Lal Krishna Advani, a BJP hawk, visited Pakistan in June 2005 and praised its founder, Mohammad Ali Jinnah, while visiting his mausoleum in Karachi. In Pakistan, Musharraf could in theory carry the army, who would pull the rest of the population along with them. Those with long memories quietly wondered if Musharraf's change of heart was merely tactical, buying time as long as the Americans were in Afghanistan. During the anti-Soviet jihad in Afghanistan Zia-ul-Haq had recognised he could not simultaneously manage conflicts on Pakistan's eastern and western borders. Thus, according to his Chief of Staff, General K.M. Arif, "to avoid facing a two-front scenario, Islamabad initiated a peace offensive with India".[12]

The Indian government judged that Musharraf was committed enough to the talk, though it had no illusions about an overnight conversion on his part. "You can't judge sincerity, but you can do an analysis of his interests," said a former Indian ambassador. "He had an interest in moving forward in some kind of relation with India. Anyone who is in power in Pakistan is driven by that logic."[13] Musharraf's promise in January 2004 not to allow territory under Pakistani control to be used against India also helped convince Delhi he was serious. "We got the impression from Musharraf that he wanted somehow to unfreeze the entire impasse on J&K," said another former Indian ambassador.[14] But to use a rather quaint South Asian expression, Musharraf had a foot in two boats. His overtures towards India were not purely tactical—his standing within and outside of Pakistan would have been bolstered by a peace deal. But nor was there a wholehearted strategic shift. Importantly, he retained the militant infrastructure set up to counter India. And while he preached "enlightened moderation", he made no dent on the ideology that drove Pakistan's competition with India. In the summer of 2005, two events within weeks of each other helped fire up this ideology and betrayed the strategic flimsiness of Musharraf's approach.

* * *

On July 7, 2005 four men blew themselves up in London, killing fifty-two people. Since three of them were connected to Pakistan, Musharraf came under tremendous pressure. The bombings raised fears about links between Pakistan-based militants and Britain, home to the largest Pakistani diaspora community, and between the Kashmir "jihad" and al-Qaeda. About a quarter of British Muslims from South Asia trace their roots to Mirpur in what used to be the kingdom of Jammu and Kashmir.[15] Like other South Asians they suffered racism in Britain, while their children struggled with the inter-generational conflicts that come with rootlessness. The decline of British industry in the 1980s and 1990s subsequently left them marooned in the British industrial towns where the first wave of migrants had sought work.

Alienation along with the Kashmir connection made the British Pakistani community fertile ground for Pakistani militant groups seeking funding and support. Among those who made the journey to Britain in the 1990s was Masood Azhar.[16] Unhappy with life in Britain and seeking a new identity in jihad, some young men used family links to travel to Pakistan hoping to fight in Kashmir. Soon they became disillusioned with the Pakistani state's role in Kashmir and, seeking a purer former of jihad, were sucked into the orbit of al-Qaeda, making them a direct threat to Britain. Mohammad Sidique Khan, who would later lead the London bombers, first became embroiled in Islamist militancy in 2001 when he and a British-Bangladeshi travelled to a camp run by the Harakat-ul-Mujahideen, a Kashmir-oriented group linked to al-Qaeda.[17] "A lot of brothers used to go to Kashmir training camps," the British-Bangladeshi, Waheed Ali, later told a court. "It's just the whole romantic idea of going there, training, helping your brothers, because we all used to just come back."[18] Khan, however, would join others on what became known as "the Kashmir escalator", starting out with hopes of fighting in Kashmir and ending up with al-Qaeda. He made several trips to Pakistan, accompanied on his last one in 2004 by Shehzad Tanweer, a friend from his home town of Beeston in northern England. He and Tanweer may have been hoping to fight in Afghanistan. Instead they were convinced by al-Qaeda to attack Britain.[19] The two of them joined up with Hasib Hussain, another British-Pakistani from Beeston, and Jamaican convert Germaine Lindsay. On the morning of July 7, 2005 they exploded bombs hidden in their backpacks on three underground trains and a bus. Khan, the young man who had set out to fight in Kashmir, died on a Circle Line train just past Edgware Road. Though Europe had suffered al-Qaeda attacks before, in the London bombings the Pakistan connection was overwhelming. The pressure on Musharraf to disarm the militant groups that began in 2001–2002 was ratcheted up further. Then further plots against the West originating in Pakistan were unravelled. In 2006, British police announced they had foiled a plot to detonate liquid explosives on seven airliners flying from Britain to the United States and Canada. The ringleader was Rashid Rauf, a British-Mirpuri from Birmingham, who had married Masood Azhar's sister-in-law and gone on to become a key player in al-Qaeda.[20] Pakistan arrested Rauf in 2006, but he escaped from Pakistani custody in December 2007. He was killed by a drone strike in November 2008.

Less than two weeks after the London bombings, President Bush and Indian Prime Minister Singh signed an agreement that implicitly accepted India as a nuclear-armed power. Under the July 18, 2005 accord, the United States agreed to resume civilian nuclear cooperation with India without requiring it to give up its nuclear weapons.[21] For its part, India committed to "assume the same responsibilities and practices" as the acknowledged nuclear weapons states. This included distinguishing India's military nuclear facilities from civilian ones and putting all civilian facilities under International Atomic Energy Agency (IAEA) safeguards. India also agreed to extend its moratorium on nuclear testing. It was a dramatic change in US non-proliferation policies that had previously tried to limit acknowledged nuclear weapons to the five permanent members of the UN Security Council. It also represented a leap forward in the post-Cold War swing towards India by the United States, driven by trade and investment opportunities and looking for an ally to address the rise of China.

The United States had begun intensive discussions with both India and Pakistan after the nuclear tests in 1998. But the dialogue with Pakistan had gone nowhere, in part because Washington had decided it could not be trusted as a responsible nuclear power. From June 1998 to September 2000, Deputy Secretary of State Strobe Talbott and Indian Minister of External Affairs Jaswant Singh met fourteen times in seven countries on three continents to discuss arms control, non-proliferation and the US-India relationship.[22] The talks began to bear fruit for India early on with Clinton's intervention in the Kargil war in 1999 and his visit to India in March 2000. The Talbott-Singh talks failed to produce an agreement, but the foundations of the India-US strategic partnership had been laid for the next administration.

Early on in the first Bush term, the United States removed the sanctions that had been imposed on India over its nuclear tests, disregarding protests from the non-proliferation community in Washington and elsewhere in the world. In January 2004, the two countries unveiled the "Next Steps in the Strategic Partnership" under which the United States would help India with its space programme, high-technology trade, missile defence and civilian nuclear trade. It was as far-reaching an agreement as it could be at the time and the main building block for the nuclear deal signed the following year. For more than a quarter of a century the United States had targeted Indian defence and scientific institutions, imposing blanket sanctions on the grounds that "dual use" technology could be diverted from civilian to military uses. Indian scientists joked that even paper clips or electric toothbrushes were likely to fall foul of US sanctions. Now Washington was ready not only to lift its embargoes but also collaborate with India in the development of missile technology to help it keep pace with China.

Pakistan found itself left in the cold. In February 2004, Pakistan's top nuclear scientist Abdul Qadeer Khan confessed on Pakistani television to proliferating nuclear technology. US and British intelligence had been watching Khan for years, piecing together the network through which he sold blueprints for uranium enrichment centrifuges and nuclear designs to Iran, North Korea and Libya. When the United States confronted Musharraf with the evidence, he forced Khan to accept sole responsibility in his public confession. Khan was disgraced and dismissed from his job. Whether he had been driven by ideological reasons to share nuclear technology with the West's enemies, or was simply after money, few believed Khan, a national hero, known for his role in developing Pakistan's nuclear weapons, had acted alone. But Washington, still betting on Musharraf's cooperation against al-Qaeda, allowed the suggestion to stand.

In July 2005, Bush and Singh announced the nuclear deal. India offered up fourteen of its twenty-two nuclear reactors for international inspections as part of the separation of its civilian and military nuclear programmes, while retaining the remaining facilities where it produced the weapons to counter China and Pakistan.[23] India could not have asked for a better deal. After declaring Iran, Iraq and North Korea as part of the "Axis of Evil" for pursuing nuclear weapons, the Bush administration had allowed India to keep and grow its military stockpile even as it gained access to technologies and fuel for its civilian reactors. While the administration contended that it served the cause of non-proliferation by bringing India into the nuclear mainstream, critics were quick to point out that its intent had been the opposite— bolstering India's capabilities, including nuclear weapons and ballistic missiles, against China. India was not required to cease producing fissile materials for weapons purposes. "This major non-proliferation failing of the agreement flows directly from the administration's priority of balancing Chinese military power," US non-proliferation expert George Perkovich wrote at the time. "As one well-placed observer explained, administration officials did not forget to ask India to stop producing bomb material; they want India to build a bigger strategic arsenal to balance China's power."[24]

Even then, forging a national consensus in India on a deal that appeared to dilute its cherished non-alignment, did not come easy. The BJP—the same one that had initiated the dialogue with the United States—was in opposition a different animal. It claimed the deal would compromise India's strategic autonomy. The Communist Party, a junior partner in the ruling coalition, was incensed at the idea of the country moving closer to the United States and withdrew support to the government. Prime Minister Singh refused to back down. He put his prime ministership on the line, threatening to resign before finally managing to push the deal through parliament in 2008. Some suggested he sacrificed the possibility of a peace agreement with Pakistan by expending all his political capital to seek allies for the nuclear deal. "He had a choice to make. Does he push the nuclear deal, or does he push on this (Kashmir)?" said a former Indian ambassador.[25]

The US sought to mollify Pakistan by designating it a "Major Non-NATO Ally" and increasing aid. It also agreed to the transfer of F-16 fighter aircraft, a sale long delayed by sanctions over Pakistan's nuclear programme. Pakistan hoped at the time that it too would eventually be offered a similar civilian nuclear deal and was therefore careful not to complain too loudly about the one given to India. It increased its efforts to safeguard its nuclear programme to prove that it too could be a responsible nuclear-armed power. Indeed, so pragmatic was Pakistan at the time that the Musharraf government even took steps to improve relations with Israel, which it saw as the most vocal opponent of it winning a nuclear deal of its own. Though Pakistan refused to give diplomatic recognition to Israel, Foreign Minister Kasuri flew to Istanbul for dinner with his Israeli counterpart Silvan Shalom in August 2005.[26]

Under the surface, however, the US-India nuclear deal and renewed pressure to curb its Islamist militant proxies after the London bombings compounded doubts within Pakistan about the wisdom of the course Musharraf had pursued since the September 11 attacks. Pakistan's grudging cooperation with the United States had been premised on the assumption it could prevent Washington allying with Delhi against it. Instead, the Bush administration had chosen to strengthen India as a counterweight to China. Bush hardly helped when during a visit to Pakistan in March 2006, he made it clear there could be no question of a civilian nuclear deal any time soon. He said Pakistan could not be compared to India—a particularly galling comment in a country that defined itself by this very comparison.[27] It was the last straw. The 2003 US-led invasion of Iraq had already been seen as evidence that the United States was at war with Muslims. By the time the Pakistan Studies textbook was published in 2011, it was confidently asserting that, "a majority of Pakistanis believe that most of the US policies are not only against the Muslims but also against Islam. For instance, some circles claim that US wants to get Pakistan destabilised, de-Islamised and denuclearized."[28] This was a view that ran through the mainstream of Pakistan. In a Pew Research Center survey of Pakistani opinion in 2007, 72 per cent of respondents said they were worried that the United States could become a military threat to Pakistan.[29]

Making matters worse, opposition to the United States was mounting just as the post 9/11 wars were beginning to go badly wrong. The nuclear deal, pushed through by a handful of officials at the top of the Bush administration without much consultation inside the United States or outside, had been a clear expression of US power. But its power had peaked. In Afghanistan, the number of deaths in the US-led coalition more than doubled to 131 in 2005 from 60 the previous year and continued to rise steadily every year thereafter.[30] By late 2005, some US generals had also begun to suspect the Iraq war was going badly. In February 2006 the bombing of a mosque in the Iraqi town of Samarra, a holy site in Shia Islam, showed the risk of sectarian war. By the end of the year Washington was planning a "surge" of extra troops for 2007. US attention was diverted from Afghanistan, and the jihadis Washington had set out to defeat in 2001 were given a new lease of life through the fighting in Iraq. The flagging of American power and possibility of its defeat in Afghanistan gave Pakistan all the more reason to hedge its bets, supporting some militant groups while fighting others. By then Pakistan was facing gun and bomb attacks by groups opposed to Musharraf's alliance of convenience with the United States. Under American pressure, the Pakistan Army had launched a military operation in South Waziristan in the tribal areas bordering Afghanistan in 2004. The blowback added to resentment within the Pakistani security establishment, as did a growing Indian presence in Afghanistan.

Musharraf was on borrowed time. His generals were restless. The post 2001–2002 curbs on infiltration, the international pressure prompted by the London bombings and the US-India nuclear deal had undone the trade-off Musharraf had made in 2001. He had claimed that if Pakistan cooperated with the United States it could preserve its most precious assets—its anti-India proxies and the strategic parity with India provided by its nuclear weapons—and been proved wrong. The talks between India and Pakistan continued; even made progress. But they were already running into the turbulence that would both poison the chances of peace and take Musharraf down.

* * *

As far as the talks themselves went, they were as imaginative as they could be within the constraints of two countries that had nurtured very different views of Kashmir since 1947. India had an interest in a peace agreement that would bolster its rise internationally, unimpeded by constant tensions with Pakistan. But since it claimed all of the former princely state and held two-thirds of it, it could fall back on the status quo without much loss to itself. Pakistan, reluctant as it was to admit or internalise this, was in greater need of an agreement. It had exhausted its options for winning control of the Kashmir Valley militarily and was losing its grip on the jihadi enterprise now turning on Pakistan. But such was the power of the noble lie that that few Pakistanis could conceive of abandoning Kashmiri Muslims to their fate. "Pakistan had suffered all that it had, not just to add territory to its own, but also for humanitarian considerations regarding the Kashmiri people," said Foreign Minister Kasuri.[31] Pakistan needed a peace agreement that would allow it to show it had extracted something from India.

Inside the former princely state of Jammu and Kashmir, opinions about how peace should be achieved were as diverse as ever. While the views of the people of J&K were not systematically sought, an opinion poll conducted on both sides of the LoC in 2009 and published by Britain's Chatham House think tank gives some indication. 43 per cent said they would vote for independence for the whole of the former princely state if offered that option. Support for independence was nearly the same on both sides of the LoC. But the preference for independence was unevenly distributed on the Indian side, with support in the Kashmir Valley outweighing opposition in Jammu. Limited to a choice between joining India or Pakistan, 28 per cent on the Indian side of the LoC said they would vote for India and only 2 per cent for Pakistan. Support for joining India was higher in Jammu and Ladakh, while in the Valley it ranged from 2 per cent to 22 per cent. Confirming anecdotal evidence that opposition to India in the Kashmir Valley did not translate into being pro-Pakistan, there was little support there for joining Pakistan. The highest it reached was 6 per cent and 7 per cent respectively in the capital Srinagar and the neighbouring Badgam district. In Azad Jammu and Kashmir, 50 per cent wanted the whole of the former kingdom to join Pakistan; only 1 per cent said they would vote to join India. Gilgit-Baltistan was not included in the poll. Only 14 per cent of those polled on both sides supported the idea of making the LoC the international border.[32] Opinion polls are never a particularly reliable gauge of what people would decide when given a real choice, all the more so in a conflict zone. The survey, based on 3,774 face-to-face interviews, nonetheless pointed to the difficulties of finding a solution that everyone would accept.

Having learned from the Agra Summit the danger of holding talks under the media glare, India and Pakistan assigned the task of devising a peace agreement to government envoys who would meet in secret.

The Indian side was initially represented by Vajpayee's National Security Adviser Brajesh Mishra, replaced after the May 2004 election by his Congress party successor J.N. Dixit. He died in office in January 2005—causing a new slowdown in the peace talks—before being replaced by veteran diplomat Satinder Lambah. Throughout, Pakistan's envoy was Tariq Aziz, a former income tax officer, political ally and close confidante of Musharraf.

The draft agreement they reached has never been made public. Prime Minister Singh gave the broad outlines as seen from India in March 2006 when he said that, "borders cannot be redrawn but we can work towards making them irrelevant—towards making them just lines on a map." Speaking in Punjabi in the city of Amritsar near the Pakistan border, he also spoke of "a situation where the two parts of Jammu and Kashmir can, with the active encouragement of the government of India and Pakistan, work out cooperative, consultative mechanisms so as to maximize the gains of cooperation in solving problems of social and economic development of the region."[33] Pakistan in its own public descriptions focused on gradual demilitarisation and the opening up of the LoC to show it was seeking to improve the lives of Kashmiris. The joint mechanism set up to coordinate issues of common interest on both sides of the LoC would also let Musharraf claim to have extracted some kind of supervisory rights over the Valley—though in reality, according to diplomats from both sides, it would have been limited to non-contentious issues like trade and tourism.

"It was my idea actually. I am very proud of the fact," Musharraf said. "The parameters were first of all demilitarising, which meant really demilitarising on the Line of Control; graduated demilitarisation from the Line of Control and also from the cities in the Indian part of Kashmir; that is what is bothering and troubling the civilians there; so therefore in first case leave the cities and go into the outskirts and then further, getting to garrisons. The second element was maximum self-governance, and the third was an over-watch of those areas not given for self-governance, and also (to) see how the self-governance is functioning. This body ... I had proposed to be of Kashmiris, Pakistanis and Indians."[34] Whether or not it was all Musharraf's idea, Singh let him take the credit, recognising it would be harder for him to win over the Pakistani public, according to his former press adviser, Sanjaya Baru.[35]

In 2006 India made an effort to help Musharraf sell the idea domestically by lifting restrictions preventing Kashmiri separatist leaders from travelling to Islamabad. Pakistan had publicly championed the rights of Kashmiris for decades; now it needed to show its people it was consulting them before relinquishing its demand for a plebiscite. Leaders from the political separatist All Parties Hurriyat Conference (APHC) duly flew to Pakistan and talked up the need for demilitarisation and autonomy. Pakistan even invited mainstream political leaders in Indian Kashmir to visit. It did so, however, when they were out of office. Among those to visit was Omar Abdullah, the grandson of Kashmiri leader Sheikh Abdullah, long blamed in Pakistan for handing the Valley to India. "Everyone, including the APHC (Hurriyat) on the Indian side and again Omar Abdullah and the leadership in Azad Kashmir, everyone was board," said Musharraf. "I am very proud of that."[36]

According to former diplomats from both sides, the outlines of an agreement were all but settled. Years later, they were enunciated by Indian envoy Lambah in a speech in Srinagar in 2014. Speaking in what he said was a personal capacity, he said, "it is essential that any agreement must ensure that the Line of Control is like a border between any two normal states. There can be no redrawal of borders." But, he said, people should be allowed to move freely across it, particularly to relieve the pain of divided families, and military forces on both sides should be kept to a minimum in populated areas. Self-governance for internal management should be granted on an equal basis on both sides of the LoC. A joint mechanism would allow people of both sides, encouraged by India and Pakistan, to cooperate on areas like tourism, travel, pilgrimages to shrines, trade, health, education, and culture.[37] The joint mechanism was never intended as joint management—an idea occasionally floated by Musharraf to dress up the agreement for a Pakistani audience. Kasuri, Musharraf's foreign minister, acknowledged in his memoirs that there could be no question of pooling issues like defence and security, which would have implied granting access to each other's troops. But by setting up a forum where Indians, Pakistanis and Kashmiris could coordinate areas of mutual interest, it would nonetheless demonstrate a softening of India's position. "The last point was absolutely essential to convince the Kashmiris and the people of Pakistan that there had been in fact a change in the status quo," said Kasuri. "The principle of the presence of Pakistan and India (in the joint mechanism) was accepted; its precise manner was still being worked out."[38]

Whether India and Pakistan might have tripped at the last hurdle in defining the final terms of the agreement was never tested. One former diplomat with access to the draft described it as non-paper five-to-six pages long and subject to political consultations.[39] It is far from clear whether Pakistan fully understood that what was on offer was a compromise covering the entirety of the former princely state, including Azad Kashmir and Gilgit-Baltistan. Its focus had been on the Kashmir Valley, and it has always been reluctant to acknowledge Gilgit-Baltistan, the strategic northern area bordering China, as part of its dispute with India over J&K. Nor was the proposed demilitarisation of the Kashmir Valley as much of a given as Musharraf suggested. Indian diplomats said that India would need to see a cessation of terrorism and violence before withdrawing its troops. "A lot of it was left grey. That's the nature of the backchannel," said a former Indian ambassador. "If someone is thinking far beyond what you have in mind, you won't correct him."[40] What is clear, however, is that it suggested a possible roadmap out of an intractable conflict while giving the people of J&K more say in managing their own affairs.

Along with talks on Kashmir, India and Pakistan made progress on the demarcation of a disputed boundary at Sir Creek, a tidal estuary on marshland between Gujarat state and Sindh province. They also dusted off a separate draft agreement on a withdrawal from Siachen first sketched out in the late 1980s. This had been intended as compromise between Indian demands that its positions in Siachen be authenticated before any withdrawal and a Pakistani refusal to acknowledge what it saw as an Indian land-grab. The two countries, according to this draft, would agree on a redeployment to positions held before the war started in 1984. An unsigned annexure would give the withdrawal schedule for the redeployment of troops from one position to another—effectively ensuring the Indian troop positions were recorded.[41]

In both India and Pakistan, hopes ran high that Prime Minister Singh would visit in late 2006 or early 2007 to sign a peace agreement. But even as the details were being finalised, Musharraf was losing patience with the talks and his grip on power. "We were almost there," said a former Pakistani ambassador. People used to say that Pakistan would

fight India to the last Kashmiri, he said; now it had come up with a plan
that provided relief to the people of Kashmir while conceding largely
to the status quo. "The formulation was intelligent enough," he said.
"The Indians missed an opportunity."[42] It was a sentiment shared by his
counterparts across the border. "There were domestic compulsions on
both sides," said a former Indian ambassador. "Broadly a framework was
agreed upon and I believe a great opportunity was missed."[43]

* * *

Had Vajpayee remained in power, he might have had the political capital
to seize that opportunity faster. Singh moved more cautiously, needing
to avoid domestic political turbulence at a time when his Congress
party was fighting state elections. But the real disruption to the talks
came not from the Indian government but from yet another act of
terrorism in India. On July 11, 2006, seven bombs placed in pressure
cookers exploded on Mumbai commuter trains, killing 209 people.
India said the bombers had help from elements in Pakistan and paused
the peace talks. Pakistan was also becoming restive with too many years
of military rule. The economy was growly strongly, as was foreign
investment. Visitors were dazzled by new shopping malls, a consumer
and construction boom, a vibrant urban scene with its burgeoning
fashion and culture and a newly liberated and frenetic electronic
media. But over time that failed to compensate for an absence of
democracy. Crucially the army was becoming restless. By 2006,
Musharraf had been army chief for eight years. In the Pakistan Army,
the chief is meant to be the first among equals with a collegiate relationship with his Corps Commanders. "The longer he was chief, the
more distant he became from everyone else. That compounds the pro-
pensity to make mistakes because there is nobody to tell you," said the
former Indian ambassador.[44] Musharraf was increasingly making con-
troversial decisions—for example in sending the army into the
Federally Administered Tribal Areas (FATA)—without taking the time
to keep the Corps Commanders fully on board. "The impression gaining ground was that he deals one-on-one with the Americans," said the
former Indian ambassador.[45]

Then in August 2006, Musharraf ordered a crackdown on a low-
level separatist insurgency that had been simmering for years in

Balochistan, fuelled by resentment over its inclusion in Pakistan in 1947 and the belief the people of the province were being cheated of their vast mineral resources. On August 26, Baloch nationalist leader Nawab Akbar Khan Bugti was killed in the cave he had used as a hideout, leading to an explosion in Baloch nationalist sentiment and a revival of the insurgency. Afterwards Pakistan would accuse India of supporting the Baloch separatists, adding yet another cause of friction between the two.

A meeting between Musharraf and Singh on the sidelines of a Non-Aligned Movement summit in Havana in September 2006—in which they agreed India and Pakistan would set up a "joint terror mechanism" to coordinate efforts to crack down on terrorism—helped salvage the peace process temporarily. "I dream of a day," Singh said in a speech to businessmen in January 2007, "while retaining our respective national identities, one can have breakfast in Amritsar, lunch in Lahore and dinner in Kabul. That is how my forefathers lived. That is how I want our grandchildren to live."[46]

By then it was too late. In March, Musharraf fired Supreme Court Justice Iftikhar Chaudhry, accusing him of using his position for personal gain. He was regarded with suspicion by many Pakistanis for his extravagant lifestyle. But Musharraf's decision to sack him was seen by the newly-assertive middle classes, liberated by economic and media reforms, as a fight between military rule and an alternative source of power in an activist judiciary. Chaudhry's sacking led to mass protests by a lawyers' movement that insisted the independence of the judiciary must not be challenged. Most assumed that Musharraf simply wanted to replace him with a more pliant judge. On the surface it appeared to be the first stirrings of civilian dissent against military rule. Many however suspected the lawyers' movement was being manipulated by Musharraf's rivals in the army and the broader security establishment. Musharraf had lost touch. He was forced to reinstate Chaudhry, and came out badly weakened.

In June, Musharraf faced a new challenge from a religious seminary and mosque in Islamabad, once a recruitment centre for fighters sent to Afghanistan and Kashmir. The Lal Masjid, or Red Mosque, had been vocal in its opposition to Musharraf's alliance with the United States and by 2007 had become a heavily armed, pro-Taliban bastion in the heart of the capital. When vigilante groups from the Lal Masjid abducted workers from a Chinese massage parlour, Musharraf was forced to act. Security forces surrounded the mosque on July 3 and hundreds of those inside surrendered. A week later commandos stormed the compound. In the fighting that followed, more than 100 people were killed. The assault on the Lal Masjid transformed the relationship between Pakistan and Islamist militants, deepening fissures present since 2001 and before.

In November Musharraf was again battling Supreme Court judges who were threatening to annul his 2007 re-election as president while he remained head of the army. On November 3, he declared a state of emergency and sacked the judges. Then facing international criticism and domestic uproar, he stood down as army chief at the end of the month. Though he remained president, his source of power as the head of the military was gone. At the end of the year, Benazir Bhutto was assassinated. She had returned to Pakistan to fight national elections—against Musharraf's wishes, say her supporters—and was killed while leaving a campaign rally for her Pakistan People's Party. (PPP). As people came out into the streets to protest, the most popular chant was, "Go Musharraf, Go!" By then, Musharraf had alienated too many different constituencies—the Islamists for ordering military action in the tribal areas and against the Lal Masjid, the lawyers, the PPP over the assassination of Bhutto, loyalists of former prime minister Nawaz Sharif who he had ousted in his 1999 coup, sections of the military for clinging on too long. His days were numbered. With him, went the possibility of a peace deal with India.

10

WAR BY OTHER MEANS

THE ATTACK ON MUMBAI

In April 2008, an American with one blue eye and one brown eye took a tourist boat out into Mumbai's large harbour, a waterway of eddying ferries, dhows, warships, fishing trawlers, tankers, speedboats and yachts. The boat trips are popular with Indian and foreign tourists alike. The ride out into the Arabian Sea on a diesel-fumed rickety and crowded boat is rewarded by magnificent views of Mumbai on the return journey. The old quays are dwarfed by the Gateway of India, the grandiose nineteenth-century arch built to commemorate the arrival by sea of King George V and Queen Mary. To the left, set slightly back from the quayside, is the 1903 luxury waterfront Taj Mahal Palace hotel with its heavy stone walls and ochre-red dome. At sunset, the view from the boat can be the most memorable image of any trip to Mumbai. But the American was unsatisfied. A second trip on a tourist boat left him equally disappointed. He decided to ask some local fisherman to organise a private boat tour. This time he sailed far out to sea. He returned to a dirty seashore next to a fisherman's slum in South Mumbai, the cove remarkable only for the extent that it cut into the land and its proximity to the main road. David Coleman Headley was finally happy. He plotted the GPS coordinates and then took them back to his handlers in Pakistan.[1] The stage was set for the biggest act of terrorism since the September 11 attacks.

* * *

The year 2008 had started out with the hope of change in Pakistan. National elections in February handed power to Benazir Bhutto's Pakistan People's Party (PPP) as it benefitted from a wave of sympathy over her death. The new army chief, General Ashfaq Pervez Kayani, drew the military back from politics to focus on building its morale and reputation. In the United States, then presidential candidate Barack Obama enthused about a new civilian-run Pakistan he believed would be more willing to take on the Taliban.[2] Washington's support for democracy was to be accompanied by diplomatic efforts to strike a grand bargain bringing peace from Kashmir to Kabul. If Pakistan's readiness to support the Taliban was due to insecurity about India, so the thinking went, peace between Islamabad and Delhi would help the United States extricate itself from Afghanistan with dignity. Pakistan's new civilian leadership jumped at the opportunity. In March, Asif Ali Zardari, Bhutto's widower and PPP leader, said India and Pakistan should focus on building trade and economic ties rather than being held hostage to the Kashmir dispute.[3]

But the early promise of 2008 overestimated Pakistan's willingness to slough off its dependence on Islamist militants and the pernicious ideology that underpinned them. Obama's strategy represented a huge challenge to the Pakistan Army—it was simultaneously being expected to abandon the Afghan Taliban, undermine its raison d'être through a peace deal with India, and cede power to civilians. Far from relations between Islamabad and Delhi being held hostage to the Kashmir dispute, Kashmir was being held hostage to the enmity between Pakistan and India, one from which the Pakistan military benefited most. Any drift by Islamabad towards better relations with Delhi without extracting concessions in return would moreover benefit India, the status quo power. If there was no tension between India and Pakistan, it would have to be created. India suspected, rightly as it turned out, that the army was steadily abandoning the peace moves made by Musharraf and easing up on the restraints he had imposed on India-focused militant groups. "When Musharraf handed over charge to Kayani, we were into a totally new ball game," said a former Indian ambassador. "Kayani was bad news."[4]

By April 2008, the Pakistani-American David Coleman Headley was taking boat trips to scout out the coast of Mumbai for a seaborne attack. It would be carried out by the Laskhar-e-Taiba after months of intensive preparations that, given their scale, could not have carried out without the knowledge of the Pakistan Army and the ISI.

* * *

The Lashkar-e-Taiba (LeT) had its roots in the Markaz ad-Dawat wal-Irshad (MDI), an organisation created in the mid-1980s to support the jihad in Afghanistan and to provide Islamic charity and spiritual guidance. It represented the Ahl-e-Hadith sect, a minority sect in Pakistan that followed the same Salafist tradition as al-Qaeda. The MDI founded by Hafez Saeed, a former professor, then split into two wings. Lashkar-e-Taiba became its military wing in 1990 and began operations in Kashmir in 1993 with support from the ISI. Its humanitarian wing, the Jamaat ud-Dawa, provided education, healthcare and disaster relief inside Pakistan. Based in Punjab, its focus was on Kashmir. But it shared the pan-Islamic ideology of al-Qaeda and had provided some of its leaders with safe houses in Pakistan as they fled Afghanistan after 2001. Though the LeT was banned after the September 11 attacks, it was unofficially tolerated and the JuD continued to operate openly, running a huge campus at Muridke outside Lahore comprising schools, houses, a mosque, a medical clinic and farmland. It also enjoyed strong support in the Pakistani diaspora.

As early as 2001, western countries had reason to worry about the LeT. In December 2001, French authorities investigated links between Richard Reid, the British convert who tried to blow up a bomb in his shoe on a flight from Paris to Miami, and the main LeT recruiter in Paris. Reid—who subsequently admitted to having been sent from Pakistan by al-Qaeda—had spent several days in Paris, going to shops and cafes run by the city's small Pakistani community[5] Among the places he visited, according to French authorities, was a Pakistani fast-food café at 80, rue de Rochechouart, in the ninth arrondissement. Opposite the café, on 83, rue de Rochechouart, was an apartment rented by Ghulam Mustafa Rama, a British Pakistani and LeT recruiter.

French authorities believed Rama was Reid's main contact in Paris. They were never able to prove that allegation in court and Rama was convicted instead of other links to terrorism. But they also discovered other connections between the LeT and global jihad. Rama had recruited men associated with the Algerian militant group, the Salafist Group for Preaching and Combat (GSPC), sending them to LeT training camps in Pakistan.

Then France began a separate investigation into a young Frenchman and convert to Islam named Willie Brigitte. Shortly after the September 11 attacks, Brigitte went to Pakistan aiming to fight in Afghanistan, but ended up instead at the LeT campus in Muridke. A man named Sajid Mir became his handler. According to former French investigating magistrate Jean-Louis Bruguière, who later questioned Brigitte personally, "he quickly understood that Sajid belonged to the regular Pakistan Army."[6] After $1^{1/2}$ months, Brigitte was taken with four other trainees to a LeT camp in the mountains. The Toyota pick-up which took them there passed through four army check-points without being stopped. During his $2^{1/2}$ month stay at the camp, Bruguière says, Brigitte realised the instructors were soldiers on attachment. Military supplies were dropped by army helicopters. Along with the other non-Pakistanis, Brigitte was told four times to hide in the mountains. Bruguière believes this was to avoid inspections by CIA officers checking that Pakistan was keeping to its word to crack down on foreign militants even as they turned a blind eye to Pakistani groups like the LeT to avoid destabilising Musharraf.[7] After leaving the camp, Brigitte was sent back to France. Mir then ordered him to Australia where he joined a cell plotting attacks there. Tipped off by French police, Australia arrested and deported Brigitte in 2003 and he was convicted by a French court. "My assessment is that Laskhar-e-Taiba has several agendas," said Bruguière. "It has a political one in close connection with military forces and the ISI in Pakistan, it was to support the actions of Pakistan against India on the Kashmir issue." Its other agenda was to support pan-Islamist militant movements, including al-Qaeda.[8]

The United States soon had its own brush with the LeT after it unearthed a network of Islamist militants in Northern Virginia who had undergone military training in an LeT camp in Pakistan. The men were convicted in 2003–2004.[9] The July 7, 2005 London bombings raised further anxieties about the Kashmir-focused groups. Under international pressure, Musharraf reined these groups in, but failed to dismantle their infrastructure, leaving them free to plot more attacks and recruit westerners sympathetic to their cause. One of the most important of those western recruits was Headley.

* * *

Born in 1960 in the United States to an American mother and Pakistani father, and originally named Daood Gilani, Headley had spent most of his childhood years in Pakistan, attending schools run by the military. After returning to America at the age of seventeen, he became a heroin addict and a drug smuggler before spells in jail convinced him to cooperate with the US Drug Enforcement Agency (DEA). He continued to work for the DEA for a short time after he decided during a visit to Pakistan to join the LeT, inspired by its commitment to the "liberation" of Kashmir. His role as a DEA informant may have initially helped him avoid suspicion. Between 2002 and 2005, he attended LeT training camps on at least five separate occasions.[10] He wanted to fight in Kashmir, but was told he could not do so because of his age.[11] Besides, as an American-passport holder with an ability to travel more easily to India than Pakistanis, he was too valuable an asset to waste as a gunman. In 2005, Sajid Mir—the same man who had been responsible for Willie Brigitte—became his handler.

Later, authorities would try to put together a description of Sajid Mir, also known as Sajid Majid. Born in Lahore, he was one of the earliest members of the LeT. Headley recalled him as being secretive and meticulous, a committed Salafist heavily influenced by religious thinking in Saudi Arabia.[12] He never fought for the LeT, instead being charged with managing western recruits. Some argue he had spent time in the Pakistan Army and, as used to be common practice, had originally been seconded by the military to the LeT. Others like Bruguière believe he was still in the army, at least when Brigitte was recruited. He was convicted in absentia by a French court along with Brigitte in 2007.[13] A subsequent Interpol notice gives only the sketchiest details along with his photograph, the name Sajid Majid, and a 1978 date of birth that seems too recent for such an early member of the LeT.[14]

In late 2005, Headley was asked by the LeT to start conducting surveillance in Mumbai.[15] That would place it right after the US-India nuclear deal was announced, but at a point when the India-Pakistan talks on Kashmir still promised to bear fruit. Before making his first visit to India, Headley returned to the United States to change his name. The Pakistani American Daood Gilani became the less noticeable David Coleman Headley. Headley subsequently told Indian investigators that he had two handlers supervising his surveillance in India. One was Sajid Mir. The other, he said, was a tall fat man with a moustache and thick hair. He knew him as "Major Iqbal" from the ISI. Sajid Mir and Major Iqbal met him separately and occasionally assigned different targets for surveillance, though Headley said the latter was aware of the former's plans throughout. He met Major Iqbal's boss only once, a baby-faced man introduced as Lt-Col Hamza. A junior Non-Commissioned Officer was assigned to teach him military reconnaissance, Headley said. It was Major Iqbal who provided the money for Headley's first trip to India.[16]

By mid-2006—around the time Indian diplomats suspected the India-Pakistan peace talks were losing momentum—Headley was ready for his mission. He used as cover the immigration consultancy of an old school-friend from his Pakistan days, Chicago-based Pakistani-Canadian Tahawwur Rana. On his first trip to India in September 2006, he was instructed to take video footage of the Taj hotel which he then brought back to Pakistan, giving copies separately to Major Iqbal and Sajid Mir. According to Headley, Sajid Mir was particularly interested in an annual conference of software professionals due to be held at the Taj. With the initial plan apparently limited to attacking this one target, Sajid Mir discussed the possibility of sending one or two attackers through Nepal or Bangladesh.[17]

But in the rapidly changing environment of late 2007, the LeT risked losing relevance if it carried out a single-target attack. The group had been straining at the seams for years, under pressure from Musharraf to limit its activities in Kashmir and losing cadres and commanders to the fighting in Afghanistan. "A debate had begun among the terrorist outfits as to whether to fight in Kashmir or in Afghanistan. The 'clash of ideology' led to splits in many of the outfits," Headley said.[18] The LeT's military commander, Zaki ur-Rehman Lakhvi, was anxious to convince LeT cadres to remain loyal to the Kashmir cause. The LeT had made its name in Kashmir and would find it harder get noticed in Afghanistan—rather like private sector companies, militant groups too depend on brand awareness for funding and support. In promoting the unity of LeT and its focus on India, said Headley, Lakhvi was reiterating the official line of the ISI.[19] The ISI was also under tremendous pressure to keep the Afghan and Kashmir-focused jihadis apart—it needed to maintain divisions between various militant groups to ensure none of them could become a serious threat to the Pakistani state. An LeT attack in India would allow it to compete with the more active front in Afghanistan, while drawing ire away from Pakistan. "I understand this compelled the LeT to consider a spectacular terrorist strike in India," Headley said.[20] The plans for an attack on Mumbai were accelerated and expanded. Whether at that point Pakistan's military leaders realised the scale of what was being prepared remains unknown—Pakistan has always denied official involvement. Given that links to militant groups were kept deliberately loose to ensure operational deniability, it is possible they signed off on plans for a single attack on Mumbai which then gathered its own momentum. Given the intensity, complexity and duration of the preparations and training that were about to follow, however, they could hardly have been unaware that something was afoot.

In March 2008, Headley attended a meeting in Muzzafarabad, the capital of what Pakistan calls Azad Jammu and Kashmir, with Sajid Mir and a man he believed to be a frogman in the Pakistan Navy. The frogman brought a sea chart, and the group discussed options for going by sea from Pakistan and landing on the coast around Mumbai. Major Iqbal, he said, supported the plan. A month later, on his seventh visit to Mumbai, Headley explored the Bhabha Atomic Research Centre, especially its staff colony, as requested by Major Iqbal. Then he began his boat rides, deciding after his third boat trip that he had found the right place to land the attackers. He also scouted out the main railway station, a mock-Gothic imperial building originally called the Victoria Terminus and subsequently renamed the Chhatrapati Shivaji Terminus (CST). At the time, Headley said, the LeT was planning to use the railway station as an escape route for the attackers. By the time of his return to Pakistan, the decision had been made. Mumbai would be attacked from the sea. The date was fixed: September 2008.[21]

* * *

In May, the young men selected to attack Mumbai began a course in advanced combat training. Among them was Mohammed Ajmal Mohammad Amir Kasab, who would become the only attacker caught alive. Born in 1987 to a poor family in the village of Faridkot in Punjab, Kasab had dropped out of school early, drifted through odd jobs and crime and quarrelled with his father over money. When he came across JuD volunteers in December 2007, he thought he had found an answer to a rootless life whose only pleasures were chewing tobacco and watching Hindi movies. He and a friend were sent to the LeT's campus at Muridke for an initial twenty-one days of training. During that time, he said, LeT founder Hafez Saeed visited to encourage them to fight for the independence of Kashmir while the group's operational commander, Zaki-ur-Rehman Lakhvi, told them the time had come to fight a war against India. Another commander told the new recruits that they planned to attack cities in India, weakening it from the inside so that it would be forced to loosen its grip on Kashmir. He later recounted these details in a lengthy confession to an Indian magistrate, a confession the Supreme Court ruled as admissible in evidence against him—not automatic given that the court quashed the confession by Afzal Guru.[22]

Kasab's three-week initiation into the LeT was followed in Feb 2008 by a further bout of combat training and in May, he was selected for an advanced combat course lasting nearly three months. Religious instruction was mixed with weapons training, from the use of AK-47s to rocket launchers and hand-grenades. The recruits were taught how to use satellite phones, GPS systems and map-reading. The physical exercise comprised staying without food for sixty hours while climbing mountains with heavy loads on their backs. Kasab said the training was so tough that ten aspiring jihadis fled the camp. During that time both Hafez Saeed and Lakhvi visited the base, as did a man who was addressed by LeT trainers as "Major-General" and welcomed with a military salute.[23]

While the recruits were trained, the plans for the attack on Mumbai expanded. In June, the LeT told Headley to add the Chabad House, a Jewish centre and hostel popular with Jewish travellers from Israel and elsewhere, to his targets for surveillance. Major Iqbal, he said, was happy about the addition of the Chabad House. In August, Headley made his eighth visit to India. He was now scouting out an ever-increasing list of potential targets. Added to the Taj Mahal Palace Hotel and the Chabad House was the Leopold Café, a restaurant popular with foreigners, and the Oberoi-Trident hotel. In considering targeting foreigners and Jews, the LeT was going further than it had ever gone before. It had always been active on the international jihadi circuit, sending volunteers to Bosnia and Chechnya. But under the restrictions imposed by the ISI it had focused on India to avoid international attention. Headley also videoed the main railway station for escape routes. When he returned to meet his LeT handlers in a camp near Muzzafarabad, he heard that the recruits for the Mumbai attacks were being trained nearby. He discussed train timetables to help them escape.[24]

* * *

By now, relations between India and Pakistan were deteriorating. In July, a suicide bombing at the gates of the Indian embassy in Kabul killed fifty-eight people, including two senior Indian officials. India saw it as an attempt by the ISI to force it to reduce its presence in Afghanistan, where it had built close ties with the US-backed government in Kabul. The US media reported that Washington believed the ISI had provided support for the attack carried out by a network led by Jalaluddin Haqqani, a veteran of the anti-Soviet jihad.[25] The attack on the embassy was followed by a spate of ceasefire violations on the Line of Control[26] and a series of bomb blasts in India believed to have links to Pakistan, prompting even the mild-mannered Prime Minister Manmohan Singh to warn that peace talks were under threat.[27] Pakistan's government made an attempt to bring the ISI under civilian control—a move it then had to hastily retract, underlining where the real power lay in the country.[28]

Obama, now the anointed Democratic candidate in the US presidential elections, doubled down on his commitment to support peace and democracy, promising his administration would triple non-military aid to the Pakistani people and "move beyond a purely military alliance built on convenience".[29] But he also said the United States would get tougher on Pakistan. "We must make it clear that if Pakistan cannot or will not act, we will take out high-level terrorist targets like bin Laden if we have them in our sights."[30] He continued to hold out hope that the

US-led campaign in Afghanistan could be made easier if the United States worked to improve trust between India and Pakistan, an assertion that caused much irritation in Delhi.[31]

In August, Musharraf—who had been only barely clinging on to power in his final year—was forced to step down as president, to be replaced by Zardari. Political parties had threatened to impeach him over his 1999 coup and subsequent handling of Pakistan. The army refused to jump in to save him—though it quietly ensured there would be no retribution against him that could humiliate the military—and he resigned on August 18, 2008. Celebrations broke out across the country, with people dancing and handing out sweets, just as they had done after his coup.

* * *

By now the LeT had realised it was going to be hard to organise an escape for the Mumbai attackers and turned the planned exit route through the railway station into a target instead. Having selected seven of the best recruits in Kasab's batch and added another three seasoned fighters, the LeT began preparing the men to accept they would not come out alive. In August, they were sent on a brief visit home before reporting back to the LeT in Lahore. They were given a *nom de guerre* by Hafez Saeed, according to Kasab's confession. A further one-month's training at the LeT campus in Muridke covered intelligence gathering and avoiding detection. During that time, the man Kasab knew only as "Major-General" visited. In September, the recruits were taken to Karachi and taught on a creek leading out to the Arabian Sea how to manage boats, read maps and use GPS at sea.[32] Throughout the preparations, according to Headley, LeT's leaders were aware of the plans. It would have been nearly impossible to carry out such intensive training without the LeT's leaders knowing about it.

The men selected for the attack were divided into five pairs. Towards the end of September, they were to set sail from Karachi, hijack an Indian boat and attack Mumbai. It would be a *fedayeen* attack—one in which the men were expected to fight to the death. Kasab in his confession said that Hafez Saeed had specifically told them to attack foreigners to undermine the financial standing of Mumbai and take revenge for the treatment of Muslims by westerners and Jews. The targets were named: the Taj Mahal Palace Hotel, the Chhatrapati Shivaji Terminus, the Leopold Café, the Oberoi-Trident Hotel, and Nariman House, also known as Beit Chabad. No detail was overlooked. The ten men were shown videos, the same ones collected by Headley, of the exact routes they should take to reach their targets. They shaved and cut their hair. They were given new clothes and told to cut the labels off, along with watches set to Indian time, half-an-hour different from that in Pakistan. They were to tie sacred threads around their wrists in the tradition of Hindus to confuse Indian authorities. Everything was being done to make it appear as though the attack came from India itself. They were given fake ID cards with Indian Hindu names. By the second half of September, they were in Karachi for a last session of maritime training in Karachi harbour.

In late September and again in October, the LeT failed in its attempts to send the attackers to Mumbai by sea as its boat ran into problems near Karachi. During that period, at least two CIA warnings were passed on to India of a seaborne attack, one mentioning the Taj by name. By now, both Britain's GCHQ intelligence agency and the Indians had found a way to intercept LeT's communications chief Zarrar Shah, according to American investigative reporter Sebastian Rotella. But they had yet to put together the pieces to recognise what was being planned.[33]

For now, attention was on events inside Pakistan. A truck bomb outside the Marriott Hotel in Islamabad in September, that killed more than fifty people and set the building on fire, provided a graphic warning of the dangers of Pakistan's policy of tolerating some militants while fighting others. Pakistan Army chief Kayani appointed a new head of the ISI, Lieutenant-General Ahmed Shuja Pasha, who took over from Musharraf confidant Nadeem Taj. For the briefest of false dawns, the possibility of a new start in the region beckoned. The Pakistan civilian government continued to talk enthusiastically about increasing trade with India.[34] Just five days before his election as president, Obama renewed his offer of help to resolve the Kashmir issue. "The most important thing we're going to have to do with respect to Afghanistan, is actually deal with Pakistan," he said in an interview with MSNBC. "We should probably try to facilitate a better understanding between Pakistan and India and try to resolve the Kashmir crisis so that they can stay focused not on India, but on the situation with those militants."[35] India resented the implication of outside interference, but had reasons of its own for optimism. It had just held state elections in Jammu and Kashmir where the turnout rose to 63 per cent from 44 per cent in the previous polls in 2002.[36] The Kashmir Valley had been hit by protests over the summer, showing that the aspiration for *Azaadi* was still very much alive. But Kashmiris were nonetheless engaging in the political process by voting in the elections, which brought the National Conference led by Omar Abdullah to power. In Pakistan, Zardari became even more expansive about peace, telling a conference in India he was ready to commit his country to a policy of no first use of nuclear weapons. His comments, made by satellite link from Islamabad, were a dramatic overturning of Pakistan's nuclear policy and guaranteed to rile the army.[37] By then, though, the wheels set in motion when Headley began his surveillance of Mumbai were turning inexorably.

* * *

On November 21, the ten gunmen were given Indian rupees, Indian SIM cards for their phones, food, weapons and explosives. The next morning they set off on a small wooden boat from a creek in Karachi. Lakhvi was there to see them off, according to Kasab. They then transferred to a bigger boat, the al-Hussaini. On the day after that, they waved down an Indian boat, the Kuber, on the pretext of seeking help, overpowered the crew and took it over. They kept only the navigator of the Kuber, to help them find their way to Mumbai, slitting his throat as they neared. By 4 pm on November 26, they were within sight of Mumbai. They transferred to an inflatable rubber speed boat they had brought with them, alighting at the fishermen's slum selected by Headley. It was around 9 pm.[38]

By then LeT communications chief Zarrar Shah had set up a system in a Karachi control room that would allow senior LeT commanders to direct the ten gunmen. They would use Voice over Internet Protocol (VoIP), routed through a company in New Jersey to disguise the Pakistan connection, along with a bank of televisions and laptops, to run an attack taking place 500 miles away. Unbeknown to them, Britain's GCHQ spy surveillance centre—which would soon realise the significance of its intercepts of Zarrah Shah and scramble to share information with American and Indian intelligence—was watching over their shoulder.[39]

Kasab and another gunman took a taxi to the railway station, leaving a bomb under the seat timed to go off later, entered the busy main concourse and sprayed everyone with machine-gun fire, tossing grenades into the crowd. Fifty-two people were killed in the railway station, the biggest single death toll in the Mumbai attacks, and 109 wounded, including women and children. Indian police, unarmed or using old weapons, were so poorly equipped to challenge the gunmen that one brave policeman resorted to throwing a plastic chair at them.[40] The elite National Security Guard (NSG), the same NSG that had failed to reach Amritsar in time during the 1999 hijacking, was once again too far away to provide any early help. Another pair of attackers took a taxi to the Leopold Café, again leaving a bomb in it timed to go off later to add to the chaos. They tossed grenades into the café and opened fire on the guests inside, killing eleven people. Then they walked over to the Taj hotel to join another two gunmen. Between them, the gunmen would manage to hold off Indian security forces for nearly three days, fighting room-to-room battles and setting fire to the hotel. Thirty-six people died in the Taj and live pictures of the hotel in flames were broadcast around the world. The last gunman was shot dead at 9 am on November 29. At Chabad, or Nariman, House, Rabbi Gavriel Holtzberg, an Israeli-American, and his pregnant wife had just finished dinner with their four guests when the gunmen burst in and took all six hostage. They were all shot dead when they lost their value as human shields. From Nariman House the gunmen fired across the street and threw hand grenades at adjoining buildings, killing and wounding more people. They would remain holed up there until the night of November 28, when they were killed by Indian security forces. Two of the Chabad House's employees survived by hiding in a storeroom, grabbing the Holtzberg's two-year-old son Moshe as they ran out. The last pair of attackers sailed the inflatable dinghy further along the coast and walked to the Oberoi-Trident. They sprayed the entrance with gunfire and then claimed more victims in a restaurant in the lobby. They held out against Indian security forces from positions on the upper floors until they were killed. Thirty-five people died in the Oberoi. Within hours of reaching the shore, the gunmen had left

Mumbai—a city of nearly eighteen million people and nerve-centre of its growing economic prowess—crippled, chaotic and terrifying. No one knew where they would strike next, where they had come from, or how many there were. People ran for safety from one attack only to be caught up in another.

Kasab and his fellow gunman, known as Abu Ismail, had run out of the railway station into a hospital opposite, killing more people as they went, and after running back out into the road ambushed a police car that was chasing them. In the exchange of fire that followed, the head of the Mumbai Anti-Terrorist Squad, Hemant Karkare, and two of his senior colleagues were killed. The loss of such senior policemen added to the chaos. Both gunmen were wounded and as they raced away in an ambushed car they ran into a police roadblock. In their final firefight, Ismail was fatally wounded. Kasab was overpowered and captured alive. He was supposed to fight to the death—his handlers in Pakistan had done everything to ensure that the origin of the attack could not be traced. Now Kasab would provide evidence against them. He made a statement from his hospital bed giving his name, age and address. He would go on to give more detailed statements and, later, a lengthy confession before a magistrate, implicating Pakistan.

By now, Indian authorities had intercepted the phones used by the gunmen to communicate with their handlers in Karachi.[41] The latter provided instructions, relayed what they could see from live television coverage of the movement of Indian security forces, and exhorted the men to die in the name of Islam. The Hindus had become too proud, the gunman at the Oberoi was told. "Let their pride be trampled in mud." Another handler told one of the gunmen at the Taj that as many as fifty fighters had entered Mumbai. "Don't get worried my friend. You do your work. By the blessing of God there is destruction all around in the whole of Bombay." He repeatedly urged the gunman to set the hotel on fire by setting alight the curtains and cushions in the rooms. Another handler, believed to be Sajid Mir, told the gunmen in Nariman House what to say to the Indian media. They should say they were from Hyderabad in India; call themselves the Hyderabad Deccan Mujahideen. If believed, the suggestion they were aggrieved Indian Muslims would have diverted attention from Pakistan and possibly triggered communal violence in India. "Give them the ultimatum that this is only the trailer and the main film is yet to come," said Sajid Mir. Then he reeled off a list of demands that bore a remarkable resemblance to the mainstream propaganda of Pakistani nationalism. India should stop mistreating Indian Muslims and release them from Indian jails; the army should be withdrawn from Kashmir and Kashmiris given their rights; an ultimatum should also be given to Israel to stop oppressing Muslims. When the hostages were no longer useful, Sajid Mir told the gunmen to kill them. The handlers also told their own recruits to fight to the death. "My brother you have to be strong. Do not be afraid," the gunmen at the Oberoi was told. "There cannot be the eventuality of arrest. You have to remember this."

By the time the last gunman was shot dead, 166 people had been killed and 238 were wounded. The dead included eighteen policemen and other security personnel and twenty-six foreign nationals.[42]

* * *

Even as the attacks were underway, India pointed at Pakistan. Kasab, arrested on the first night of the assault, told Indian police the gunmen had come by sea from Karachi. The military tactics and *fedayeen* style of attack bore all the hallmarks of the Laskhar-e-Taiba, the militant group closest to the Pakistan Army and one that, unlike Jaish-e-Mohammed and al-Qaeda, eschewed suicide bombings. Prime Minister Singh said in a televised address to the nation on November 27 that the group behind the attacks was based outside India and promised "the strongest possible measures to ensure that there is no repetition of such terrorist acts."[43] Pakistan condemned the attack and the civilian government took the unprecedented step of offering to send the head of the ISI to exchange information. But the offer was quickly retracted. Pakistan's Foreign Minister Shah Mehmood Qureshi, on a prescheduled visit to Delhi meant to review the peace process, packed his bags after the Indian government cancelled meetings with him.

Over time the Indian government, helped by other countries whose citizens had been targeted, turned up ever-increasing evidence of Pakistani involvement. The British intercepts on Zarrar Shah helped piece together the LeT's role. Indian authorities found the Indian boat hijacked by the gunmen drifting offshore—the attackers were meant to have sunk it but in their haste had failed to do so. DNA from the dead gunmen was matched with sweat stains on clothes they had left behind on the Kuber. Forensic help from the FBI established that a GPS device found on the boat, along with those retrieved from the dead gunmen, had been used to mark waypoints from Karachi to Mumbai. The FBI also traced the serial number on the Yamaha outboard engine of the dinghy the gunmen used to reach the shore—it had been sold to a buyer in Karachi in January 2008. Calls made between the gunmen and their handlers in Karachi were tracked to the New Jersey company that had provided Voice over Internet Protocol services. The FBI established that payments for the service had been made from Pakistan. The Nokia mobile phones used by the gunmen had also been shipped to Pakistan.[44] But there was little India could do to retaliate. All the same limitations that had confronted it in 2001–2002 remained. Instead, India relied on international diplomacy, and particularly the diplomatic might of the United States, to put pressure on Pakistan to close down the Lashkar-e-Taiba and the Jamaat-ud-Dawa (JuD) once and for all.

The pressure on Pakistan was intense. The sophistication of the attack and the training of the gunmen pointed to the involvement of the Pakistani military. "Mumbai was war by other means," said a former Indian intelligence official. "These were not terrorists. They were commandos."[45] Senior officials in the outgoing Bush administration flew to the region to demand Pakistan take action. Even Pakistan's old ally China refused to support it, voting with the other permanent members of the UN Security Council to blacklist the JuD. "What could we say after Mumbai?" a Chinese expert was quoted as saying by Andrew Small, author of a book on Pakistan's relations with China. "They obviously had military training. We couldn't defend that."[46] Hafez Saeed, Lakhvi and two other LeT leaders were added to a list of a list of people and groups facing sanctions for ties to al-Qaeda or the Taliban, including a freeze on assets and travel ban.[47] After initially denying that the attackers had come from Pakistan, authorities arrested Lakhvi and five others in a raid on an LeT camp in the hills above Muzzafarabad. Dozens more were detained across the country. Pakistan said it would abide by the UN decision blacklisting Hafez Saeed, and put him under house arrest. Police also raided JuD offices around the country, A spokesman for Pakistan's central bank said directives had been issued to banks to freeze JuD accounts.[48] Government officials took control of the LeT compound in Muridke. It was enough to avert a war between India and Pakistan. Prime Minister Singh eventually tried to revive talks about the draft agreement on Kashmir that had been so laboriously constructed. But Indian public opinion after Mumbai was solidly against Pakistan, and he would make no headway. In Pakistan, without the possibility of peace with India, the space for the civilian government to outmanoeuvre the military shrank further.

The United States stopped short of accusing the Pakistani military leadership of directly ordering the Mumbai attacks, instead seeking refuge in the grey area that allowed it to overlook Pakistani support for militants in exchange for its cooperation in Afghanistan. If the military leadership knew some kind of attack was planned, so this thinking went, it probably did not anticipate the scale of it—in the final months of preparation, the plans had expanded from an assault on the Taj to the siege of a city by multiple gunmen. Privately, Pakistani officials pointed to the amount of money needed to prepare the attack to insist that no ISI officer could have helped without authorisation from their superiors.[49] It was an assertion, if true, that cut both ways: either none were involved or the payments were approved all the way up the chain of command to the top. Either way, the United States—caught during the handover from the Bush to the Obama administration—continued to hope Pakistan could be convinced to change course. In 2009, Obama authorised the US military to deploy additional troops in Afghanistan. It would take a while for Washington to realise the diplomatic plank of its strategy had disappeared. The fondly imagined Kashmir to Kabul peace deal was off.

Pakistan gradually lifted the restrictions on the JuD. Of the 100 or so LeT members rounded up in the aftermath of the Mumbai attacks, most were released in the following months.[50] Five were eventually put on trial for involvement in the attacks, including Lakhvi, but never convicted as Pakistan insisted it did not have enough evidence against them. A court ordered the release of Hafiz Saeed. The asset freeze mandated by the United Nations made little difference—before it took effect, the group transferred its funds into other bank accounts under a different name.[51] The JuD compound at Muridke continued to function as before. When American researcher Stephen Tankel, author of a book on the LeT, visited Muridke in May 2009, he was told by a JuD administrator that the provincial government made only weekly visits. The government continued to fund its provision of services, including its schools and hospital.[52] Pakistan also chipped away at the Indian version of Mumbai to undermine any suggestion that the LeT and Hafez Saeed were involved. The United States would eventually offer a $10 million reward for information leading to the conviction of Hafez Saeed, saying he participated in the planning of the Mumbai attacks.[53] But inside Pakistan, after a brief pause, he was allowed to resume his old activities in public, as was the JuD. By 2010, the ISI was confidently asserting that Mumbai had been a false flag operation conducted by India to discredit Pakistan. Journalists were invited to briefings at ISI headquarters—a modern building in the Aabpara district of Islamabad—for a detailed exposition of the Indian threat. They were led past a room unabashedly marked "psy-ops" to be told of alleged Indian involvement in violence in Balochistan and the Federally Administered Tribal Areas (FATA). No documentary evidence was provided. The ISI did, however, distribute a book purporting to prove that Hemant Karkare, the Indian police chief killed in the Mumbai attacks, had been shot dead by the Indian Hindu right—evidence, it said, that called into question allegations of Pakistani involvement.[54] The deliberate obfuscation over Mumbai further confused a bewildered Pakistani public about the threat from Islamist militancy, even as they faced a fresh spate of gun and bomb attacks at home.

Kasab was tried and convicted by an Indian court and hanged on November 21, 2012. Headley's role was initially overlooked. He claimed that before the assault on Mumbai, he had discussed with both Sajid Mir and Major Iqbal the possibility of attacking the Danish *Jyllands-Posten* newspaper over its publication of cartoons of the Prophet Mohammed in 2005. After the Mumbai attacks, however, the pressure on the LeT was so great that it was no longer interested in such an operation. Major Iqbal told him not to contact him again. Headley turned to Ilyas Kashmiri, a senior commander in al-Qaeda, to support the plot. In 2009, using his cover as an immigration consultant, Headley travelled to Copenhagen and visited the offices of the *Jyllands-Posten*, while also taking video footage of restaurants, hotels, the French embassy and the main railway station. The plans were for a Mumbai-style attack that would also include the beheading of staff at

Jyllands-Posten. By now, however, Headley's trail had been picked up by British intelligence after he met with two British Pakistanis. British intelligence tipped off the Americans who began to track him. He was arrested in October 2009 at Chicago's O'Hare International Airport as he was about to travel to Pakistan. He immediately began bargaining with US authorities, offering to turn prosecution witness and provide information in exchange for being spared the death penalty. He was sentenced to thirty-five years in jail in January 2013.[55] Tahawwur Rana, the Pakistani Canadian whose immigration consultancy Headley had used as cover, was convicted for providing support to Headley and jailed for fourteen years.[56] Sajid Mir was not arrested. Headley identified photos of him and confirmed to Indian investigators that his was the voice giving instructions from the Karachi control room to the gunmen in the Chabad House. He also said Sajid Mir had undergone plastic surgery, though it did not much change his appearance. Indian officials believe he continues to live in Pakistan under ISI protection. The man known as Major Iqbal was subsequently detected directing intelligence and terrorism operations in other cases. US and Indian officials also said phone and e-mail evidence had corroborated Headley's contact with him.[57] Pakistan denies all knowledge of him.

11

ANATOMY OF MURDER

PAKISTAN'S RELATIONSHIP WITH ITS NORTH-WEST FRONTIER 1947–2011

In the photos that are all that remain of her, she is a large woman with a heavy-set face already turning jowly. She wears red lipstick and a violet dress embroidered with red-and-gold butterfly flowers and matching headdress. A certain coarseness to her appearance hints at poverty; a seriousness in her eyes offsetting the gaiety of the dress. Shabana is, or was, a "dancing girl", one of many women in the Swat Valley who performed at weddings, engagements or private parties to celebrate the birth of a child. They were born into the profession, the daughters of singers and musicians, and often supported their families. In recent years, they had begun to make music CDs where groups of four or five girls performed simple dances to Pashto songs on love, separation and exile. Some dreamed of becoming film stars. One night in January 2009, the Pakistani Taliban broke into Shabana's house in the town of Mingora and dragged her outside. Neighbours heard her screaming for her life, her cries joined by the shrieks of her mother. Shabana bargained with them, promising never to dance again. The Taliban dragged her by her hair to the main square in Mingora. Her wailing mother ran after them. Then the anguished appeals of the two women became plaintive. They were no longer bargaining for her life, but negotiating the manner of her death. They begged the Taliban not to behead her. The gunmen relented. They shot Shabana at point-blank range, flung her CDs onto her bullet-ridden body and left her in the square as a warning to others.[1]

Shabana was one of thousands to die in Pakistan's turbulent north-west after 2001. Her death attracted more attention than usual in the media, perhaps because Swat, an Alpine region less than five hours' drive from Islamabad, was popular with tourists throughout Pakistan. But the reasons for her murder were widely misunderstood. In Pakistan's urban heartland, many assumed she was the unfortunate victim of a conservative Pashtun culture that infused the inhabitants of Pakistan's north-west periphery. The Pakistani Taliban were assumed to be a Pashtun problem, an overspill of the US-led war in Afghanistan. As described by one influential Pakistani report published in 2011, the unrest in the north-west was the result of "an upswing in Pashtun nationalism seeking to support their Afghan brethren in a tussle against non-Pashtuns in Afghanistan".[2] The narrative suited the Pakistani security establishment well, allowing it to portray the Afghan Taliban as a Pashtun liberation movement fighting a foreign-backed government. When Shabana was murdered, she was seen as the outlier, the Pakistani Taliban a cruel but authentic expression of Pashtun nationalism.

Those assumptions were wrong. Shabana far more typified the local culture, one that celebrated music, poetry and dance and treated the dancing girls with courtesy albeit without honour. The Pakistani Taliban were the aberration. Far from representing ancient Pashtun traditions, they were a product of the influences of the modern world, some international, many the result of policies adopted by Pakistan's central-ised, militarised state. Pakistan wrongly assumed that conflict moved east from Afghanistan, spilling into the north-west and towards the Pakistani heartland. But in reality, rather than the conflict moving inwards from the periphery, it radiated outwards from the centre. It was Pakistan that had exported the Afghan Taliban to Afghanistan in the first place, and continued to offer them safe haven after 2001 as a hedge against Indian influence in Kabul. It was Pakistan that had encouraged the growth of radical Islamist groups to suppress ethnic Pashtun nation-alism. President Pervez Musharraf had then created the political condi-tions in the north-west that allowed Islamist groups to flourish and paved the way for the rise of the Pakistani Taliban. Blinded by competition with India and an unwillingness to recognise the changes wrought in part by its own security policies, Pakistan never formed a coherent, clear-sighted strategy towards Afghanistan and the north-west. The result was a muddled, reactive policy that exacerbated the upheaval caused by the Afghan war, led to thousands of deaths and accelerated its slide into defeat in the Great South Asian War.

* * *

Pakistan's understanding of the Pashtun tribes who lived on its periphery was inherited from the British, who after their two invasions of Afghanistan in the nineteenth century decided the best solution was to keep them at bay. With Afghanistan turned into a buffer state against Russia, the Pashtuns on the frontier were to become a secondary buffer and excluded from the "civilising" benefits of empire. They would also be stereotyped as primitive, wild tribes—a common enough practice by all states and empires that draw people into the comforts of centralised power by painting the periphery as dangerous. The Frontier, and Afghanistan beyond it, became seen as an ungovernable space, too steeped in tradition to benefit from the "modernising" influences of colonialism. This space was managed through a series of concentric lines across which British authority gradually tailed off. The outermost line separated Afghanistan from the Raj and was agreed in the treaty negotiated with Afghanistan in 1893 by the British Foreign Secretary of India, Sir Mortimer Durand. The Durand Line was never intended as a formal border, instead indicating spheres of influence beyond which the other should not interfere.[3] Between Afghanistan and the settled areas, the British established "the Frontier". This was not, as its name suggests, a border, but a deliberately created no-man's land. The 1901 Frontier Crimes Regulation (FCR) decreed that the mainly Pashtun inhabitants should be managed as tribes, subject to collective punishment, rather than treated as individuals entitled to the rule of law. The idea of frontier tribes frozen in time through their own resistance to modernity—the archetype of the "noble savage"—was thus actively encouraged by the British to maintain the boundaries of the empire. In reality, like many people from peripheral regions deprived of economic opportunity, the Pashtuns travelled extensively. In the eighteenth century, tens of thousands migrated east to settle as farmers, soldiers and traders, many of them northeast of Delhi in the Rohilkhand region.[4] During the Raj, thousands more joined the British Indian Army, travelled overseas as indentured labourers to commercial plantations or were recruited for the colonial police in other parts of the empire. Indeed, towards the end of British rule, those among the British who interacted with Pashtuns had begun to soften their stereotypes of an immutable people rigidly following an ancient code of conduct known as "Pashtunwali". A 1938 edition of the British *Handbooks for the Indian Army* cautioned against such stereotypes of what it called the "Pathans". Instead it spoke respectfully and sympathetically of their history and poetry, commended them as soldiers and noted their respect for democracy and justice. It also stressed the need for political reform to provide a more settled form of governance.[5]

In 1947, Pakistan not only adopted the British stereotypes but hardened them. Barring the Pashtun elite who joined the army and bureaucracy in disproportionate numbers, Pashtuns were regarded from the drawing rooms of Lahore with the same kind of wary bigotry common to the Clubs of the Raj. Faced with the uncertainties of the Durand Line that Afghanistan refused to recognise, Pakistan retained the British system for managing the Frontier. Before the Pakistani Taliban emerged to threaten the state, urban Pakistan remained largely indifferent to the inhabitants of the Federally Administered Tribal Areas (FATA) and the broader Pashtun belt. This was partly the result of Pakistani state priorities that focused on rivalry with India, partly due to the fact that in the Punjabi heartland people had far more in common culturally, ethnically and linguistically with Indians than with Pashtuns. FATA was neglected, useful only as a source of prestige or wealth from bribery for political agents appointed by the Pakistani state to run it, or as a producer of cannon fodder for Pakistan's proxy wars in Afghanistan. Pakistan continued to assume an immutability about the region even as a fresh wave of migration in the 1970s brought significant economic and social changes to the tribal areas and the broader Pashtun belt. Thanks to a rise in oil prices and a conscious decision by Pakistan to develop links with the Middle East following the loss of East Pakistan, Pashtuns travelled in large numbers to the Gulf, Libya and Iraq to work. By 1984, some two million Pakistanis were working outside the country, including hundreds of thousands of Pashtuns from Peshawar and the border areas.[6] Local networks, a reputation for hard work and economic underdevelopment at home meant that in the boom years of the 1970s–1980s, Pashtuns were recruited to the Middle East at a rate of two to three times their population per centage within Pakistan.[7] Others migrated to cities in Pakistan, including Karachi. The impact of this migration took a generation to sink in, upending social structures as the possessors of new wealth undermined traditional sources of class and tribal authority. The migrant workers also brought back the hard-line Islam of the Gulf. In some areas of the Pashtun belt, as many as one out of every three or four working age males were working in Middle East. High migration districts were particularly susceptible to the post-2001 upheaval. Among them was Swat. The Soviet invasion of Afghanistan in 1979 and the use of the tribal areas as a launch-pad for the Pakistan-run insurgency brought further turmoil to the region, as did a flood of Saudi money to fund madrasas across the Pashtun belt. By the 1990s, when Pakistan projected its Afghan Taliban allies as an authentic product of Pashtun tradition, Pashtun society on both sides of the Durand Line had been transformed and fissured by the very modern influences of industrialised jihad and migration.

* * *

After the September 11 attacks, Pakistani stereotypes of Pashtun culture melded conveniently into the Pakistan Army's covert support for the Afghan Taliban. Publicly Pakistan claimed the Afghan Taliban insurgency was a Pashtun nationalist rebellion against the US-backed government of President Hamid Karzai, which it complained was dominated by non-Pashtuns and overly close to India. Its position had a grain of truth. Many Afghans also believed the United States had blundered by excluding the Afghan Taliban from the political process after 2001. Pakistan's motivation, however, was never about upholding Pashtun interests, but about countering Indian influence in Afghanistan, which it assumed was designed to weaken Pakistan. "Obviously we were looking for some groups to counter this Indian action against Pakistan," Musharraf admitted years later in an interview with *The Guardian*.[8] As early as the start of October 2001, even before the Afghan Taliban were overthrown, Musharraf had begun to dress this up as support for

Pashtuns in Afghanistan. In private meetings with the Americans he said he preferred to drop "Taliban" as a descriptive term and instead refer to the Pashtun majority.[9] Within a year or so of their overthrow, the Afghan Taliban were regrouping with Pakistani support. Musharraf kept relations with the United States smooth by arresting and handing over al-Qaeda leaders—among them September 11 mastermind Khaled Sheikh Mohammed, detained in Rawalpindi in 2003. "Towards the autumn of 2003, the Pakistani game plan became abundantly clear and yet the Americans chose to ignore it," said a retired Indian ambassador. "The CIA on the ground in southern Afghanistan were quite clear the Pakistanis had activated the Taliban."[10] Pakistan would pay a particularly high price for that decision, all the while blaming the blowback it faced in its north-west on the US-led war in Afghanistan.

Musharraf's own domestic political imperatives, and use of Islamist political parties to shore up his support, muddied the waters further. The Pashtun belt had never been a strong supporter of Islamists—mullahs were generally looked down upon as occupying a lower status in society. Though more socially conservative than Pakistan's urban heartland, it retained a leftist tradition handed down from Abdul Ghaffar Khan, the anti-colonial Pashtun leader who had become known as the Frontier Gandhi. Unlike Punjab—which had coalesced around various shades of the right-wing—it was also politically split between the secular left and the right. But after these two strands were briefly united in opposition to the 2001 invasion of Afghanistan, Islamist support for the Afghan Taliban melding into the anti-Americanism of the left, Islamist parties gained popularity. In 2002, Musharraf needed political allies in national and provincial elections. Determined not to allow mainstream political parties to challenge him, he prevented them from campaigning, while their leaders were out of the country. This paved the way for the rise to power of the Muttahida Majlis-e-Amal (MMA), an alliance of religious parties that won control of the provincial government in Peshawar. Among them were the Jamaat-e-Islami, Pakistan's biggest religious political party, which had strong ideological linkages with the Pakistan Army. The MMA also included two factions of the Jamiat-ul-Ulema-e-Islam (JUI), whose leaders had been mentors to the Afghan Taliban movement. Some argue Musharraf deliberately installed the MMA government to provide a supportive environment for the Afghan

Taliban; others that it was a by-product of his decision to allow only the religious parties to campaign openly. Either way, by sin of omission or commission, he ensured that Islamist hardliners were in the ascendancy in the north-west from 2002–2007. The MMA government quickly began a campaign of Talibanisation. Music was banned, singers beaten up and theatres closed. Billboards in Peshawar with women's faces were torn down or defaced. The government disingenuously claimed it was applying the will of the people.[11] The MMA government created an environment in which Islamist militant groups could flourish. Among those hiding in the area under their control was bin Laden.

At first Pakistan barely registered the transformation in the north-west, focused as it was on Indian influence in Afghanistan. India had moved quickly to build its presence in Afghanistan after 2001, using the soft power of economic development projects. It opened two new consulates in Herat and Mazhar-e-Sharif and reopened two others in Kandahar and Jalalabad, a geographical spread that it said was meant to show it was not favouring one part of the country over another. It became one of Kabul's leading donors and had close ties with the government—Karzai had gone to university in India—while the post-2001 political settlement had brought to prominence men from the old India-backed Northern Alliance. India's readiness to help Afghanistan was very much in pursuit of its own interests. For decades it had aimed to minimise Pakistan's influence in Afghanistan, while Kabul in turn looked at India as a balancer against Pakistani interference. The 1999 hijacking of Indian Airlines Flight IC-814 had given India all the more reason to work to prevent a return to power by the Taliban. By matching its development projects to specific requests from the Afghan government, India won an acceptance that eluded Pakistan with its security-oriented agenda. Funds were committed for education, health, power and telecommunications. Among India's flagship projects was a new parliament building in Kabul. It also built roads, including a highway in south-west Afghanistan near the Iranian and Pakistan borders.

Pakistani officials claimed the Indian consulates in Afghanistan were staffed mainly by intelligence officials. Road construction was carried out by the Border Roads Organisation, run by the Indian Army and thus bringing its military close to the Pakistan border. Pakistan accused the Indian intelligence agency, the Research & Analysis Wing (R&AW), of using its presence in Afghanistan to support a separatist insurgency in

Balochistan. It also suspected R&AW of working with Afghan intelligence agency the National Directorate of Security (NDS), to destabilise Pakistan. Its allegations may have contained a grain of truth. Indian intelligence agencies operated with far less oversight than their western counterparts. With their roots in British organisations designed to counter Indian nationalism, they inherited a tradition from the British of secrecy and non-accountability. Shielded from parliamentary oversight and public debate, and supported by a consensus that India's security remained vulnerable, they had a certain amount of leeway in what they did in Afghanistan. Indian intelligence agencies were certainly not above giving money to Baloch separatists in exchange for influence and information. But Pakistan's claims were overstated—if India had seriously wanted to run a full-blown insurgency, it would have been able to hand over far more substantial sums to Baloch exiles in Dubai or London.

Pakistan exaggerated India's intelligence capabilities by making a false equivalence between the ISI and R&AW. Though the exact workings of the two intelligence agencies are shrouded in secrecy, they reflect their countries' cultures and history. The ISI, led and dominated by serving army officers, grew strong through years of military rule. It ran one of the largest covert operations in history in the anti-Soviet jihad. It had a staff of at least 8,000[12] to 10,000[13] and possibly many more. The domestic power of the Pakistan Army, and the use of intelligence agencies for political ends, gave the ISI access to a huge network that made up the Pakistani establishment. On top of that were the army's linkages with Islamist groups that it used as a force multiplier both domestically and against India. In contrast, the staff in R&AW came mainly from the civil service and lacked political influence. Estimated to have 5,000 personnel, R&AW suffered from severe skills and staff shortages.[14] Its covert capabilities had been reportedly wound down in the late 1990s by a government keen to promote better relations with Pakistan.[15] Whatever remained of covert R&AW operations were dwarfed by those run or influenced by the ISI. Such was the power of the ISI inside Pakistan, however, that many Pakistanis assumed Indian intelligence must be equally potent, making them susceptible to military propaganda about the supposed threat.

As Pakistan had done throughout its history, it overstated an external threat while underplaying its self-created domestic problems. Its centralised security state, grown strong through years of competition with

India, had the perverse effect of weakening Pakistan by alienating those on the periphery, from the Baloch to the Pashtuns. In Balochistan, heavy-handed military crackdowns had only spurred Baloch separatism. "We have a culture of fishing in each other's troubled waters," said one former Pakistani ambassador of the rivalry between India and Pakistan. In 1971, he said, India took advantage of the civil war in East Pakistan to divide the country. "But the political blunder was our own. We have committed blunders everywhere." He estimated that only 10 to 20 per cent of the unrest in Balochistan was due to Indian interference with the rest Pakistan's own doing. "We have mishandled Balochistan."[16]

The security establishment appeared to believe its own propaganda. "They (India) want to create an anti-Pakistan Afghanistan and in the process they are using Afghanistan to destabilise Pakistan and maintain us in a weak, destabilised state," Musharraf said in a 2011 interview. "That is their intention so that they can have their own designs for the whole region, their own aspirations of dominance over the whole region without any opposition from anyone because Pakistan is the only thorn in their side." After assuming an unremittingly hostile Indian intent, it became easier to reach for a military rather than political or diplomatic solution. "I do believe in offensive action. If someone is against me or doing harm to Pakistan, we have to take counter-measures," said Musharraf. "India should not take us for granted. If they think they can come and punish us or attack us, we'll pay them back in the same kind."[17]

Having promised the United States to turn against the Taliban, Pakistan embarked on a suicidal course in seeking to regain its influence in Afghanistan. Such was the weakness of its diplomatic links with Afghanistan that the only players it had access to who could provide that influence after an assumed eventual American withdrawal were Islamist insurgents. Among them were the Afghan Taliban and fighters loyal to Jalaluddin Haqqani, a veteran of the anti-Soviet jihad. As the influential Pakistani policy report, produced in 2011 by Islamabad's Jinnah Institute, argued, "these groups provide Pakistan leverage in the end game and are still Pakistan's friendliest option in Afghanistan in any post-transition scenario."[18] The choice would have profoundly damaging effects on Pakistan's tribal areas and the Pashtun belt.

* * *

After the overthrow of Taliban in 2001, foreign and Afghan fighters fleeing Afghanistan set up mini-emirates in the tribal areas, swamping the local culture. Among them was Haqqani who had set up a base in Miram Shah in North Waziristan during the anti-Soviet jihad, used locals as recruits, forged a relationship with bin Laden and the Inter-Services Intelligence (ISI), and built links with the Gulf, where he raised donations. Through his family, he expanded his influence into a group that became known as the Haqqani network, with business interests in Pakistan, Afghanistan and the Gulf.[19] After 2001, the network's leaders were widely assumed to be operating from safe houses in Rawalpindi and Peshawar. Others setting up in FATA included jihadis from Central Asia and the Middle East, among them those from al-Qaeda. Militants from Punjab-based groups also began to move into FATA to escape crackdowns in the heartland. Over time the various militant groups set out to destroy traditional power structures in FATA, killing tribal elders who might challenge their authority.[20]

Under pressure from the United States to go after militants holed up in the tribal areas, Musharraf launched a series of on-and-off military forays starting in 2004. At first Pakistani security forces, designed to fight India in the plains, did badly. The army operations also galvanised opposition from those who had once been used as cannon fodder to fight for the Afghan Taliban, bringing to the fore new leaders who had previously not enjoyed positions of authority. A selective approach by Musharraf that aimed to shelter forces friendly to the Pakistani state while fighting others undermined the Pakistani military operations further, as did a series of peace deals struck by military appointees with various groups in FATA. The "good Taliban, bad Taliban" approach meant that thousands of Pakistani troops would die chasing hostile forces from one part of FATA to another. To explain successive failures, the Pakistani establishment played up the narrative that Pakistani Taliban violence in FATA was the result of traditional Pashtun resistance to outsiders, ignoring the deep social changes underway. "Being tribal they see things in black and white. For them any outsider is the infidel," said one Pakistani diplomat. "It is incumbent on them to fight the infidel."[21] Since Musharraf had portrayed the Afghan Taliban as a Pashtun nationalist movement against foreign occupation, the militants on the Pakistani side of the Durand Line were assumed by urban

Pakistanis to share similar sentiments. When Musharraf ordered troops to storm the Lal Masjid in Islamabad in 2007, unrest in FATA turned into a full-blown insurgency. Militant groups coalesced into the Tehrik-e-Taliban Pakistan (TTP), or Pakistani Taliban, under the leadership of Baitullah Mehsud. Underlining how different they were from local tribal traditions, the TTP produced much of their written material in Urdu or Arabic rather than Pashto. Ideologically, they were close to Pakistani militant groups based in the Punjabi heartland and al-Qaeda. In the broader Pashtun belt, militants also gained ground, helped by the pro-jihadi sympathies of the provincial government. There too, traditional symbols of Pashtun culture were attacked. Among the targets of the TTP was the marble mausoleum on the outskirts of Peshawar of a seventeenth-century Sufi poet, blown up in 2009. The poet, Abdul Rehman, commonly known as Rehman Baba, believed in the importance of music, poetry and dancing as a path for reaching God and was loved by Pashtuns for his mystical verse.

Swat, to the east of FATA, was one of the first regions outside of the tribal areas to succumb to the Pakistani Taliban. The causes of its vulnerability are contested and, like much else in Pakistan's north-west, more a reflection of the political preconceptions of outsiders. Most versions agree on a basic historical context. In 1992, a cleric named Sufi Muhammad had launched a protest movement to demand the enforcement of sharia, which he claimed would provide greater justice for the poor. His movement was crushed when paramilitary forces opened fire on its supporters. In 2001, Sufi Muhammad led thousands of poor, untrained supporters into Afghanistan to defend the Taliban against the "infidel" Americans. Most were killed or died after being detained by Afghan anti-Taliban forces. Sufi Muhammad fled to Pakistan and was briefly arrested. After that, explanations for the rise of the Taliban diverge. Some emphasise the marginalisation of the poor. Though relatively socially liberal—girls' education, for example, had long been encouraged in Swat—the region was one of the more class-bound parts of Khyber-Pakhtunkhwa. The social impact of migrant workers in the Gulf combined with poor administration by the Pakistani state encouraged increased resentment among those lower down the class hierarchy. Others blame a regional environment created by the Pakistan military's provision of sanctuary and support to the

Afghan Taliban and Haqqani network, and the MMA government for enabling hardline Islamists. Either way, Swat suffered. After Sufi Muhammad was arrested, his son-in-law, Fazlullah, took over the leadership of his movement and began using pirate FM radio to denounce girls' education, polio immunisation, music, singing and dancing. Pro-sharia members of the MMA provided logistical and financial support to him. With Fazlullah named by the TTP as their leader in Swat, and energised by the assault on the Lal Masjid, the TTP began a ruthless campaign to assert their authority. The involvement of other jihadis from Pakistani militant groups and those linked to al-Qaeda added an even harder edge. While the local Pashtun culture might have compelled Fazlullah to show restraint due to his family and clan ties, these jihadis had no such qualms.[22] Police officers, politicians and security personnel were murdered, their bodies strung up in Mingora's Green Square. Fazlullah captured public attention, but the person driving the campaign of beheadings was a different man, known as Bin Yameen.[23] Though born in Swat, bin Yameen had fought with the Afghan Taliban in the 1990s and had been captured and jailed by the Northern Alliance before being released in 2001. According to the late Pakistani journalist Saleem Shahzad, he had then joined the Jaish-e-Mohammed, the group set up by Masood Azhar, before it splintered into pro- and anti-Pakistan factions. Arrested by Pakistan security forces, he was freed in time to drive the campaign of terror in Swat.[24] Videos were produced of beheaded bodies and uploaded by disaffected young men on their cell-phones. With many men working abroad, women with teenage children became easy prey for Islamist militants seeking recruits. They manipulated the women and convinced them they would have more rights under Taliban rule, or forced them to send one son to them as a form of protection. Those who joined were then categorised according to their ability. The least educated were used for menial chores. Those one step up were destined to become suicide bombers. Fighters and commanders were higher up the pyramid. Untold numbers of young men were too frightened to leave for fear of being killed.[25] The Islamist militants attacked video, music and cosmetics stalls. Girls' schools were closed. The tourism industry, central to the livelihood of thousands in the Alpine region, collapsed. The militants also killed anyone who once held traditional authority, including elders, along with those whose religious views rivalled their own. Ordinary people were too frightened to speak out against them. In January 2009 they dragged Shabana from her house and killed her.

A month after Shabana's death, the Pakistan government promised to introduce sharia law into Swat to appease the Pakistani Taliban. Blinded by their failure to understand the multiple currents driving the violence in Swat, Pakistanis in the urban heartland hoped the introduction of sharia would be enough to keep the supposedly regressive inhabitants of Pakistan's north-west periphery quiet. The silence of the terrified inhabitants of Swat was taken as acquiescence when the peace deal was agreed with the Tehrik-e-Taliban Pakistan in February 2009. It was signed by a more secular provincial government that had taken over in 2008, who by then found it impossible to roll back the damage done by the MMA. Then the TTP overran more territory east of Swat, forcing the army to launch an offensive to drive them out. They fled to other regions on either side of the Pakistan-Afghanistan border while Fazlullah went on to become the head of the overall Pakistani Taliban movement. By the time the Taliban were driven from Swat, hundreds of its people had been killed and thousands turned into refugees. Even then, the people could not live without fear as fighters crept back into remote parts of the region. Three years later, the TTP ordered the shooting of Swat schoolgirl Malala Yousafzai in the main town of Mingora.

The trauma of the TTP's reign of terror in Swat, and the frisson of fear that ran through urban Pakistan as they advanced east towards the Pakistani heartland, might have shocked another country into re-examining both its policies and its view of events on its periphery. Yet even when confronted with evidence that the Pakistani Taliban were hated by the people and that far from representing Pashtun tradition they set out to crush it, the dominant narrative persisted that violence in Afghanistan and the north-west was the product of indigenous Pashtun nationalism. So too did an assumption that violence moved from the periphery to the heartland and could therefore be blamed on the US-led war in Afghanistan and Indian interference.

* * *

The Obama administration that took office in 2009 inherited a war that was going badly in Afghanistan and an increasingly unstable Pakistan.

Obama promised to send more US troops to Afghanistan and initiated a new diplomatic outreach, appointing Richard Holbrooke—who had helped broker a peace deal in Bosnia in 1995—as Special Representative for Afghanistan and Pakistan. Obama also promised more civilian aid to Pakistan and support for its fragile democracy. But the American approach ran aground on all fronts. In Afghanistan the United States struggled to impose order in a country facing problems of governance and where its own war economy had fuelled corruption, crime and a violent settling of scores that melded into the ongoing Taliban insurgency. In a BBC interview in March 2009, Holbrooke compared the position of NATO forces to "putting your fist into water. Pull out your fist. The water re-forms."[26] A US bill to triple civilian aid to Pakistan to $1.5 billion per year hit opposition from the Pakistan Army. The Kerry-Lugar bill stipulated that US aid would cease if Pakistan did not help fight Islamist militants and provided for an assessment of civilian control over the military. The Pakistan Army under General Kayani responded by issuing a strongly worded statement rejecting interference in Pakistan's internal affairs.[27]

Washington also inadvertently reinforced Pakistan's worldview by suggesting its security concerns about the Indian presence in Afghanistan should be assuaged. "While Indian activities largely benefit the Afghan people, increasing Indian influence in Afghanistan is likely to exacerbate regional tensions and encourage Pakistani counter-measures in Afghanistan or India," US commander in Afghanistan General Stanley McChrystal wrote in a leaked assessment in August 2009.[28] India quietly began to scale back its activities in Afghanistan around that time in what its officials said was a deliberate attempt to bring down tension. No major new infrastructure projects were initiated and Delhi turned down requests from Kabul for military aid. But Pakistan's reliance on Afghan insurgents to project its influence in Afghanistan remained unchanged.

Perhaps one of the biggest mistakes of the Americans was to assume Pakistan actually had a strategy for Afghanistan and the north-west. Pakistan had detailed policies on India, right down to which Bollywood films should be allowed to be screened. Its retired diplomats held extensive "Track Two" talks with their counterparts in India. In contrast, its approach to Afghanistan and the Pashtun belt on its side of the Durand

Line was muddled and reactive. Concerned about the multinational collection of militants in the tribal areas, some plotting attacks on the west, Obama in March 2009 called the border region "the most dangerous place in the world".[29] But other than prodding the Pakistan Army to clear out militant sanctuaries in the tribal areas, Washington struggled to find a way of turning the situation around. In the middle of 2009, the Pakistan Army announced plans for a military operation in South Waziristan, the largest and most populous of the seven tribal agencies, and since 2001, a refuge for thousands of Arab and Central Asian militants. In August 2009, the United States helped Pakistan by killing Baitullah Mehsud in a drone strike, one of the few deaths by drone celebrated in Pakistan. He was replaced by his one-time aide Hakimullah Mehsud. But both the United States and Pakistan were drifting along in the original untruth—that the origins of the violence lay in the periphery rather than the heartland. When in October the Pakistan Army finally moved into South Waziristan, it succeeded only in dispersing the Pakistani Taliban, who took refuge in North Waziristan, other parts of FATA and the ungoverned spaces in Afghanistan created in part by Pakistan's own support for Afghan insurgents.

The Obama administration went just far enough to accommodate Pakistan as to reinforce its worldviews, and not far enough to satisfy it. In January 2010, an international conference on Afghanistan in London endorsed the possibility of holding talks with the Afghan Taliban, offering them a share of power if they agreed to break with al-Qaeda, renounce violence and respect the Afghan constitution. The US endorsement of talks, which began half-heartedly and gathered momentum through the year, had the unintended consequence of encouraging Pakistan to believe that Washington was desperate for an exit strategy from a war that was going badly. As one Pakistani officer serving in the tribal areas remarked in the middle of 2010, "The Pashtun areas (of Afghanistan) are slipping out of the hands of ISAF and NATO, and everybody knows it."[30] Pakistan had all the more reason to hedge its bets and support the Afghan Taliban in the hope of retaining leverage after the Americans left. "American and NATO disengagement is making everyone nervous," said a senior Pakistani diplomat. "Everyone is increasing their involvement as they expect to see a political vacuum."[31] Although Pakistan did in fact nudge the various Afghan militant groups into talks, these made no serious progress.[32] Holbrooke, the man Obama had once hoped would be able to pull off a grand bargain from Kashmir to Kabul, died in December 2010. His diplomatic legacy survived long enough for the Americans to hold their first face-to-face contacts with the Taliban in late 2010.[33] Yet though talks continued on-and-off—the Taliban would even go on to open an office in Doha in 2013—they were never able to gain momentum. The United States was limping badly in the longest war in American history. But the failure was not just one of diplomacy or military tactics. It was also one of geography. In February 2011, then US Secretary of State Hillary Clinton would repeat the same wrong assumptions about the centre of militancy. "We've made progress," she said, "but the tribal areas along the border between Afghanistan and Pakistan remain the epicentre of violent extremism that threatens Americans and peace-loving people everywhere."[34]

* * *

Even before the United States embarked on its tentative talks with the Afghan Taliban, it was becoming clear that Obama's efforts to persuade Pakistan to change course were failing. The total number of deaths in the US-led coalition in Afghanistan had reached a peak of 711 in 2010, including 499 American soldiers[35] and the United States and Pakistan became increasingly embroiled in a propaganda war over who was responsible. Later that year, the Pakistan Army flew groups of foreign and Pakistani journalists by helicopter from Islamabad to Bajaur, in the north-ernmost part of FATA, to show that it was doing more than its fair share in fighting militants. The region is one of the more prosperous in FATA, thanks in part to earnings sent home by migrant workers. Compared to Kiplingesque stereotypes of the tribal areas, where the savagery of the terrain is emphasised to underline the supposed wildness of their inhabit-ants, Bajaur comes across as a remarkably green and pleasant land. While some parts of the tribal areas are bleaker, the terrain here is hilly rather than rugged, although the mountains rise higher towards the Afghan border. Around Bajaur's main town of Khar, the land is well-tended and fertile. Here in what is supposedly part of "the most dangerous place in the world" are neatly laid out fields, the lush farmland either terraced or marked out with fruit trees.[36] Having been used as a base for the mujahi-deen during the anti-Soviet jihad, Bajaur also became a sanctuary for fighters fleeing Afghanistan in 2001. They had grown so powerful that the army presence had been limited to the fort at Khar while outside, militants ran their own checkpoints, collected revenue, beheaded prisoners in the bazaar and convinced every family to offer up one male child to the cause. In 2010, the army decided to launch a full-scale military operation. It cleared out the last of the main militant strongholds in Bajaur after months of intense fighting that destroyed villages, left gaping wounds in buildings, and sent villagers fleeing.

In what became a standard tour for visiting journalists, the army was now able to take them to inspect an abandoned Taliban stronghold, some twenty-five km (sixteen miles) from the Afghan border. Here at Damadola, local militant leader Fakir Mohammad once held court, settling disputes brought to him by the people. For safety, the militants could retreat through a low narrow tunnel into a warren of caves so well dug into the hillside that no aerial bombing could damage them. The region had been the target of early US drone strikes in the belief al-Qaeda deputy Ayman al-Zawahiri was hiding there. At least one strike, in October 2006, reportedly went wrong, killing eighty students in a madrasa.[37] The Pakistan Army had had to clear the caves one by one, throwing in smoke grenades and then opening fire. But by then many of the militants had escaped, either across the mountains into Afghanistan or back into the local population. All that remained was a name scrawled onto the wall of a cave and some abandoned belongings. A single flip-flop lay in the dirt at the low narrow entrance to one of the caves.

The Pakistani military in Bajaur complained that at the other side of the border, the Americans were not doing enough to stop the Pakistani Taliban from fleeing and then regrouping to return to attack Pakistani forces. The United States had largely pulled out of Kunar province on the Afghan side after deciding to concentrate its troops on population centres. It was a reasonable complaint, though one that obscured a deeper problem. Unlike Pakistan, the US-led forces were not deliberately giving safe haven to militants. Locals in Bajaur also accused Pakistani security forces of secretly colluding with the militants to enlist their support for the war in Afghanistan.[38]

A military briefing in the fort at Khar unwittingly offered up evidence of how much Pakistan had clung to its stereotypes of the Pashtun tribes.

This was a region, journalists were told, that was run according to a 6,000-year-old tribal system where each individual was so clear about his or her obligation to society that it worked perfectly in its own way. The old order broke down with the jihad against the Soviet Union, and it nearly collapsed altogether with the flood of fighters fleeing the US-led invasion of Afghanistan in 2001.[39] That description was untrue. The particular tribal system Pakistan inherited was only 100 years old. It was the product of a colonial system of management, including the collective punishment of tribes prescribed by the Frontier Crimes Regulation, which deliberately codified the behaviour of the people into a more rigid one that would make them easier to control. That order had begun to break down with the rise in migration to the Gulf and other Pakistan cities before the anti-Soviet jihad. This was the heart of Pakistan's problem in the north-west. It was fighting a war it did not itself understand, one that originated in its own heartland, whose Islamist militant ideology it had then projected onto the Pashtun periphery.

* * *

Towards the end of the first decade of the twenty-first century, Punjab province had also come under increasing attack. In October 2009, gunmen attacked the headquarters of the Pakistan Army in Rawalpindi, leading to a twenty-two-hour-long siege and hostage-taking in which eleven people were killed. Pakistani security officials blamed the Punjab-based Lashkar-e-Jhangvi, an anti-Shia group linked to al-Qaeda and based in southern Punjab. In May 2010, gunmen killed more than eighty people in two mosques in Lahore of the minority Ahmadi community, a revivalist sect officially denounced as heretical by the Pakistani state. People distributed sweets in the street to celebrate. In January 2011, Punjab governor Salman Taseer was gunned down by his own bodyguard in the centre of Islamabad after he took up the case of a Christian woman who had been unfairly convicted of blasphemy. His killer was garlanded with flowers.

Pakistan had backed itself into too tight a corner to change course. It dared not turn against militants fighting in Afghanistan for fear these would unite with other jihadi groups against the Pakistani state. It also relied on them to keep the Pakistani Taliban in check while ignoring significant overlaps between different militant groups. The Haqqani network was closest to the Pakistan Army and therefore the one that could be most trusted to project Pakistani influence into Afghanistan and help rein in the Pakistani Taliban. However, the Haqqani network also had close historical links with al-Qaeda. The Afghan Taliban led by Mullah Omar regarded Pakistan with suspicion. Their links with the Pakistani Taliban meant they could use them to put pressure on Pakistan if it turned too strongly against them. According to the influential foreign policy report produced by Pakistan's Jinnah Institute in 2011, many feared an ineffective campaign against sanctuaries in the tribal areas could lead Afghan insurgent groups, especially the Haqqani network, to back the TTP against the Pakistani state. "Those wedded to this argument doubt the Pakistan military's ability to manage such an onslaught. They believe a massive backlash in Pakistan's heartland to be inevitable," said the report, titled "Pakistan, the United States and the End-Game in Afghanistan".[40]

Ever conscious of its standing in the eyes of the people, the Pakistan Army turned to its friends in the media to whip up public opinion against the United States while absolving itself of any blame for the country's predicament. The media duly played up conspiracy theories that blamed India, Israel and the United States for covert operations designed to destroy Pakistan. In one typical example in late 2010, Pakistani media published fake WikiLeaks cables that purported to be from the US embassy blaming India for the violence in FATA and Balochistan. They had based their articles on a report from the Online Agency, an Islamabad-based news service that frequently ran pro-army stories.[41] Since the fake WikiLeaks cables also parroted arguments made in briefings by the ISI—including that the Mumbai attacks were a false flag operation by India to discredit Pakistan—many assumed that they were a Pakistani intelligence plant.[42] The newspaper articles were later retracted, but the allegations largely stuck with a population looking for simple answers to the bewildering rise in violence in Pakistan. *Dawn* columnist Cyril Almeida said the fake WikiLeaks cables showed the extent to which the military aimed to use public opinion to ward off American pressure to "do more" against the Taliban. The army would then be able to tell the United States the people would not tolerate any more military action. "All true enough—until you stop to ponder how exactly 'public opinion' decides it is in favour of something or against it," he wrote.[43] Conspiracy theories that non-Muslims were out to destroy the Islamic world's only nuclear-armed state gained further credence when in January 2011 an American contractor working for the CIA was arrested after shooting dead two Pakistanis in Lahore. Raymond Davis was released after spending weeks in a Pakistani jail under a US-Pakistan deal that allowed the payment of blood money to the relatives of the dead men in exchange for his freedom. Far from looking for Pakistan's nuclear weapons, he was reportedly part of a group of Americans seeking information on Lashkar-e-Taiba, an operation prompted by its attack on Mumbai.[44]

Nowhere did the propaganda war have a more damaging impact on Pakistan's view of its north-west periphery than over the issue of American drone strikes in the tribal areas. US secrecy over its drone strikes, the contradictions of Washington's policies towards Pakistan, public anxiety about a new weapons system and Pakistani resentment about the apparent challenge to its sovereignty combined to make it both intractable and emotional. The CIA had initially coordinated secretly with Pakistan on its drone campaign but in July 2008 it told Kayani it would no longer seek advance permission for all drone strikes.[45] It suspected the Pakistani military of tipping off in advance those militant groups friendly to the Pakistani state. The drone strikes were ripe for exploitation by anyone who wanted to whip up anger against the Americans. The drone was a signifier of Pakistani weakness that fitted into the rumours of foreign agents running around Pakistan to prevent it from emerging as a major Muslim nuclear power. Encouraged by Urdu-language newspaper columnists and a booming television media dominated by religious and political talk show hosts, the notion of a country being attacked by foreign powers gained ascendancy. With little access to FATA for independent journalists and human rights investigators, and the people of the tribal areas themselves deprived of a voice, it became easy to argue that the drone strikes were indiscriminate and producing multiple civilian casualties.

Circumstantial evidence suggested the anti-drone sentiment was encouraged by the Pakistani security establishment, or pro-Taliban elements within it. In December 2010, the CIA station chief in Islamabad was named by lawyer Shahzad Akbar in a legal complaint about Pakistanis killed by US drone strikes. The name of the station

chief then began appearing on websites believed to have a close association with the ISI. He received death threats and had to be rushed
out of the country. Akbar was representing Kareem Khan, a resident of
North Waziristan who said his son and brother were killed in a drone
strike and was seeking $500 million in compensation. Since the CIA
station chief's name was not known in public, the United States assumed
the ISI had a hand in revealing his identity. The *New York Times* quoted
western and Pakistani intelligence officials as saying the drone strike also
killed Haji Omer, a senior commander allied with the Haqqani network
and al-Qaeda.[46] Subsequent "witness" testimony supplied by Akbar's
Foundation for Fundamental Rights (FFR) on behalf of the British-based
charity Reprieve to journalists and academics visiting Pakistan reinforced suspicions that elements of the anti-drone campaign had military
support. The "witnesses" provided by FFR in Islamabad invariably criticised only the American drone strikes while ignoring the Pakistan
Army's own role in bringing violence to the tribal areas.

In the absence of independent access to FATA, the impact of drones
was almost impossible to assess. In principle, they have the technologi-
cal capacity to cause fewer civilian casualties than other forms of warfare because of their ability to hover over a target before a strike. As
such they compare favourably to Pakistani military operations or airstrikes, or the indiscriminate violence inflicted on local populations by
the Pakistani Taliban. Research carried out by Amnesty International
found evidence of more civilian casualties from drone strikes than
admitted to by the United States.[47] A separate Amnesty report also
documented human rights abuses by the Pakistan Army.[48] Most other
testimony on drone strikes came from witnesses supplied by Akbar's
FFR in Islamabad. This was then relayed by foreigners who rushed to
criticise US military policy while ignoring the basic principles of
reporting: witnesses supplied by an activist group, military or intelligence agency in a capital city are never a reliable indicator of conflict
on the periphery. A survey of FATA residents carried out by the New
America Foundation criticising drone strikes showed unexpectedly
high favourability ratings for the Pakistan Army,[49] raising questions
about whether respondents believed it was safe to speak freely. A
Pakistani military commander in FATA was quoted by Pakistani media
as saying that most of those killed in drone strikes were "hardcore ele-

ments, a sizeable number of them foreigners".[50] A survey carried out among the people of North Waziristan who had been forced to flee their homes by Pakistani military operations found that a majority endorsed drone strikes as a means of weakening the Taliban.[51]

Whatever the truth, the losers in what became a heated international debate about the merits of drone strikes were the people of FATA. With their voices largely submerged within the heartland of Pakistan, they were wrongly equated with the Pakistani Taliban. Opponents of drone strikes argued, anachronistically, that the Pakistani Taliban were merely angry tribesmen seeking revenge for American drone strikes. It was an assumption that slotted easily into the old prejudices that portrayed Pashtuns as inherently primitive and violent.[52] Large numbers of urban Pakistanis began to believe that if only the drone strikes were ended and peace talks held with the Pakistani Taliban, the violence would stop. That Pashtuns were among the primary victims of Taliban violence went largely unremarked; while concern for the welfare of those caught up in the war rarely extended to those fleeing it. At least 1.8 million people became internal refugees,[53] many of them discovering they were unwelcome in other Pakistani provinces and ending up stranded in makeshift camps.

Nearly ten years after the overthrow of the Afghan Taliban, the Jinnah Institute report, *Pakistan, the United States and the End-Game in Afghanistan*, showed that most of the assumptions made by Musharraf remained intact. The report was based on consultations with the country's "foreign policy elite". India continued to loom large in the calculations, though the report allowed that as the biggest economy in the region, it could not be kept out of Afghanistan. "There is also a fairly candid admission that the Pakistani security establishment exhibits paranoia when it comes to Indian activities in Afghanistan," it said. But India was to be limited to economic development, and made to provide fact-sheets of its activities. Any attempt to exclude the Afghan Taliban from a political settlement in Afghanistan, it said, would be seen as an effort to sideline Pakistan.

The report suggested that the security establishment was still clinging to the idea that the best way of securing Pakistani interests in Afghanistan was through the militant groups whose ideological brethren had brought such mayhem to Pakistan. Participants expressed a range of views on ISI support for these Afghan groups, from toleration, to occasional tactical support to active equipping and funding. But they settled on the idea that the Pakistan Army's refusal to target their sanctuaries fell somewhere between lack of capacity and lack of will. "Project participants were also of the view that Pakistan will not cease a certain level of interference in Afghanistan until a credible reconciliation process takes off." Crucially, it continued to conflate the militants on both sides of the Durand Line with Pashtun nationalism. The report stressed the need to stabilise Afghanistan through an inclusive government recognised by all ethnic and political stakeholders. Such a settlement, it said, "should not lead to a negative spillover such that it contributes to further instability in Pakistan or causes resentment among Pakistani Pashtuns…" Afghan Pashtuns—as represented in the Pakistani view by the Afghan Taliban—were assumed to be the key to any settlement. "Pakistani policy elite we spoke with tended to believe that a genuine intra-Afghan dialogue will inevitably allow a significant share of power to the Pashtuns and thus produce a dispensation in Kabul that is sensitive to Pakistani interests." But if the Afghan Taliban were excluded, the report said, "Pakistani Pashtuns would also be resentful of the outcome and the TTP may use this sentiment to increase recruitment and justify continued attacks against the Pakistani state."[54]

On May 2, 2011, US forces found and killed Osama bin Laden in Abbottabad, a town on the fringes of the Pashtun belt that is also home to the Pakistan Military Academy. Far from being in the tribal areas as many had believed, he was hiding in a safe house just 110 km (68 miles) from Islamabad. Faced with accusations that the Pakistan Army had been deliberately hiding him all along, the military settled for a plea of incompetence over complicity. Whether the military leadership knew where he was is unlikely to be settled for years, if ever. What is undeniable is that bin Laden's ability to hide in Pakistan was made possible by the policies pursued over the previous decade. Many of the leading players in the Kashmir-focused militant groups had been moved to Abbottabad to escape scrutiny by the West. If the military leadership really did not know where bin Laden was hiding, it would only have been because it assumed the safe house he was using was occupied by one of its own favoured militants. If bin Laden had escaped detection while on the run from Afghanistan after 2001, it would only be because of the help of Islamist sympathisers in the MMA government. If Pakistan and much of the rest of the world had assumed bin Laden was hiding in the tribal areas thanks to traditional Pashtun notions of hospitality, it was because the Pakistani description of unchanging society in FATA and the broader Pashtun belt was fundamentally flawed. Some of the men who helped bin Laden were indeed Pashtuns, but they were not the product of the mores of an unchanging village life—they had been raised in the Gulf, the children of migrant workers.[55]

When Shabana was murdered, she was the victim of a movement produced by Pakistani security state policies, the political manipulation of the north-west to shore up a military ruler, and the unnoticed social upheavals caused by migration. All the elements that allowed bin Laden to survive for so long were there, in the anatomy of the murder of a dancing girl. India, the supposed cause of all of Pakistan's problems, had remarkably little to do with it.

12

PURSUIT OF PARITY

THE CLOSING YEARS: INDIA AND PAKISTAN FROM 2009 TO 2016

The bespectacled bearded young man leads the way to a black dinghy at the edge of a vast shimmering new lake, moored near the point where the road disappears under the water. He is a college student and volunteer for the Jamaat-ud-Dawa, the charitable wing of the Laskhar-e-Taiba, helping to bring relief supplies to villages marooned by Pakistan's worst floods in living memory. It is August 2010, two years after the Mumbai attacks should have put the JuD/LeT out of operation once and for all, and a year before American forces find bin Laden in Abbottabad. By the side of the submerged road, the JuD has pitched a small tent. Sacks of relief supplies to help the villagers celebrate the upcoming Eid festival are stacked next to it. They are labelled as coming from the Falah-e-Insaniyat, the new name adopted by the JuD to evade its international ban. "They are meant to express our goodwill. We are trying to share the celebration with these people," says Abdul Ghafar, who is in charge of relief operations in the district. The young volunteer steers the black dinghy out in the water, heading for the village of Kalar Wali, some twenty minutes away by boat and turned into an island by the floodwaters that cover the surrounding farmland. Army-issue life jackets lie ignored at the bottom of the boat. When travelling on a similar boat with the Pakistan Army during the floods, the wearing of life-jackets is compulsory. The proxies are more reckless. As Kalar Wali comes into sight, a black flag flying above its mosque marks it as a Shia village. The JuD aims to provide relief to people of all sects as it seeks converts to its own Ahle-e-Hadith beliefs. Arriving at the village, local elder Sayed Raiz Hussain says his family had taken care of the villagers' welfare for generations and when the floods came, he told them to stay, promising food and shelter. But after fifteen days his stocks had dwindled and he phoned the local politician to appeal for help. "He said, 'I don't have any way to reach you people. I'll drop some food at the road and you will have to make your own arrangements to collect it," says Hussain.

It is a familiar story, repeated across the region, of politicians failing to rise to the challenge of floods that swept down from the north-west, killing nearly 2,000 people and forcing some 20 million to flee their homes. As the extent of the disaster unfolded, President Zardari went ahead with an ill-judged visit to Europe. Pakistani media angrily played up images of him visiting a family chateau in France. The pictures harmed a man haunted by corruption allegations, and the lack of a visible sense of government urgency during the floods undermined Pakistan's fragile civilian democracy. In contrast, all too keen to be visible, the JuD—which had already earned popularity for its rescue work during a 2005 earthquake—grabbed the opportunity to raise its standing in the eyes of the public.

"The first people to come here were the Falah-e-Insaniyat," says Hussain, the village elder in Kalar Wali. "Thanks to these men, we were given food in a very respectable manner. They came to our homes to see what we needed." Villager Alamdar Hussain adds that the JuD volunteers had never talked about religion. "We are lucky they came," he says. "They are supporting us when no one else does."[1] Here in a Shia village under the searing August sun is one of the reasons why Pakistan's Islamist groups prove so resilient. They are woven into the system. If money collected for the JuD finds its way to the Lashkar-e-Taiba, the group also has a welcoming front door that promises help to those in need. Volunteers from the JuD are not out in large numbers during the floods, but they are active enough to rehabilitate the group after the post-Mumbai ban. Some 200 miles to the north, in a basement of the

JuD headquarters in Lahore, a compound housing a mosque, a library and a warehouse, men are working around the clock to prepare flood relief. It is piled high with sacks, ghee, towels, oil, crockery, pots and clothes. Lime green dresses for girls, pale cream for the women, spill out of sacks also containing food, household supplies and shoes intended as a gift for Eid. "We don't have the resources to meet their demands or get their houses rebuilt or give compensation for their crops," says JuD spokesman Yahya Mujahid. "So this idea came up … let's give them this package so that they can forget their problems for at least one day." The Eid packages also include 3,000 rupees ($35) per family so elders can follow an Eid tradition of giving money to children. The JuD has similar warehouses in every province and some 5,500 volunteers. With many of the goods in its warehouse coming from donations, Mujahid points to high-quality blankets to be distributed to families in the winter, proof, he says, that donors trust the JuD to make sure goods go to those in need rather than being pilfered by corrupt officials. In the corner of the warehouse in Lahore are large sacks of flour. They are marked "Government of Punjab".[2]

If groups like the JuD are rehabilitating themselves during the floods, they are not the biggest winners. That prize is claimed by the Pakistan Army, which has seized on the disaster as an opportunity to shake off the damage to its image of the final years of Musharraf's presidency. It is the only national institution with the manpower, the organisational skills and the equipment to reach those who are stranded. Soldiers' leave is cancelled and rations cut in half, the other half going to flood relief. Men work around the clock to assemble and deliver relief packages. The army accompanies its rescue operations with a public relations exercise that makes it clear that rather than working under the orders of the civilian government, as would have happened elsewhere, it is stepping in to save the people. On gaily-painted trucks packed with relief supplies are banners reading, "The Pakistan Army and the people are together." White sacks of supplies for flood relief carry a message in black Urdu lettering: "In tough times, the Pakistan Army is with you."[3] Both deliberately and by default, the Pakistan military is the face of disaster relief while civilian politicians are either invisible or too visibly elsewhere.

Across the country, military briefings to journalists include such concerted criticism of the civilian government that it becomes hard to believe it does not have approval from the top. The "bloody civilians", as the military call them, have once again failed to rise to the challenge. But if civilians have failed, it is because they have been emasculated by decades of on-and-off military rule, while money that might have been spent on infrastructure to cope with floods has been diverted into defence spending. As usual, the army explains its position in security terms, claiming its concerns are about the potential for unrest given the failure of the civilian government to provide adequate flood relief.[4] But in places affected by the floods, there is no sign of unrest. People queue patiently behind relief trucks and talk in practical terms of what they need to rebuild their lives—material to repair their houses and seeds to replant crops. Sometimes they proffer ID cards with that look of hopeful anticipation and respect for authority that you often see in South Asia when poor people mistake you for an official who might be able to help. It is hard to escape the conclusion that, rather than ordinary people threatening unrest, it is the army that, like its British colonial predecessors, distrusts the people.

By the time the flood relief operation was over, the popular refrain in the last years of Musharraf's rule—that "the worst democracy is better than the best dictatorship"—had well and truly lost its sheen. The Pakistan Army had no desire to take over. A new diarchy was being forged in which the civilian government took the blame for everything that went wrong while the military retained power without accountability. The civilian government had been destabilised and the hopes of progress towards building a real democracy that began with Musharraf's departure had been crushed. Groups like the JuD had been given a new lease of life, in a symbiotic relationship with the military that would ultimately keep Pakistan permanently off balance. India could be every bit as chaotic in a disaster. But whereas in Pakistan the army complained about politicians while the charitable wing of a jihadi group spread out across the country to deliver flood relief, in India you always felt the civilian government, even when incompetent, remained in charge. It was this difference between the two countries that ultimately lost Pakistan the Great South Asian War. Pakistan was convinced its main threat was India. Even during the floods, military officers and an anxious-to-please media suggested they were caused by India releasing water from dams on its side rather than a consequence of a heavy monsoon and poor land management and irrigation. Pakistan's real threat was not India, but its own internal weakness. In a centre set up by UNICEF to help children who had fled the floods, one child had drawn a picture in black crayon showing a small house floating away on giant waves.[5] It could have been a metaphor for the entire country, washed along by forces its people were not able to control.

* * *

Twelve years earlier, India and Pakistan had declared themselves nuclear-armed powers, offering an opportunity to reset their tortured relationship. Pakistan had believed its nuclear weapons would restore strategic parity with India, helping it to counter Indian influence in the region and prevent Kashmir from slipping from its grasp. Politicians in both countries had hoped the nuclear tests would lead to talks on a lasting peace settlement. Instead, the nuclear weapons had made it easier for Pakistan to support Islamist militant proxies against India without fear of punishment. As had happened between the United States and the Soviet Union during the Cold war, the nuclear weapons helped prevent the outbreak of all-out war. But just as Pakistan had feared being beaten by its bigger neighbour in war, it turned out that India also won the peace. Nuclear weapons were not in themselves the decisive element. As had been the case with the United States and the Soviet Union, the country with the greater domestic political stability and economic strength came out ahead. Unlike the Soviet Union, Pakistan had not begun to break up, but it had just as badly let down its own citizens. India had used its nuclear-armed status to win international respect. Pakistan had frittered away the security it might have gained from being protected from invasion, instead engaging in suicidal proxy wars that ultimately threatened the Pakistani state. Pakistan's inherent political weakness relative to India had been apparent before the 1998 tests; its behaviour after them made its standing significantly worse. Economically, diplomatically and politically, it fell too far behind India ever to have any hope of catching up.

* * *

On the economic front, India had pulled ahead of Pakistan in income per head in 2009. For decades, Pakistan had been the more prosperous state, thanks to its more open economy and foreign aid. Indian visitors returned home with envious tales of plentifully stocked shops and better roads and infrastructure. Pakistanis were able to boast that while they might be the smaller of the two countries, they were the more successful. But years of violence had taken their toll, slowing investment and growth. India finally began to pull away, thanks to the economic reforms initiated in the early 1990s and its greater political stability. In 2009, India's income per capita, measured in terms of purchasing power parity, overtook that of Pakistan for the first time in recent history and then continued rising.[6] Both countries still faced problems of poverty, the social strains of inequalities between the rich urban elite and the rural poor, and chaotic urbanisation. But India, with its more stable political system, was better placed to cope. In Pakistan a thriving black economy helped insulate the elite within a bubble of wealthy gated communities and upmarket shopping malls, while also building a pool of illegal funding in which violent non-state actors thrived. Moreover, Pakistan's legitimacy as a state depended on its ability to show it could do better than, or keep pace with, India. In 1947, Pakistanis had hoped a Muslim country would build a fairer society than one dominated by the Hindu caste system. United Nations indicators of development showed Pakistan falling behind there too. In the UN Human Development Index—a composite measure covering life expectancy, education and income per capita—Pakistan fell to 147th place in 2015, compared to 130th place for India.[7] Unlike India, Pakistan was also dependent on foreign aid. Occasionally Pakistanis would point to the fact that the Indian economy was dwarfed by that of China. But Pakistan's ambition had been to prove itself equal to India, not to see another country do better. By 2016, India was one of the world's fastest growing economies, outstripping even China in its rate of growth.[8] Indian economic growth was estimated at 7.3 per cent in 2015–2016, according to the International Monetary Fund, strengthening its advantage over Pakistan, with growth of 4.5 per cent.[9] A World Economic Forum assessment of global competitiveness showed India jumping to thirty-ninth place in 2016.[10] Pakistan trailed in 122nd place and was the only country in South Asia to have failed to improve its levels of health and primary education.[11]

* * *

On the international front, Pakistan had alienated potential allies and angered its enemies. Relations with the United States soured over the discovery of bin Laden in Abbottabad in May 2011 and perceived Pakistani double-dealing in the Afghan war. In September 2011, Admiral Mike Mullen, the outgoing chairman of the US Joint Chiefs of Staff, complained that the Haqqani network acted as "a veritable arm" of the ISI after a truck bomb attack on a US base in Afghanistan and an assault on the US embassy in Kabul which led to a twenty-hour siege.[12] It was the most forthright assertion yet by the United States that the Pakistani military was not merely turning a blind eye to militant groups based on its border with Afghanistan but actively encouraging them to attack American interests. Then in November 2011, a NATO airstrike killed twenty-four Pakistani soldiers on the Afghan border in what Washington said was a mistaken incident of friendly fire. Pakistan responded by closing supply lines used by the Americans to bring equipment from the Pakistani port of Karachi to its troops in Afghanistan. The United States and Pakistan eventually patched up their differences enough to allow the reopening of US supply lines into Afghanistan after a seven-month closure. But the deep distrust remained. In western capitals, officials and diplomats who had once talked hopefully of being able to turn Pakistan around, spoke privately in tones of weary frustration if not outright hostility. The United States belatedly began to scale back aid to Pakistan.[13] It continued to provide funding, fearing a full suspension of aid would leave it in the same position as it had been in the 1990s, without influence or leverage. Pakistan was also still able to win international largesse because of fears about Islamist militants gaining access to its nuclear weapons. But it was the attention accorded to a blackmailer. Goodwill had run out.

Within the region, Pakistan's support for the Afghan Taliban and the Haqqani network had so enraged the people of Afghanistan that it had lost all hope of exerting influence there except through the use of subterfuge and force. Afghan views of Pakistani perfidy were hardened further when the Afghan government announced in 2015 that Taliban leader Mullah Omar had died in Karachi two years earlier.[14] His successor, Mullah Akhtar Mohammad Mansour, was killed a year later in a US drone strike while on his way to the Pakistani city of Quetta.[15] Pakistani officials no longer bothered to deny that the Afghan Taliban and their families were using Pakistan as a base, but claimed their influence over them was limited. They were partly correct. Had Pakistan turned aggressively against the Afghan Taliban at that point, they might ally with the Pakistani Taliban to threaten the Pakistani state. But Pakistan was trapped in a vicious circle of its own making. The continued instability in Afghanistan opened up ungoverned spaces that the Pakistani Taliban used as a base from which to attack Pakistan.

Having lost one of its old certainties—the trope that it could be defined by the three A's of "Army, Allah and America"—Pakistan turned to China for help. In 2015, China pledged to invest up to $46 billion in Pakistan, dwarfing aid provided by the United States. The plan, known as the China Pakistan Economic Corridor, was meant to open up trade and transport routes from western China to the Pakistani port of Gwadar on the Arabian Sea. From there goods were to be shipped back and forth to the Gulf.[16] The scale of the investment, however, was contingent on Pakistan being able to restore domestic security, something that had so far eluded it. China, moreover, had little sympathy for Islamist militants, fearing their spread to its Xinjiang region, home to Muslim Uighurs who had a history of unrest against Beijing. It also had no patience for Pakistani risk-taking against India, as shown by its reactions to the Kargil war, the 2001–2002 standoff and the Mumbai attacks. China, as a neighbour of both countries, had good reason to fear an escalating conflict that might lead to nuclear war between India and Pakistan. Nor was a partnership with Beijing any more likely to ease Pakistani discontent than one with the United States if the fate of the people of North Korea, another country sheltering under China's wing, was anything to go by. And as Egyptians had discovered when the Suez Canal was built in the nineteenth century, hosting a crucial transport route was no guarantee for increasing a country's prosperity and autonomy. Having spent years chafing against US pressure, Pakistan was setting itself up to face the same from China. Pakistanis muttered quietly that this might also come with shoddier goods—the made-in-China products sold on the Pakistani market were considered inferior to those from the west.

In contrast to Pakistan's continued dependence on foreign paymasters, India had raised its stature on the world stage by concentrating on domestic development. This was partly a legacy of pre-1998 decisions.

Pakistan had looked outwards for strength, ending up in damaging foreign entanglements like its Cold War alliance with the United States, while trying to project its influence into Afghanistan, Kashmir and the Middle East. India had largely focused on defending its own borders rather than projecting power outwards.[17] It had good reason to do so: such was India's size that it had 15,000 km of land borders, a coastline including its islands of 7,516 km, and it shared its borders with nine countries. India's undoubted aspirations towards regional hegemony, a major source of Pakistani anxieties, were thus constrained by its need to prioritise self-defence. A disastrous intervention in Sri Lanka's civil war in the late 1980s had left India even warier of military adventurism.[18] Delhi also made a virtue of necessity in giving priority to domestic stability. As a large, multi-ethnic, pluralist state, its main threat in the early decades after independence had been of internal fracturing. It had addressed this by seeking domestic cohesion through democracy and indigenous economic development where Pakistan had relied on military rule and foreign aid. In the period after the nuclear tests, these choices began to bear fruit as the requirements of Indian democracy encouraged a pragmatic approach to international relations. In Pakistan, foreign and security policies continued to be monopolised by the military and driven by an obsession with India. In India, antagonism towards Pakistan, important as it was to the shrill and patriotic national media, was diluted by the millions of voters who had more practical economic concerns. Indeed despite a Pakistani conviction that the India-Pakistan obsession was mutual, there was little evidence from state or national elections since 1998 that Indian voters could be galvanised by India's policies, whether hawkish or dovish, towards its smaller neighbour. India's inward focus on domestic economic strength, combined with its sheer size, ultimately made it a more attractive partner internationally than Pakistan.

Within the region, the possibility of access to the Indian market helped Delhi reach a reasonable accommodation with many of its neighbours, with Pakistan the most obvious exception. Notably, though India's border with China remained disputed, leading to occasional spikes in tension, rising trade between the two Asian giants cushioned antagonism. An agreement between India and Bangladesh over their border was reached in 2015.[19] Outside the region, India built ties with the Gulf states, Pakistan's traditional stamping ground, helped by Indian energy needs and trade. Most importantly, India's growing economy and relative political stability wooed the United States away from its traditional Cold War ally, Pakistan. While Pakistan gambled away the advantages of its nuclear status with the Kargil War, India showed enough restraint then and in 2001–2002 to suggest it could be trusted. It was rewarded with the US deal that acknowledged it as a nuclear-armed power. By the second decade after the nuclear tests, India still faced significant security threats, among them Islamist militancy in Afghanistan, Pakistan and Bangladesh. The American embrace of India as a counterweight to China made it more vulnerable to Chinese hostility. But compared to where it was in the late 1990s, India's position internationally had been transformed. Back then, it had faced international opprobrium and economic sanctions over its nuclear tests. Nearly two decades later it was building a relationship with the United States that was often defined—to a degree unimaginable in 1998—on Indian terms. Though it had offered Washington the use of Indian military bases to support the US campaign in Afghanistan in 2001, it had refused, after much debate within the BJP-led government of the time, to support the 2003 US invasion of Iraq. As economic and political power shifted towards Asia, India was well placed to position itself as an American strategic partner. In January 2015, President Obama visited Delhi as the guest of honour at India's Republic Day ceremonies on January 26. He was the first American president to be the chief guest at the ceremonies. After being sanctioned by world powers over its nuclear tests, India had not only survived but come of age.

* * *

On the domestic front, Islamist groups who had thrived in Pakistan under Musharraf's military rule were given yet another burst of oxygen as the security establishment turned to them to assert its authority over the civilian government that succeeded him. A new alliance of Islamist groups known as the Difa-e-Pakistan (Defence of Pakistan) began holding rallies in cities around the country at the end of 2011. It included the Jamaat-e-Islami religious political party, the rehabilitated Jamaat-ud-Dawa, and the anti-Shia Sipah-e-Sahaba, whose militant offshoot, the Lashkar-e-Jhangvi, had been involved in a string of attacks inside Pakistan. Hafiz Saeed, founder of the Lashkar-e-Taiba, was a leading player, as was Sami ul-Haq, a religious leader closely associated with the Afghan Taliban. The alliance brought a pathological antipathy towards India and the United States onto the same platform. Since the army had encouraged Islamist street protests to rouse public opinion behind its agenda in the past, the Difa-a-Pakistan was seen as a stalking horse for the military. It served as a warning to the United States not to push Pakistan too hard on the Afghan Taliban and a shot-across-the-bows of the civilian government lest it become too bold about making peace with India. This was the "Deep State" in action. An agglomeration of sympathetic militants, bureaucrats, diplomats and the security establishment, the Deep State was bigger than the military alone. It could be manipulated by the army to enhance its power domestically, or for megaphone diplomacy. But as shown during Musharraf's foray into peace talks with India, it also ensured that an ideology based on enmity with India would outlive the actions of any individual leader or general. At one typically inflammatory Difa-e-Pakistan rally in Karachi in 2012, JuD leader Ameer Hamza vowed to make "mincemeat" of India and called on those present to "break the legs of any whore who went to India to sing and act in films".[20]

The Islamist groups embodied the hyper-nationalism, militancy, sectarianism and faith-based politics that underpinned the Pakistani security state. Between them they continued to indoctrinate the population in favour of jihad, diverted attention away from the domestic threat posed by militancy and bolstered a vision of a country besieged by external enemies. Conveniently for the security establishment, they also promoted a widely held view that Pakistan's main domestic problem was the corruption of its politicians, whose greed, they said, had drained the country of resources. Though nobody would deny the prevalence of corruption in Pakistani politics, the allegations obscured the army's powerful role in the economy. The armed forces not only consumed more than a quarter of the annual budget[21]—and possibly more since some of its costs were covered elsewhere—but also ran large businesses designed to provide welfare for former soldiers. Among them, the army's Fauji Foundation was one of the biggest conglomerates in Pakistan, its interests extending into the production of fertilisers and cornflakes. Various branches of the armed services also occupied large tracts of prime real estate, where they built comfortable bungalows for retired officers. The Pakistan Army had set itself up as a neutral arbiter in the country; but its huge economic interests meant that it was also a political player, channelling resources for its own institutional gain.[22] Such was its dominant political and economic role that the army squeezed the space for civilian politicians, leaving little room for disputes to be negotiated peacefully. In turn, in a country where Islam was used both to enforce power and to contest it, Islamist groups became one of the few means through which the poor and lower social classes could seek access to scarce resources. The result was a vicious circle that further eroded the legitimacy of the state, left Pakistan creaking under a militarised economy, and made it all the more vulnerable to jihadis looking to exploit its divisions.

National elections in May 2013 offered Pakistan its first chance in history of a democratic transfer of power from one elected government to another. Former prime minister Nawaz Sharif faced stiff competition from former cricketer-turned-politician Imran Khan. A right-winger who demanded "Islamic" social justice—he prayed on stage at one of his political rallies to demonstrate his religiosity—Khan had been struggling in the political wilderness since launching his Tehrik-e-Insaf (PTI) party in the late 1990s. But as he picked up support from a young urban elite tired of the old political parties, he began to be seen as the favoured choice of the security establishment. His party attracted high-profile figures who had been close to the army and gained sympathetic coverage from analysts and media known to back the military. Khan garnered public support by tapping into a popular but simplistic theme that all of Pakistan's ills could be blamed on a corrupt political elite "bribed" by the United States into cooperating in its war in Afghanistan. He campaigned against US drone strikes, wrongly equating the Pakistani Taliban with the people of the tribal areas, and called for peace talks with them. His critics dubbed him "Taliban Khan". Sharif won the elections with a 100-seat majority, helped by the strong political base of his PML-N party in Pakistan's biggest province, Punjab. But when he tried to assert his authority over the military, putting a recently returned Musharraf on trial and setting out to make peace with India, Khan stepped forward to challenge him. In 2014, Khan led protests in

Islamabad complaining that the elections had been rigged and calling on Sharif to resign. His own party's president, Javed Hashmi, broke with Khan to accuse him of acting on the behest of the army in the hope of forcing fresh elections.[23] After weeks of drama, the protests fizzled. Sharif however had been chastened. The military reasserted its control of foreign and security policy and Musharraf was eventually allowed to leave Pakistan. Sharif remained as a fig-leaf for the democratic process while the army got on with running the country.

During these years of domestic political torment, Pakistani casualties from Taliban attacks continued to mount. Prodded by Khan, and keen to keep the peace in the heartland Punjab province which was his main political fiefdom, Sharif had offered talks with the Pakistani Taliban in 2013. Khan and Sharif, both based in Lahore, had fallen for the old lie equating jihadi violence with Pashtuns living on the periphery. They wrongly assumed the Pakistani Taliban could be contained if, for example, the tribal areas were left alone to run under sharia. But like al-Qaeda, the Pakistani Taliban were more interested in spreading mayhem; and in any case, their sights were set on the Pakistani state as a whole. They drew their strength not from the hapless foot soldiers recruited from the people living on the periphery but from the web of jihadi networks emanating from the heartland of Pakistan. Unsurprisingly, the talks failed, but not before they gave even more space and legitimacy to the jihadis threatening Pakistan.

Nearly 60,000 people died in Pakistan between 2003 and 2015, more than half of them alleged insurgents, along with nearly 21,000 civilians and more than 6,000 members of the security forces, according to figures collated by the Delhi-based South Asian Terrorism Portal.[24] On December 16, 2014, gunmen from the Pakistani Taliban stormed the Army Public School in Peshawar. They killed 144 people, most of them children. The youngest was a six-year-old girl.[25] It was the worst act of terrorism in Pakistan's history. Deeply shocked, Pakistan adjusted its approach to the Pakistani Taliban while retaining its overall framework of tolerating or encouraging some Islamist militants while fighting others. It was akin to changing gear while driving off a cliff. The army attacked Pakistani Taliban sanctuaries in the tribal areas, driving thousands of ordinary people from FATA into makeshift refugee camps in the process. Military courts were introduced across Pakistan, a moratorium on the death penalty abandoned and hundreds hanged, many of them ordinary convicted criminals too poor to pay a lawyer to secure their release. The army chief appointed in 2013, General Raheel Sharif, took the lead in driving the response to the Peshawar school attack and, like his predecessors before him, became Pakistan's most powerful man. The military operations in the tribal areas, combined with a clean-up in urban Pakistan, brought down the level of violence in the country. But the Pakistan Army had a history of achieving short-term reductions in violence, including, for example, in East Pakistan in 1970 before the civil war that erupted the following year. It confused the presence of silence with the presence of peace. Attacks by the Pakistani Taliban and other militants picked up again. On Easter weekend in 2016, a suicide attack next to a playground in a park in Lahore killed at least seventy-five people, mostly women and children.

On the domestic front in India, Prime Minister Manmohan Singh had returned to power with an increased mandate in national elections in 2009. His ability to do so despite his perceived weakness in responding to the Mumbai attacks the previous year underscored the relative unimportance accorded to Pakistan by Indian voters. But a temporary deceleration in Indian economic growth, corruption scandals and the sluggish pace of reforms left Indian voters weary of a prime minister who was too weak to rein in the powerful satraps in the Congress Party. In national elections in 2014, voters turned instead to the BJP and its new leader, Narendra Modi, who came to power promising to unleash the economy, clean up tainted and dynastic politics and fix India's infrastructure problems. As Chief Minister of Gujarat, Modi had overseen the communal violence there in 2002. The rise to power of a man who many blamed for that violence worried Indian secularists who saw it as paving the way for the imposition of a hardline Hindu agenda. It was perhaps coincidental, and certainly ironic, that at a time when India had proved its own system of secular democracy to be so much more robust than that of Pakistan, it began to let it fray at the edges. Indian newspapers filled up with anguished columns about sporadic incidents of violence against Muslims. Modi's critics also fretted about what they saw as an authoritarian streak that suppressed dissent and challenged some of the basic underpinnings of democracy, among them freedom of speech[26] and academic freedom.[27] Some even began to draw parallels with Pakistan, and the damage done to it by its mixing of politics and religion. All that said, India retained the brakes to stop any slide into extremism that had been sorely missing in Pakistan. Its diffuse, chaotic and deep-rooted democracy was likely to limit any drift into democratic authoritarianism. So too was its devolved federal structure that gave state governments considerable power, diluted the influence of the national government and made it easier to challenge the BJP at a regional level. In contrast, such was the power of the military in Pakistan that many of its civilian politicians tended to amplify rather than challenge its worldview. Pakistan was also overwhelmingly dominated by Punjab, its biggest province and its political and military heartland. Moreover, Indian voters at both state and national level had tended to put their economic interests first, constraining any drift into religious or nationalist extremism. During Modi's election campaign, though he had promised a harder line on terrorism and Pakistan, his overwhelming focus had been on economic development. Having won voters across the political spectrum on a promise to drive economic growth, his success depended on him maintaining the political stability that would allow the economy to flourish. A year into his tenure, he was still popular with Indian voters, according to a Pew survey of opinion, though they remained wary of his management of relations between different religious groups.[28]

* * *

As for the direct relationship between India and Pakistan, repeated attempts since the nuclear tests to find a basis for lasting peace had come to nothing, undermined by the Kargil War and a string of militant attacks, from the 2001 raid on parliament to the 2008 assault on Mumbai. Prime Minister Singh had tried to revive talks after the 2009 elections, and held a couple of meetings with Pakistani civilian leaders on the fringes of international conferences.[29] But Pakistani inaction on the Lashkar-e-Taiba after the Mumbai attacks and the very public role played by Hafiz Saeed in the Defa-e-Pakistan left Singh with little room for manoeuvre. In Delhi, hawks whipped up media and public opinion against any softening of India's position. "Prime Minister Manmohan Singh does want to move forward," said one senior Indian diplomat at the time. But for that India needed not only action against Pakistan-based militant groups, but that justice should be seen to be done over Mumbai.[30] Singh had also thought that by reaching out to the civilian government in Pakistan, he might bolster its position relative to the army and make peace more possible. The deliberate stalling of the democratic process in Pakistan put paid to such hopes. Having once believed a settlement on Kashmir was within his grasp, Singh left office without achieving his dream of visiting Pakistan as prime minister to sign a peace deal. Modi in turn made some erratic attempts to revive peace talks, inviting Nawaz Sharif to his inauguration in Delhi in 2014, and making an unexpected flying visit to Lahore in December 2015. But like his BJP predecessor, Vajpayee, and Singh, he made no headway. Attacks on India by Pakistan-based militant groups continued.[31]

Yet for all the failure of peace talks in the period that followed the nuclear tests in 1998, India's reluctance to start a war had served it well. Born out of a combination of necessity, pragmatism and indecision, this reluctance was relabelled as "strategic restraint". Not only did it allow India to portray itself as the more responsible power, but it left it the space to develop its economy. Its willingness to persevere with talks even in the face of attacks by Pakistani militant groups also strengthened Delhi's hand diplomatically, helping to convince the international community that the unwilling partner in peace was not India but Pakistan.

Pakistan, meanwhile, became a cause of increasing international anxiety as it ramped up its nuclear programme while clinging on to its Islamist militant proxies. Despite its acquisition of nuclear weapons, the Pakistan Army continued to be haunted by a fear that any Indian invasion could cut Pakistan in half, just as India had done in 1971. It defended its expanding nuclear programme by pointing to what it said was India's superiority in conventional weapons, an assertion that did not stand up particularly strongly to scrutiny of Indian military capabilities.[32][33] India's sheer size and its need to defend its lengthy borders meant it would always be hard for it to muster the speed, strength and agility for a full-scale attack on Pakistan that stayed below the nuclear threshold.

In the 2001–2002 military standoff, India's conventional weakness had been clear. India realised it took too long to mobilise its army and decided it needed to be able to conduct punitive but limited operations against Pakistan quickly. Thus was born what became popularly known as "Cold Start"—a means of rapid deployment while integrating military operations with those of the air force and to a lesser extent the navy. Most experts on Indian defence reckoned it would neither win approval politically nor work, given the historical divisions between the different branches of the Indian armed forces.[34] But the Pakistan Army responded by developing tactical, or "battlefield" nuclear weapons that could be used over short distances to stop an Indian armoured advance. In April 2011, Pakistan tested a new missile, the Hatf-9 Nasr, designed to deliver nuclear warheads to targets within a 60-km range. Pakistani decision-makers had decided there was a gap in their deterrence posture that India sought to exploit, and "therefore, the idea of Nasr was born, that we need to plug this particular gap," Khalid Kidwai, the long-time head of Pakistan's Strategic Plans Division which is responsible for its nuclear weapons, told an audience in Washington in early 2015.[35] The development of nuclear weapons for use on the battlefield was the culmination of a nuclear programme that had perversely made Pakistan more insecure. It had become trapped in the path of dependency offered up by technology. The tactical nuclear weapons, since they were intended to block an Indian invasion, were designed for use inside Pakistan. In other words, it was threatening to use nuclear weapons on its own soil. Since operating battlefield nuclear weapons required a loosening of the chain of command, it was also raising the risk of these being seized by Islamist militants or a disaffected pro-jihadi officer. As Hillary Clinton said in early 2016 of Pakistan's drive for tactical weapons, "we live in fear that they're going to have a coup; that jihadists are going to take over the government, they're going to get access to nuclear weapons, and you'll have suicide nuclear bombers."[36]

The Pakistan Army's enthusiasm for tactical nuclear weapons underscored how far the security state worldview blinded it to alternative approaches. India was expected to attack Pakistan only in the event of a major Mumbai-style attack. It had no interest otherwise in taking over a mainly Muslim country of 200 million people, risking its own internal cohesion. The most effective way for Pakistan to head off the risk of Indian retaliation would have been to disarm its militant groups. Instead it doubled down on nuclear weapons. The battlefield nuclear weapons were expected to be used mainly in Pakistan's less populated desert rather than near urban areas. Nonetheless the principle stood. Nearly two decades after the nuclear tests, Pakistan was turning its own country into a suicide bomb.

* * *

The dispute over Kashmir remained as intractable as ever, but one that continued to cause more harm to Pakistan than India. If in Pakistan it helped bolster the position of the Pakistan Army and the jihadi groups, in India, such was the size of the country that few cared about a region that for most Indians was too far away, out of sight and out of mind. The roadmap for a comprehensive settlement on Kashmir sketched out by envoys of Musharraf and Singh was a tragically lost opportunity. Though the terms of a settlement had yet to be fleshed out, and may well have run into political resistance in both India and Pakistan, it offered the most promising basis for agreement in years. Among its greatest merits was that it treated Jammu and Kashmir as a whole, including Ladakh, the Kashmir Valley, Jammu, Azad Kashmir and Gilgit-Baltistan, rooting the settlement in the historical origins of the former princely state and preventing the Balkanisation that would come with any fresh partition. By granting maximum autonomy to both sides and allowing the people to travel freely within the state, it would also have given them the political space they had been denied for centuries. At the same time, neither India nor Pakistan would have seen any real dilution of their territorial ambitions for the state since there was to be no exchange of territory. The lion's share of the blame for the failure of this plan rested with Pakistan. Though India may have been slow in grabbing the opportunity for a peace deal when Musharraf was in office, it was the combination of the Mumbai attacks and Pakistan's subsequent refusal to take action against the Lashkar-e-Taiba that drove it out of reach. The Pakistani security establishment had yet to learn the lessons of 1965 and the Kargil War—that India did not, in fact, negotiate better under pressure. When Musharraf left office, Pakistan returned to its old focus on the Kashmir Valley and rhetorical demands for the implementation of the defunct UN resolutions. It was a policy stance that fed its sense of grievance, provided fuel to fire up jihadi groups, and did nothing to address the complexities of the dispute. India, meanwhile fell back on its status quo position under which it publicly claimed all of the former princely state while privately accepting its division along the Line of Control. It also reaffirmed its insistence that Kashmir was an integral part of India, effectively closing the door to any revival of the plan mooted under Musharraf and Singh.

As for the Kashmir Valley, Pakistan lost it without India truly gaining it. When the insurgency first erupted in Kashmir, many ordinary Kashmiris, driven by resentment of India, regarded Pakistan with admiration. But its backing for pro-Pakistan militants in the Valley, its Kargil folly in 1999, and its own slide into instability and violence, made it increasingly clear Pakistan could do little for Kashmir, while making it less and less attractive as a country. Pakistan also lost international support for its position on Kashmir. The United States had once been sympathetic to Pakistan's argument that the dispute over Kashmir was the cause of all its problems. Right up to the Mumbai attacks, and for a while afterwards, Washington had been willing to push for a Kashmir settlement. That sentiment evaporated as the United States, burned by its experience in Afghanistan and steadily uncovering evidence of the Pakistani role in Mumbai, decided Pakistan, rather than Kashmir or India, was the cause of problems in the region.

India made good progress at first in drawing Kashmiris into participatory democracy by holding a series of fair state elections in Indian Jammu and Kashmir. With turnout rising to 63 per cent in polls held in 2008 from 44 per cent in 2002,[37] Kashmiris in the Valley became more optimistic about the political process. The opinion poll published by Britain's Chatham House think-tank in May 2010 showed that 52 per cent of the population in Indian Jammu and Kashmir thought the state elections had improved the chances of peace. Crucially, only 20 per cent thought militant violence would help solve the dispute, compared to 39 per cent who thought it would make a solution less likely. Support for militant violence was, unsurprisingly, higher on Pakistan's side of the Line of Control, where 37 per cent thought it would be more likely to solve the dispute, against 31 per cent who thought it would make it less likely.[38] The elections, however, were not enough in themselves to bring lasting peace. The Valley was hit by weeks of summer unrest in 2008–2010, when youths throwing stones in protest against the killing of civilians by Indian security forces replaced the former gunmen of a previous generation. Tear gas, curfews and razor wire briefly came back to haunt the region. The protests ebbed away again and soon tourists, once the mainstay of the economy, were flocking back to the Valley in numbers not seen since before the insurgency began. By 2011, record numbers of tourists were visiting Kashmir, including more than one million Indians and 32,000 foreign tourists.[39] Indian security forces thinned out their presence in the towns and the sandbags that used to be piled up everywhere against bomb attacks disappeared. Kashmir's once heavily militarised capital Srinagar returned to being a normal bustling city, its streets safer to walk in than those of many a Pakistani or Indian city.[40] From a high-intensity conflict—919 civilians were killed in 2001—the number of violent incidents fell steadily to the more manageable levels of a low-intensity conflict. Twenty-eight civilians were killed in 2014. The numbers of militants killed dropped sharply from 2,020 in 2001 to 110 in 2014.[41] Conversations in the Valley that once centred on violence were replaced by talk of frustration with poor governance by the state government. "Hartals", shutdown protests by separatists, became increasingly unpopular for keeping people away from work, children away from school, and day labourers out of money. At the end of 2014, India held another state election in Jammu and Kashmir, with turnout of 65 per cent. For the first time, the BJP, thanks to voters in Jammu, gained a share of power in the state in a coalition led by the Kashmir Valley-based People's Democratic Party (PDP).

But like Pakistan, the Indian state confused the presence of silence with the presence of peace. Fair elections were a necessary but not sufficient condition for addressing deep-rooted historical grievances, while Delhi's tight management of Kashmiri political parties left them little space to develop mature, sophisticated responses. The aspiration for *Azaadi* in the Kashmir Valley remained, as did resentment at human rights abuses by Indian security forces. Poor state governance, indifference from Delhi and the absence of any hope of progress in broader peace talks between India and Pakistan continued to chafe below the surface. So too did suspicion among many Kashmiri Muslims of the perceived anti-Muslim agenda of the BJP, whose inclusion in the J&K state government rankled in the Valley.

When Indian security forces killed the Kashmiri commander of the Pakistan-backed Hizb-ul-Mujahedeen in the summer of 2016, protests erupted anew in the Valley. The commander, Burhan Wani, had made a name for himself on social media as the poster boy for a new breed of educated Kashmiri youth who had taken up arms against India. Numbering barely 100 men, they were too few to be a serious threat to Indian security, but visible enough on the internet to capture public imagination. Wani's death was the catalyst for an explosion in long-simmering resentment; thousands turned out for his funeral, leading to protests which caught India off-guard. A heavy-handed response by poorly-equipped and poorly-trained Indian police inflamed sentiment further. Nearly 100 people were killed in the unrest, while many more were blinded by pellet-guns used to tame stone-throwing protesters. But the protests were largely leaderless and had no clear political articulation beyond an ill-defined aspiration for *Azaadi*. Individual Kashmiris would often tell reporters that what they wanted was independence rather than to join Pakistan. Even if India had been willing to contemplate this, and it was not, the old conundrum remained: an independent Kashmir Valley sandwiched between hostile states was non-viable and would lead to a fresh partition; a broader settlement covering all of the former princely state required peace between India and Pakistan. In the absence of any political mechanism for channeling the protesters' anger, the main people to suffer were Kashmiris themselves.[42] Pakistan's attempts to persuade the international community to condemn the Indian crackdown fell on deaf ears—for too long it had used outrage over Kashmir to justify jihadi violence. Politicians in Delhi began again to talk of improving the political and economic situation in the Valley. If past performance was anything to go by, they would soon forget and the presence of silence would once more become a substitute for the presence of peace. Indian security forces started to re-establish control and the protests petered out. Over the very long term, better relations between India and Pakistan might create the space for a new generation of Kashmiris to reassert their desire for independence. But in the short term, as long as Pakistan continued to support Islamist militants against India, there would be no such political space. Kashmir's best hope was that new political leaders might emerge who could steadily expand the scope of participatory democracy, challenge the use of violence by all sides. including the state, and stake a claim to greater autonomy. Otherwise, the Valley would likely be condemned to a cycle of sporadic summer protests followed by a return to normality in which the only lasting impact would be on those who died.

Pakistan's own efforts to wrest control of the Kashmir Valley had come to nothing. In all its years of trying, it had sacrificed the interests of its citizens while propping up an overly powerful army and spawning a dangerous collection of jihadis on home soil. The nuclear weapons it had believed would prevent the Valley slipping out of its grasp had instead encouraged a recklessness that drove a Kashmir settlement permanently out of reach.

* * *

In a letter to Pakistan's founder, Mohammad Ali Jinnah, on May 28, 1937, the country's ideological father, the poet Muhammad Iqbal, had written about the potential of a homeland for South Asian Muslims. India would struggle to become a democracy, he said, because of its Hindu caste system; while a Muslim country would flourish. "... it is clear in my mind that if Hinduism accepts social democracy, it must cease to be Hinduism," he wrote in his letter from Lahore. "For Islam, the acceptance of social democracy in some suitable form and consistent with the legal principles of Islam is not a revolution but a return to the original purity of Islam."[43] His prediction proved wrong, not because of any inherent problem with Islam—many Muslims are also secularists and democrats—but because of the nature of the Pakistani state. It was India that became the world's biggest democracy. Where Pakistan had sent gunmen to wrest control of Kashmir, India had offered an, albeit limited, managed democracy to try to pacify it. As India became the world's fastest-growing economy, Pakistan was calcifying into a militarised state dependent on nuclear weapons and Islamist proxies. After 1971, Pakistan had recovered and prospered. Its slide relative to India from 1998 onwards, however, appeared to be irreversible. Pakistan had lost the Great South Asian War.

EPILOGUE

A JAW FOR A TOOTH

India Crosses the Line of Control

The Indian Army's brigade headquarters at Uri lies beneath the forested slopes of the Pir Panjal mountain range that separates the Kashmir Valley from the plains of Jammu and Punjab. It is one of the more vulnerable army bases on the Line of Control, almost surrounded on three sides by territory held by Pakistan. To the south, the LoC juts eastwards into Indian-held territory, following a large U-shape that then curves back towards the west. Before Partition, it was possible to cross the mountains to the south of Uri through the Haji Pir Pass to reach the town of Poonch in Jammu. But since 1947, the mountains contained within that large U-bend have been held by Pakistan, a sore subject for the Indian Army which captured the Haji Pir Pass in the 1965 war only to see the government hand it back in a subsequent peace agreement. With its forested slopes and hidden gullies, the area around the Haji Pir is one of the main routes for infiltrators sent from Pakistan into the Kashmir Valley and the Jammu region. On September 18, 2016, four gunmen, heavily armed and carrying incendiary ammunition, attacked the Indian camp at Uri, killing nineteen men. The base was unusually full at the time as two battalions were rotating in and out, and tents and temporary shelters set up to accommodate them caught fire during the attack. Soldiers who had enlisted expecting to fight were burned alive or died of asphyxiation. It was the deadliest assault on an Indian Army camp in Jammu and Kashmir since 2002. Such was the method of the attack and apparent link to infiltration through the Haji Pir, that India immediately blamed Pakistan. Denying involvement, Pakistan argued that the attack was an overspill of the protests against Indian rule that had erupted in the Kashmir Valley in July. But its assertion was unconvincing. People in the small town of Uri had largely stayed away from the uprisings elsewhere the Valley due to its more remote location and heavy military presence.[1] By the time of the Uri attack, India had begun to get a grip on the protests. Little evidence existed to suggest that local Kashmiris had the sophistication, training and weaponry to carry out the assault. Nor would they have had any reason to travel as far as Uri to attack Indian security forces. Intelligence on the timing of the battalion rotation also appeared likely to have come from the Pakistan Army—typically both militaries keep close track of troop movements on the other side. Indian assessments said the use of specialised incendiary ammunition, along with apparent help in intelligence and logistics, all pointed to the involvement of Pakistan. Poor Indian security at Uri had then contributed to the death toll.[2] Whatever the actual truth of the Uri attack—those prone to conspiracy theories claimed it was a false flag operation by India to discredit Pakistan and the Kashmir protesters—it definitely looked as though it carried the fingerprints of the Pakistan Army. The United States condemned it as a "cross-border attack", indicating that it had no doubt the gunmen had come from Pakistan.[3]

In the immediate aftermath, Prime Minister Narendra Modi promised that "those behind this despicable act will not go unpunished."[4] BJP General Secretary Ram Madhav suggested that "for one tooth, the complete jaw" should be India's policy.[5] His choice of language echoed that used in an attack on a Pakistani village across the LoC in May 1998, where Indian forces reportedly avenging a massacre of civilians on their side left a leaflet saying, "Ten eyes for one eye, one jaw for a single tooth".[6] It was also an indication of what was to come. During his election campaign, Modi had pitched himself as a strongman who would stand up to Pakistan. Though economic issues had mattered far more to Indian voters, his own political leanings and demands for reprisals from his core constituency in the Hindu right made retaliation for Uri almost inevitable. But even leaving aside Modi's own views, arguably any other Indian prime minister would have been compelled to act. The army wanted revenge. Indian public opinion, in part whipped up by a jingoistic national media, had been nursing its wrath since Mumbai. Like other prime ministers before him, Modi had tried his hand at peace-making with Pakistan after he took office in May 2014, inviting Prime Minister Nawaz Sharif to his inauguration and visiting him in Lahore in December 2015. But the drip-drip of attacks by jihadis from Pakistan—big enough to be irritating, small enough not to provoke Indian retaliation—continued. In 2015, a police station in Gurdaspur in Indian Punjab was attacked. Then, a week after Modi made his surprise visit to Lahore, gunmen attacked an Indian Air Force base at Pathankot in Punjab, near the border with Pakistan. India said its investigations pointed to the involvement of Jaish-e-Mohammed and demanded Pakistan curb the group and its founder Masood Azhar.[7] As usual, Pakistan promised to take action but did little. Jaish continued to operate openly from its base in Bawahalpur in south Punjab, apparently relaxed enough to press on with building a large new madrasa outside the town.[8] Masood Azhar, released by a previous BJP government after the 1999 Kathmandu to Kandahar hijacking, and Jaish, the group behind the 2001 attack on the Indian parliament, were as active as ever. Even then India and Pakistan might have continued in a state of uneasy managed conflict—Modi's priority was economic growth—had it not been for Uri. It was one attack too many and appeared to be a classic case of the overreach and miscalculation that had blinded the Pakistan Army at Kargil. After Mumbai, and even more so after Pathankot, the Uri attack made it nearly impossible for India not to respond. As ever, the same limitations that had defined Indian "strategic restraint" since the 1998 nuclear tests applied. An all-out military attack or air strikes across the border with Pakistan risked escalating into a nuclear exchange. Covert operations would do nothing to satisfy public opinion. The use of Indian artillery or special forces to attack militant camps in Pakistani Kashmir might quench public thirst for revenge, but would have little impact on Pakistan's strategic culture of supporting some jihadis while fighting others. Nor would it make any dent on the jihadi infrastructure in places like Bawahalpur, or on the Lahore-based Lashkar-e-Taiba. Yet for all these limitations, the international environment had changed dramatically since 1998. India's economic and diplomatic clout had risen. The international community had become increasingly wary of Pakistan's support for jihadis and was more inclined to sympathise with Indian complaints about it. In deciding its response to the Uri attack, India exploited this change to the maximum.

The Indian government started off by flexing its diplomatic muscles. It announced it was pulling out of a summit of the South Asian Association for Regional Cooperation (SAARC) due to be held in Islamabad in November. Underlining Pakistan's growing isolation within the region, Afghanistan, Bangladesh and Bhutan quickly said they too would not attend.[9] India also began to consider other diplomatic and economic means of putting pressure on Pakistan, for example, by trying to dissuade countries and companies from trading with it.[10] It suggested it might build more dams on rivers on its side of the LoC before they flowed into Pakistan—a largely impractical and rhetorical threat that nonetheless served notice that it was willing to consider all measures, including tightening water supplies, to drive home its case. Then on September 29, 2016, the Indian foreign ministry summoned journalists to an unscheduled news conference that was as hastily convened as the one in 1998 when Prime Minister Vajpayee announced India's nuclear tests. In a sign of changing times, the 2016 summons came via a WhatsApp group. The news conference would be held, not in the garden of the prime minister's bungalow, but in a plush new foreign ministry building, itself emblematic of India's aspirations as a rising global power. Shortly before calling the media to the news conference, the foreign ministry circulated—via the same WhatsApp group—a White House statement on an overnight phone call between Indian National Security Adviser Ajit Doval and his US counterpart Susan Rice. Condemning the Uri attack as "cross-border terrorism"; the Americans reiterated US demands that Pakistan take action against the Lashkar-e-Taiba and Jaish-e-Mohammed and reaffirmed "the robust US-India partnership".[11] It was one of the strongest official statements in favour of India ever from Washington, which for years had tried to balance pressure on Pakistan over its support for Islamist militants with quiet diplomacy to nudge Delhi on Kashmir. Notably it made no mention of Kashmir; nor called for India and Pakistan dialogue. The entire onus was on Pakistan to disarm its jihadi proxies. The US statement set

India up well for the announcement at the media briefing, where the main speaker was, unusually, the Indian Army's Director-General of Military Operations (DGMO). In an overnight operation, Lt-General Ranbir Singh said, the Indian Army had conducted "surgical strikes" against Pakistan-backed militants preparing to infiltrate into Indian Kashmir. These strikes on launch-pads along the LoC had inflicted "significant casualties". India had no plans for further military operations, he added, and had already contacted the Pakistan Army to inform it formally of its action.[12] The DGMO read his statement in English and Hindi, took no questions and saluted the media on his way out. Other military officials were on hand to tell journalists the Indian Army had crossed the LoC in several different places to target would-be infiltrators. For the first time since 1971, India had announced military action across the LoC.

For all of India's insistence on the sanctity of the LoC during the Kargil War, Indian forces had carried out covert strikes across the LoC before.[13] These had happened even under the dovish Prime Minister Manmohan Singh, including in 2011, 2013 and 2014, according to the Congress Party.[14] But Modi's government was the first to announce these publicly. Even more remarkably, it did so without any objection from the international community—indeed Washington had given India considerable diplomatic cover with its own statement blaming Pakistan for cross-border terrorism. The details of the cross-LoC raids, conducted under the nose of the Pakistan Army, remained murky. Pakistan flat out denied they had taken place at all while some of Modi's critics in India accused his government of exaggerating them for political gain. Indian media reports by reliable military and security journalists said Indian Special Forces had crossed the LoC in at least four different places, some going as far as 4 km (2.5 miles) deep, to kill dozens of militants. Indian artillery fire was used to distract the Pakistan Army and allow them to cross and return safely.[15] Another version said that nearly 100 Special Forces from India's Parachute Regiment had crept across the LoC forty-eight hours earlier to identify sites where Pakistan-backed militants were waiting to infiltrate into Kashmir. On receipt of a signal, they attacked six launch-pads along a wide stretch of the LoC near-simultaneously before making their way back safely to the Indian side.[16] It was the stuff of action movies, details in the various accounts possibly embellished by some sources for dramatic effect, or distorted in the telling as they were relayed from the frontline to army superiors, politicians and journalists in Delhi. Exactly what happened might never be known for sure. What could not be disputed, however, was the Indian announcement and the international reaction. That in itself pointed to a new unpredictability in relations between the two countries—an unpredictability the Indian government said it was deliberately cultivating to keep Pakistan off guard.[17] The Pakistan Army would be forced to look again at its assumptions that international anxiety about nuclear war gave it impunity to conduct small-scale attacks on India without fear of retaliation. Washington had publicly taken India's side. China was reportedly pressing Pakistan quietly behind the scenes for a change of course,[18] in line with the wariness at Pakistani adventurism it had shown in previous India-Pakistan crises, even as it continued to defend it in public.

India had come a long way from the lonely humiliation of the Kathmandu to Kandahar hijacking in 1999 to the public announcement of cross-LoC raids into Pakistan-held territory in 2016. The cross-LoC raids were a tactical rather than strategic success, since the old rules stood. Pakistan was unlikely to abandon its strategy of supporting some jihadis while fighting others—the ideology of confrontation with India had become too deeply embedded to be uprooted. Nor had India escaped the requirements of "strategic restraint". Beyond skirmishes on the LoC, more significant Indian military action still faced the risk of escalation into a nuclear exchange. Inside the Kashmir Valley, India still needed to find the political means of addressing Kashmiri resentment. In the event of further attacks from Pakistan, moreover, India's options for further unpredictable retaliation remained limited. If it had international support for its cross-LoC raids, it was precisely because Indian responses to attacks by jihadis from Pakistan had been so carefully controlled since 1998, thanks to Prime Minister Modi's predecessors. It could not continue seeking ever more forceful retaliation without putting that at risk. Nor could it rely on international impatience with Pakistan—it was too useful a country for China and too worrying for the United States to abandon. Pakistan's defeat in the Great South Asian War contained a warning for India too. Pakistan had been brought low by hubris, a chauvinist nationalism and an unhealthy obsession with its neighbour. As it emerged as the far stronger power, India needed to be wary of succumbing to similar sentiments, lest it neglect the need to tend to the domestic stability and restraint that had served it so well.

Nonetheless, in the short-run, India had added a new twist to the old rules. It had announced its cross-LoC raids without international objection and acted quickly to reassure both Pakistan and the outside world that it intended no further escalation. It had added this new twist using the very weapons that Pakistan, with its nuclear weapons and jihadis lacked—India's diplomatic and economic strength. That it was able to do so was a product of multiple factors, many outside India's control. Pakistan had failed to adjust to the more fertile environment for jihadis that emerged at the end of the Cold War and then to the international opposition to Islamist militants that coalesced after the September 11 attacks. After 2001, it had made the mistake of trying to take on India and the United States simultaneously. Preoccupied with its own domestic power struggles, and fixated on an ideology that required it to seek parity with India, Pakistan was blinded to the ways in which the world around it was changing. After their nuclear tests in 1998, the UN Security Council had issued a statement urging India and Pakistan "to avoid threatening military movements" and resume talks to remove tensions between them. "They were encouraged to find mutually acceptable solutions that address the root causes of those tensions, including Kashmir," the Security Council said.[19] By 2016, Kashmir had been dropped from the international agenda, while India's announcement of what once would have been condemned as a threatening military movement had been greeted with sympathy and support. The progress India has made between 1998 and 2016 is a victory that has many fathers. In Pakistan, torn between blaming its external enemies and the "traitors" of its internal power struggle, defeat is an orphan.

NOTES

PROLOGUE: THE SPIDER'S WEB

1. Captain Devi Sharan with Srinjoy Chowadhury, *Flight Into Fear.The Captain's Story*, New Delhi, Penguin Books New Delhi, 2000 (pp. 5–7).
2. Interview with the author, 2014.
3. Captain's comments are in an interview with the author unless otherwise stated (2014).
4. KPS Gill, *Faultlines:Writing on Conflict and Resolution* (Vol 4), Edited by K.P.S. Gill and Ajai Sahni, The Institute of Conflict Management, New Delhi, 2000.
5. Indian Airlines IC-814 Hijack. National Geographic documentary https://www.youtube.com/watch?v=7mIUOZsrIUc
6. Josy Joseph, "NSG Crack Team was Ready on Dec. 24", Rediff, Dec 28, 1999. http://www.rediff.com/news/1999/dec/28josy1.htm.
7. Josy Joseph, "They were called Burgher, Doctor, Duphtar", Rediff, Dec 26, 1999. http://www.rediff.com/news/1999/dec/26ia16.htm.
8. Interview with the author.
9. K.P.S. Gill, *Faultlines:Writing on Conflict and Resolution*, The Institute of Conflict Management, New Delhi, 2000.
10. Interview with the author.
11. Interview with the author.
12. Onkar Singh and Josy Joseph, "Released Hostages Return to Delhi", Rediff, Dec 25, 1999. http://www.rediff.com/news/1999/dec/25free.htm
13. Jaswant Singh, *India At Risk: Mistakes, Misconceptions and Misadventures of Security Policy*, Rupa, New Delhi, 2013 (p. 211).
14. Ibid. (p. 211).
15. Onkar Singh and Josy Joseph, "Released Hostages Return to Delhi", Rediff, Dec 25, 1999. http://www.rediff.com/news/1999/dec/25free.htm

16. Praveen Swami, 'Masood Azhar, in his own words', *Frontline*, vol. 18—Issue 21. Oct 13—26, 2001. http://www.frontline.in/static/html/fl1821/18210190.htm

17. Innes Bowen, *Medina in Birmingham, Najaf in Brent: Inside British Islam* (p. 32), Hurst, London, 2014.

18. Innes Bowen, 'Masood Azhar: The man who brought jihad to Britain', I, BBC, April 5, 2016. [http://www.bbc.co.uk/news/magazine-35959202]

19. *The Army of Madinah in Kashmir*, Esa al Hindi, Maktabah al-Ansar Publications, Sparkhill, Birmingham, 1999.

20. *Medina in Birmingham, Najaf in Brent*, p. 32.

21. Daniel Flynn, "Omar Sheikh, a childhood friend turned Pakistani militant", Reuters, Sept. 25, 2008. http://blogs.reuters.com/pakistan/2008/09/25/omar-sheikh-a-childhood-friend-turned-pakistani-militant/

22. Interview with the author.

23. Bernard-Henri Levy, *Who Killed Daniel Pearl?* UK edition, Melville House Publishing, London, 2003 (p. 349).

24. Ibid., pp. 246–7.

25. All comments by Doval are from an interview with the author.

26. Interview with the author.

27. Alex Strick van Linschoten and Felix Kuehn, *An Enemy We Created, The Myth of the Taliban/al Qaeda Merger in Afghanistan, 1970–2010*, Hurst, London, 2012, p. 203.

28. Interview with the author.

29. Bruce Riedel, *Deadly Embrace: Pakistan, America and the Future of the Global Jihad*, Brookings Institution Press, Washington, DC, 2012, p. 51.

30. "RAW agent on board seized Airbus, says FO," Pakistan News Service, Dec. 28, 1999. http://indianterrorism.bravepages.com/Nepal3.htm

31. For a full account of the kidnapping see: Adrian Levy and Cathy Scott-Clark, *The Meadow: Kashmir 1995—Where the Terror Began*, HarperCollins, London, 2012.

32. Husain Haqqani, *Between Mosque and Military*, Carnegie Endowment for International Peace, Washington, DC, 2005, p. 300.

33. Interview with the author.

34. Interview with the author

35. *Flight Into Fear: The Captain's Story*, p. 114.

36. *India At Risk*, p. 212.

37. Ibid., p. 211.

38. "154 hostages exchanged for 3 militants," Rediff, Dec. 31, 1999. http://www.rediff.com/news/1999/dec/31ia12.htm

39. Sumatra Bose, *Kashmir, Roots of Conflict, Paths to Peace*, Harvard University Press, Cambridge, MA, 2005, p. 126.

40. Indian Airlines IC-814 Hijack, National Geographic documentary https://
www.youtube.com/watch?v=7mIUOZsrIUc
41. *India At Risk*, p. 213.
42. Ibid.
43. *India At Risk*, p. 215.
44. Neena Haridas, "Where is he? Why isn't he here to see me"?Rediff, Jan.
1, 2000. http://www.rediff.com/news/2000/jan/01rachna.htm
45. Declassified State Department cable. http://foia.state.gov/searchapp/
DOCUMENTS/9-30-FY2013/F-2011–03409/DOC_0C17640550/
C17640550.pdf
46. *An Enemy We Created*, p. 200.
47. *India At Risk*, pp. 214–15.
48. Interview with the author.
49. Interview with the author.

1. SETTLING A SCORE: FROM 1947 TO THE NUCLEAR TESTS

1. For YouTube video of announcement https://www.youtube.com/
watch?v=DIi1U—FzC0
2. For YouTube video of announcement https://www.youtube.com/
watch?v=BRxIDFr_duM
3. John Ward Anderson and Kamran Khan, "Pakistan Sets Off Nuclear Blasts",
Washington Post, May 29, 1999 http://www.washingtonpost.com/wp-
srv/inatl/longterm/southasia/stories/pakistan052998.htm)
4. Sartaj Aziz, *Between Dreams and Realities; Some Milestones in Pakistan's
History*, Oxford University Press, Karachi, 2009, p. 28.
5. Text of UN Resolution. [http://www.un.org/en/ga/search/view_doc.
asp?symbol=S/RES/47(1948)]
6. Carey Sublette, The Nuclear Weapon Archive, Pakistan's Nuclear Weapons
Program, January 2, 2002. [http://www.nuclearweaponarchive.org/
Pakistan/PakOrigin.html]
7. *Between Dreams and Realities*, p. 36.
8. Alastair Lamb, *Kashmir, A Disputed Legacy, 1846–1990*, Roxford Books,
1991, p. 253.
9. Carey Sublette, *The Nuclear Weapon Archive, Pakistan's Nuclear Weapons
Program*, January 2, 2002. [http://www.nuclearweaponarchive.org/
Pakistan/PakOrigin.html]
10. Simla Agreement. July 2, 1972, Indian Ministry of External Affairs.
[https://mea.gov.in/in-focus-article.htm?19005/Simla+Agreement+
July+2+1972].
11. Katherine Frank, *Indira, The Life of Indira Nehru Gandhi*, Harper Collins,
London, 2001, pp 344–347.

12. J.N. Dixit, *Across Borders: Fifty Years of India's Foreign Policy*, Picus Books, New Delhi, 1998, p. 116.

13. Scott D. Sagan, "Why Do States Build Nuclear Weapons?: Three Models in Search of a Bomb", *International Security*, Vol. 21, No. 3 (Winter 1996–1997) [http://faculty.maxwell.syr.edu/rdenever/PPA%20730–11/Sagan.pdf]

14. Yogesh Joshi, *The Imagined Arsenal; India's Nuclear Decision-Making, 1973–1976*, Nuclear Proliferation International History Project, Woodrow Wilson International Center for Scholars, June 2015. [https://www.wilsoncenter.org/sites/default/files/WP6—The%20Imagined%20Arsenal_2.pdf]

15. Ibid

16. Andrew Small, *The China-Pakistan Axis: Asia's New Geopolitics*, Hurst, London, 2015, p. 31.

17. Ibid., pp. 34–35.

18. The Kargil Committee Report[http://fas.org/news/india/2000/25indi1.htm]

19. *The China-Pakistan Axis*, p. 40.

20. Feroz Khan, *Eating Grass: The Making of the Pakistani Bomb*, Stanford University Press, 2012, pp. 175–190.

21. Assessment of international nuclear experts provided to the author.

22. The Kargil Committee Report[http://fas.org/news/india/2000/25indi1.htm]

23. Shuja Nawaz, *Crossed Swords: Pakistan, Its Army, and the Wars Within*, Oxford University Press, 2008, pp. 490–491.

24. Assessment of international nuclear weapons experts, as given to the author

25. Farrukh Iqbal, "What's really going on with income trends in India and Pakistan?", Brookings. July 15, 2015. http://www.brookings.edu/blogs/future-development/posts/2015/07/15-income-india-pakistan-iqbal

26. The Kargil Committee Report[http://fas.org/news/india/2000/25indi1.htm]

27. C. Raja Mohan, *Crossing the Rubicon: The Shaping of India's New Foreign Policy*, Penguin Books India, New Delhi, 2003, p. 6.

28. India's Nuclear Weapons Program. 2001 [http://nuclearweaponarchive.org/India/index.html]

29. Ibid.

30. *Between Dreams and Realities*, pp. 191–193.

31. Kenneth Cooper, "Key Indian Official Warns Pakistan", Washington Post, May 19, 19998. [http://www.washingtonpost.com/wp-srv/inatl/longterm/southasia/stories/indiawarn051998.htm]

32. Tom Mintier, "Pakistan holds off on nuclear tests for now", CNN, May 19 1998. [http://edition.cnn.com/WORLD/asiapcf/9805/19/pakistan. test.folo/index.html]

33. Ibid.

34. *Pakistan's Nuclear Weapons Program*. [http://www.nuclearweaponarchive. org/Pakistan/PakOrigin.html]

35. *Between Dreams and Realities*, p. 194.

36. *Pakistan's Nuclear Weapons Program* [http://www.nuclearweaponarchive. org/Pakistan/PakOrigin.html]

37. YouTube footage [https://www.youtube.com/watch?v=IhygFzpyxyI]

38. Eqbal Ahmad, "When Mountains Die", June 1, 1998 [https://www.tni. org/en/archives/act/478]

39. Full text of Sharif's press statement [http://www.nuclearweaponarchive. org/Pakistan/SharifAnnounce.txt]

40. Asim Yousafzai, "Environmental fallout from nuclear tests", Daily Times, August 2, 2014. [http://www.dailytimes.com.pk/opinion/02-Aug-2014/environmental-fallout-from-nuclear-tests]

41. United Nations press release. June 6, 1998 [http://www.un.org/press/ en/1998/sc6528.doc.htm]

42. *Crossing the Rubicon*, p. 186.

43. *"Pakistan and India Under the Nuclear Shadow"*. Documentary produced in 2010 for the Eqbal Ahmad Foundation. [https://www.youtube.com/ watch?v=EeBRVFxe5oQ])

44. Ibid.

45. *India At Risk*, p. 175.

46. Ibid., p. 176.

47. YouTube video: [https://www.youtube.com/watch?v=I0iIqnw6fLw]

48. *Between Dreams and Realities*, p. 223.

49. *India at Risk*, p. 178.

50. Lahore Agreement. [http://www.stimson.org/research-pages/lahore-summit/]

51. *Between Dreams and Realities*, p. 223.

2. "A BRILLIANT TACTICAL OPERATION": PAKISTAN'S DEFEAT IN THE KARGIL WAR OF 1999

1. For full details on the Siachen War, see Myra MacDonald, *Heights of Madness: One Woman's Journey in Pursuit of a Secret War*, Rupa, New Delhi, 2007.

2. Ibid., p. 142.

3. Copy of handwritten notes given to the author on condition of anonymity.

4. Accounts differ on exactly when the plan was approval, ranging from within weeks of Musharraf becoming army chief in October 1998 to mid-

January by Musharraf's own account. See *Crossed Swords: Pakistan. Its Army and the Wars Within*. Shuja Nawaz. Oxford University Press. 2008, p. 507, and *In the Line of Fire*. Pervez Musharraf. Simon & Schuster UK. 2006, p. 90.)

5. General V.P. Malik, *Kargil: From Surprise to Victory*, Harper Collins, New Delhi, 2006 (2010 edn, p. 66).
6. *In the Line of Fire*, p. 90.
7. Shireen Mazari, *The Kargil Conflict 1999: Separating Fact from Fiction*, Institute of Strategic Studies, Islamabad, 2003, pp. 14–15.
8. *In the Line of Fire*, p. 90.
9. Hasan-Askari Rizvi, *The Lessons of Kargil as learned by Pakistan. Asymmetric Warfare in South Asia. The Causes and Consequences of the Kargil Conflict*, Edited by Peter R. Lavoy. Cambridge University Press, 2009, p. 338.
10. The Kargil Committee Report. [http://fas.org/news/india/2000/25indi1.htm]
11. Ibid.
12. Ibid.
13. John H. Gill, *Military Operations in the Kargil conflict. Asymmetric Warfare in South Asia. The Causes and Consequences of the Kargil Conflict*, Edited by Peter R. Lavoy. Cambridge University Press, 2009, p. 96.
14. *Kargil: From Surprise to Victory*, p. 87.
15. Ibid.
16. Ibid., p. 160.
17. Ibid., p. 244.
18. *Between Dreams and Realities*, p. 254.
19. Ibid., pp. 256–257.
20. The Kargil Committee Report. [http://fas.org/news/india/2000/25indi1.htm]
21. Interview with the author, 2015.
22. *Kargil: From Surprise to Victory*, p. 140.
23. *India at Risk*, p. 185.
24. *The Kargil Committee Report* [http://fas.org/news/india/2000/25indi1.htm]
25. *Between Dreams and Realities*, p. 258.
26. *The Kargil Committee Report* [http://fas.org/news/india/2000/25indi1.htm]
27. *Military Operations in the Kargil Conflict; Asymmetric Warfare in South Asia*, p. 102.
28. "India Agrees to Kashmir Talks", May 31, 1999. CNN. [http://edition.cnn.com/WORLD/asiapcf/9905/31/india.pakistan.01/]
29. Barry Bearak, "2 Indian Warplanes Lost Over Pakistan's Part of Kashmir", *New York Times*, May 28, 1999 [http://www.nytimes.com/1999/05/28/world/2-indian-warplanes-lost-over-pakistan-s-part-of-kashmir.html]

30. Peter R. Lavoy. *Introduction: the importance of the Kargil conflict. Asymmetric Warfare in South Asia, pp 10–11*.

31. *In the Line of Fire*, pp. 88.

32. *Kargil: From Surprise to Victory*, p. 259.

33. Timothy D. Hoyt. *Kargil: the nuclear dimension. Asymmetric Warfare in South Asia*, p. 159.

34. *Between Dreams and Realities*, pp. 264–265.

35. Transcripts are included in Jaswant Singh's *India At Risk*. pp 189–196.

36. Ibid., p. 202.

37. Ibid., p. 197.

38. *Between Dreams and Realities*, p. 272

39. *Kargil: From Surprise to Victory*, p. 289.

40. John. H. Gill, *Military Operations in the Kargil Conflict; Asymmetric Warfare in South Asia*, p. 123.

41. *Kargil: From Surprise to Victory*, p. 157.

42. John H. Gill, *Military Operations in the Kargil Conflict, Asymmetric Warfare in South Asia*. p. 114.

43. Ibid.

44. *Kargil: From Surprise to Victory* p. 147.

45. Bruce Riedel, "On The Brink", extracted from *Avoiding Armageddon: America, India and Pakistan to the Brink and Back*, HarperCollins, p. 248. [http://www.telegraphindia.com/1130428/jsp/7days/story_16836328.jsp#.VnnnqPmLSM-]

46. *Kargil: From Surprise to Victory*, p. 147.

47. *Military Operations in the Kargil Conflict; Asymmetric Warfare in South Asia*, p. 114.

48. Thomas W. Lippman, "India Hinted At Attack In Pakistan", *Washington Post*, June 27, 1999. [http://www.washingtonpost.com/wp-srv/inatl/longterm/southasia/stories/kashmir062799.htm]

49. Zinni's account is quoted by Husain Haqqani in, "When Image is truth and truth is an image", Carnegie Endowment for International Peace. [http://carnegieendowment.org/2004/06/10/when-image-is-truth-and-truth-is-image].

50. *India At Risk*, p. 200.

51. *The China-Pakistan Axis*, pp. 58–59.

52. Ibid.

53. *Between Dreams and Realities*, p. 277.

54. *Avoiding Armageddon*, p. 248. [http://www.telegraphindia.com/1130428/jsp/7days/story_16836328.jsp#.VnnnqPmLSM-]

55. *Between Dreams and Realities*, p. 278.

56. Praveen Swami, *The Kargil War*, LeftWord Books, New Delhi, 2000 (2005 edn, p. 37).

57. *Kargil: From Surprise to Victory*, pp. 342–343.
58. Ibid.
59. *Military Operations in the Kargil Conflict; Asymmetric Warfare in South Asia*, p. 122.
60. *Crossed Swords*, p. 523.
61. *The Kargil Conflict 1999, Separating Fact from Fiction*, p. 68.
62. Ibid.
63. Praveen Swami. *The impact of the Kargil conflict and Kashmir on Indian politics and society, Asymmetric Warfare in South Asia*, p. 259, p. 264.
64. Benazir Bhutto, *Daughter of the East. An Autobiography*, Simon & Schuster UK, London, 2007, p. 425.
65. Brian Cloughley, *War, Coups & Terror. Pakistan's Army in Years of Turmoil*, Pen & Sword, 2008, p. 114.
66. *In the Line of Fire*, pp 12–13.

3. THE GENERAL AND THE POET: FROM THE KARGIL WAR TO THE AGRA SUMMIT

1. Ibid., p. 45.
2. Ibid., p. 80.
3. *Crossed Swords*, p. 500.
4. Atal Bihari Vajpayee, *Twenty-One Poems*, English translation, Penguin, New Delhi, 2001, p. xi.
5. Ibid., p. xiii.
6. *Crossing the Rubicon*, p. 49.
7. Celia W. Dugger, "Clinton Fever: A Delighted India Has All the Symptoms", *New York Times*, March 23, 2000. [http://www.nytimes.com/2000/03/23/world/clinton-fever-a-delighted-india-has-all-the-symptoms.html]
8. White House: President Bill Clinton, New Delhi. India Parliament Speech. AP Archives. [http://www.aparchive.com/metadata/WHITE-HOUSE-PRESIDENT-BILL-CLINTON-NEW-DELHI-INDIA-PARLIAMENT-SPEECH/2504f6b5ee7e471297d84503049b5049]
9. Jonathan Marcus, "Analysis: The world's most dangerous place?", BBC, March 23, 2000. [http://news.bbc.co.uk/1/hi/world/south_asia/687021.stm]
10. *Deadly Embrace*, pp. 60–62.
11. US Department of State [https://foia.state.gov/searchapp/DOCUMENTS/5-FY2014/F-2011–03409ER/DOC_0C17641284/C17641284.pdf]
12. Ibid.
13. South Asia Terrorism Portal. Responses to India's Offer of Cease-fire. [http://www.satp.org/satporgtp/countries/india/states/jandk/documents/papers/Response_Ceasefire.htm]

14. Atal Behari Vajpayee, "My musings from Kumarakom—I: Time to resolve problems of the past", The Hindu, Jan 2, 2001. [http://www.thehindu.com/2001/01/02/stories/02020001.htm]

15. South Asia Terrorism Portal. Responses to India's Offer of Cease-fire. [http://www.satp.org/satporgtp/countries/india/states/jandk/documents/papers/Response_Ceasefire.htm]

16. Praveen Swami, "An Audacious Strike", Frontline, Oct 13–26 2001. [http://www.frontline.in/static/html/fl1821/18210200.htm]

17. Kargil, From Surprise to Victory, p. 372.

18. "Musharraf wants one-to-one with Vajpayee" The Hindu, Feb 7, 2001. [http://www.thehindu.com/2001/02/07/stories/01070008.htm]

19. US Department of State [https://foia.state.gov/searchapp/DOCUMENTS/5-FY2014/F-2010–03412/DOC_0C05192720/C05192720.pdf]

20. In the Line of Fire, pp. 12–13.

21. Satish Jacob, "Musharraf's family links to Delhi", BBC, July 13, 2001. [http://news.bbc.co.uk/1/hi/world/south_asia/1436723.stm]

22. NDTV, via YouTube. [https://www.youtube.com/watch?v=a10A957kw28]

23. "I was supposed to be the hidden hand: Advani." Excerpts from My Country My Life by Lal Krishna Advani carried by Times of India, March 17, 2008 [http://timesofindia.indiatimes.com/india/I-was-supposed-to-be-the-hidden-hand-Advani/articleshow/2872224.cms]

24. Crossing the Rubicon, p. 177.

25. In the Line of Fire, p 298.

26. Excerpts from My Country My Life by Lal Krishna Advani carried by Times of India. [http://timesofindia.indiatimes.com/india/I-was-supposed-to-be-the-hidden-hand-Advani/articleshow/2872224.cms]

27. Prabhu Chawla, Raj Chengappa and Shishir Gupta,"Hit and Run", India Today cover story, July 30, 2001. [http://indiatoday.intoday.in/story/indo-pak-agra-summit-positions-of-delhi-and-islamabad-remains-incompatible/1/230813.html]

28. Transcript of Musharraf's comments. [https://presidentmusharraf.wordpress.com/2008/01/20/agra-summit-editors-for-breakfast/]

29. Excerpts from My Country My Life by Lal Krishna Advani carried by Times of India. [http://timesofindia.indiatimes.com/india/I-was-supposed-to-be-the-hidden-hand-Advani/articleshow/2872224.cms]

30. India At Risk, p. 224.

31. Ibid., p. 227.

32. In the Line of Fire, pp. 297–299.

33. Crossing the Rubicon, p. 180.

34. In the Line of Fire, p. 299.

35. Ibid.

36. India At Risk, p. 228.

4. THE ASSASSINS FROM AFAR: PAKISTAN AND AFGHANISTAN

1. Television footage from YouTube. [https://www.youtube.com/watch?v= gM6IY9uoZc0]
2. Ibid.
3. Jean-Louis Bruguière, *Ce que je n'ai pas pu dire: Entretiens avec Jean-Marie Pontaut*, Paris, Robert Laffont 2009, p. 357.
4. Mustafa Hamid and Leah Farrall, *The Arabs at War in Afghanistan*, London, Hurst, 2015, pp. 39–40.
5. Thomas Barfield, *Afghanistan: A Cultural and Political History*, Thomas Barfield, Princeton University Press, 2010, p. 253.
6. *The Arabs at War in Afghanistan*, p. 299.
7. Husain Haqqani, *Magnificent Delusions. Pakistan, the United States, and an Epic History of Misunderstanding*, Public Affairs, 2013, p. 273.
8. Interview with the author, 2009.
9. *Afghanistan: A Cultural and Political History*, p. 258.
10. Carlotta Gall, *The Wrong Enemy: America in Afghanistan 2001–2014*, Houghton Mifflin Harcourt, 2014, pp. 48–49.
11. *Between Dreams and Realities*, p. 211.
12. Eqbal Ahmad, "In a Land Without Music", Reproduced Oct 27, 2009. [https://secularpakistan.wordpress.com/2009/10/27/in-a-land-without-music/]
13. See for example Sebastian Junger on "Afghanistan's Slain Rebel Leader", *National Geographic*. [http://www.nationalgeographic.com/adventure/0111/junger.html]
14. J.N. Dixit, *Across Borders: 50 Years of India's Foreign Policy*, Picus Books, New Delhi, 1998, p. 143.
15. Author interviews with retired diplomats and officials.
16. Compilation of Usama bin Ladin Statements. 1994–Jan 2004. Foreign Broadcasting Information Service. (pp 53–54) [http://fas.org/irp/world/para/ubl-fbis.pdf]
17. *The Army of Madinah in Kashmir*, 'Esa al Hindi (Dhiren Barot), Maktabah al-Ansar Publications, Birmingham, 1999.
18. Interview with the author, 2015.
19. *The 9/11 Commission Report* (p 73) [http://www.9–11commission.gov/report/911Report.pdf]
20. "Algerian Is Found Guilty of Terrorism", Associated Press, April 7, 2001. [http://www.nytimes.com/2001/04/07/world/07TERR.html]
21. *Jihad Against Jews and Crusaders: World Islamic Front Statement.* [http://fas.org/irp/world/para/docs/980223-fatwa.htm]
22. Declassified archives. [http://nsarchive.gwu.edu/NSAEBB/NSAEBB97/tal28.pdf] Quoted by Bruce Riedel in *Deadly Embrace*.

23. *Between Dreams and Realities*, pp. 212–213.
24. Ibid., p. 214.
25. *The 9/11 Commission Report*. [http://www.9–11commission.gov/report/911Report.pdf]
26. *The Army of Madinah in Kashmir*.
27. *The 9/11 Commission Report*. [http://www.9–11commission.gov/report/911Report.pdf]
28. Ibid.
29. Ibid.
30. Ibid.
31. Obituaries. Ahmad Shah Massoud. *The Telegraph*, Sept. 17, 2001. [http://www.telegraph.co.uk/news/obituaries/1340726/Ahmad-Shah-Massoud.html]
32. Ibid.
33. Television footage from YouTube. [https://www.youtube.com/watch?v=gM6IY9uoZc0]
34. "Le commandant Massoud a Bruxelles", Sonuma (video). [http://www.sonuma.com/archive/le-commandant-massoud-%C3%A0-bruxelles]
35. United States District Court. Reporter's Transcript of Proceedings. [http://seattletimes.nwsource.com/art/news/nation_world/terrorist-within/testimony16.pdf]
36. "Algerian Is Found Guilty of Terrorism", Associated Press, April 7, 2001. [http://www.nytimes.com/2001/04/07/world/07TERR.html]
37. United States District Court. Reporter's Transcript of Proceedings. [http://seattletimes.nwsource.com/art/news/nation_world/terrorist-within/testimony16.pdf]
38. Ibid.
39. *The 9/11 Commission Report*. [http://www.9–11commission.gov/report/911Report.pdf]
40. *Ce que je n'ai pas pu dire*, p. 363.
41. Ibid. (p 366).
42. "Masood Murder Plotters Convicted", BBC. May 17, 2005. [http://news.bbc.co.uk/1/hi/world/south_asia/4555633.stm]
43. *The Arabs at War in Afghanistan*, p. 281.
44. *Ce que je n'ai pas pu dire*, 364.
45. Email to the author from Amrullah Saleh, aide to Massoud and former head of Afghan intelligence
46. Interview with the author, 2014.
47. Email to the author. Assertion based on cables found in Pakistan embassy in Kabul after 2001.
48. *Ce que je n'ai pas pu dire*, p. 365.
49. "Belgium convicts eight on terrorism charges", BBC, May 10, 2010. [http://news.bbc.co.uk/1/hi/world/europe/8673229.stm]

50. "America's Bush no whiz on foreign quiz", Nov. 6, 1999 BBC [http://news.bbc.co.uk/1/hi/506298.stm]

51. K.J.M. Varma, "Editors' meet makes Musharraf a hero back home", Rediff, July 18, 2001. http://www.rediff.com/news/2001/jul/18in pak4.htm

52. *The 9/11 Commission Report.* [http://www.9–11commission.gov/report/911Report.pdf]

53. *An Enemy We Created*, p. 191.

54. *The 9/11 Commission Report.* [http://www.9–11commission.gov/report/911Report.pdf]

55. Declassified cable. July 2001. [https://foia.state.gov/searchapp/DOCUMENTS/5-FY2014/F-2011–03409ER/DOC_0C17641136/C17641136.pdf]

56. Piotr Balcerowicz, "The Last Interview with Ahmad Shah Masood", August 2001. [http://www.orient.uw.edu.pl/ balcerowicz/texts/Ahmad_Shah_Masood_en.htm]

57. Interview with the author, 2014.

58. YouTube footage from television documentary. [https://www.youtube.com/watch?v=ZHVVJ8zIUXc]

59. Craig Pyes and William C. Rempel, "Slowly Stalking an Afghan 'Lion'". *Los Angeles Times*, June 12, p. 202. [http://articles.latimes.com/2002/jun/12/world/fg-masoud12/2]

60. Thomas Harding, "Blast survivor tells of Massoud assassination", *Daily Telegraph*, Oct. 26, 2001. [http://www.telegraph.co.uk/news/world-news/asia/afghanistan/1360632/Blast-survivor-tells-of-Massoud-assassination.html]

5. "SOMEBODY'S GOING TO PAY": FROM THE SEPTEMBER 11 ATTACKS TO THE END OF 2001

1. *In the Line of Fire*, pp. 199–200.

2. Interview with the author

3. Described to the author by an official at the meeting.

4. *The 9/11 Commission Report.* [http://www.9–11commission.gov/report/911Report.pdf]

5. Ibid.

6. Ibid.

7. George W. Bush. Address to the Nation on the Terrorist Attacks. [http://www.presidency.ucsb.edu/ws/?pid=58057]

8. *Crossing the Rubicon*, p. xi.

9. India Offers US Military Backing. Sept. 14, 2001. BBC. [http://news.bbc.co.uk/1/hi/world/south_asia/1544149.stm]

10. Ibid.

11. *The 9/11 Commission Report*. [http://www.9–11commission.gov/report/ 911Report.pdf]

12. *In the Line of Fire*, p. 201.

13. *The National Security Archive*. [http://nsarchive.gwu.edu/NSAEBB/ NSAEBB358a/doc02.pdf]

14. *The National Security Archive*. [http://nsarchive.gwu.edu/NSAEBB/ NSAEBB358a/doc03–1.pdf]

15. *The National Security Archive* [http://nsarchive.gwu.edu/NSAEBB/ NSAEBB358a/doc05.pdf]

16. *In the Line of Fire*, p. 206.

17. Khurshid Mahmud Kasuri, *Neither a Hawk Nor a Dove*, Oxford University Press, Karachi, 2015, p. 567.

18. *Deadly Embrace*, pp. 66.

19. *In the Line of Fire*, p. 202.

20. "Musharraf Rallies Pakistan", BBC, Sept. 19, 2001. [http://news.bbc. co.uk/1/hi/not_in_website/syndication/monitoring/media_ reports/1553542.stm]

21. US Department of State [https://foia.state.gov/searchapp/DOCU- MENTS/5-FY2014/F-2010–03412/DOC_0C05192743/C05192743. pdf]

22. Interview with the author, 2015.

23. Interview with the author, 2014.

24. Ibid.

25. Farrukh Iqbal, "What's really going on with income trends in India and Pakistan?", Brookings. July 15, 2015. http://www.brookings.edu/blogs/ future-development/posts/2015/07/15-income-india-pakistan-iqbal

26. Ahmed Rashid, *Descent into Chaos. The US and the Disaster in Pakistan, Afghanistan and Central Asia*, London, Penguin Books, 2009, pp. 30–31.

27. Rod Norland, "Prejudice in Pakistan", *Newsweek*, Sept. 14, 2001. [http:// europe.newsweek.com/prejudice-pakistan-152341?rm=eu]

28. *In the Line of Fire*, 2006, p. 216.

29. *An Enemy We Created*, p. 229.

30. *The Wrong Enemy*, p. 54.

31. Abdul Salam Zaeef, *My Life with the Taliban*, edited by Alex Strick van Linschoten and Felix Kuehn, Hurst, London, 2011, p. 147.

32. US Department of State. [https://foia.state.gov/searchapp/DOCU- MENTS/9-FY2013/F-2010–03784/DOC_0C17522039/C17522039. pdf]

33. *The Arabs at War in Afghanistan*, p. 283.

34. *An Enemy We Created*, p. 225.

35. Ibid., p. 226.

36. Interview with the author, 2015.
37. Praveen Swami, "An Audacious Strike", *Frontline*, Oct. 13–26 2001. [http://www.frontline.in/static/html/fl1821/18210200.htm]
38. Husain Haqqani, *Between Mosque and Military*, Carnegie Endowment for International Peace. 2005, p. 303.
39. Praveen Swami, "An Audacious Strike", *Frontline*, Oct 13–26 2001. [http://www.frontline.in/static/html/fl1821/18210200.htm]
40. Text of Prime Minister Vajpayee's letter to President Bush. Rediff. Oct 2, 2001. [http://www.rediff.com/us/2001/oct/02ny9.htm]
41. "Kashmir Central to Indo-Pak Relations", says Powell. The Hindu. Oct 16, 2001. [http://www.thehindu.com/thehindu/2001/10/17/stories/01170001.htm]
42. "The Fears in Kashmir", *The Economist*, Oct 17, 2001. [http://www.economist.com/node/821462]
43. Briefing for foreign journalists, attended by the author. 2001.
44. Indian officials in interviews with the author. 2014
45. Dexter Filkins and Carlotta Gall, "Pakistanis Again Said to Evacuate Allies of Taliban", *New York Times*, Nov 24, 2001. [http://www.nytimes.com/2001/11/24/international/asia/24AFGH.html]
46. *The Wrong Enemy*, p. 8.
47. Seymour Hersh, "The Getaway", *The New Yorker*, Jan 28, 2002. [http://www.newyorker.com/magazine/2002/01/28/the-getaway-2]
48. Interview with the author. 2014.

6. THE ATTACK ON THE INDIAN PARLIAMENT: THE TRIAL OF AFZAL GURU

1. Unless otherwise stated, details of the attack are taken from Indian Supreme Court documents. Copy with the author. Supreme Court of India. Judgement on Appeal by Guru. August 5, 2005.
2. Ibid.
3. Sanjeev Miglani,"Twelve Die in Indian Parliament Attack," *Reuters* (taken from *The Guardian* website, dated Dec 14, 2001) [http://www.theguardian.com/world/2001/dec/14/kashmir.india].
4. Supreme Court of India. Judgement on Appeal by Guru. August 5, 2005.
5. "Twelve Die in Indian Parliament Attack".
6. "Indian parliament attack kills 12", BBC, Dec. 13, 2001. [http://news.bbc.co.uk/1/hi/world/south_asia/1707865.stm]
7. Celia W. Dugger, "Suicide Raid in New Delhi: Attackers Among 12 dead", *New York Times*, Dec 14, 2001. [http://www.nytimes.com/2001/12/14/world/suicide-raid-in-new-delhi-attackers-among-12-dead.html]
8. Ibid.

pp. [122–129]

9. B. Muralidhar Reddy, "I am Shocked: Musharraf", *The Hindu*, Dec. 14, 2001. [http://www.thehindu.com/2001/12/14/stories/20011214 00340100.htm]

10. "Government blames LeT for Parliament attack: asks Pak to restrain terrorist outfits", Rediff, Dec. 14, 2001. [http://www.rediff.com/news/2001/dec/14parl12.htm]

11. "Pakistan forces put on high alert: Storming of parliament", *Dawn*, Dec. 15, 2001. [http://www.dawn.com/news/10821/pakistan-forces-put-on-high-alert-storming-of-parliament]

12. "Confrontation: India and Pakistan", *PBS Newshour*, Dec. 26, 2001. [http://www.pbs.org/newshour/bb/asia-july-dec01-confrontation2_12–26/].

13. Statement of Mohammad Afzal to the Court. [http://www.revolutionarydemocracy.org/afzal/azfal6.htm]

14. "I Hope My Forced Silence Will Be Heard", Mohammad Afzal's letter to his lawyer. Oct 21, 2004. [http://www.outlookindia.com/article/i-hope-my-forced-silence-will-be-heard/225472]

15. Vinod K. Jose, "Mulakat Afzal, Mohammad Afzal interview from Tihar jail", *Caravan Magazine*, Feb. 1, 2006. [http://www.caravanmagazine.in/reportage/mulakat-afzal?page=0%2C1]

16. Ibid.

17. Statement of Mohammad Afzal to the Court. [http://www.revolutionarydemocracy.org/afzal/azfal6.htm]

18. Ibid.

19. Supreme Court of India, Judgement on Appeal by Guru, August 5, 2005.

20. Statement of Mohammad Afzal to the Court. [http://www.revolutionarydemocracy.org/afzal/azfal6.htm]

21. "I Hope My Forced Silence Will Be Heard. Mohammad Afzal's letter to his lawyer. Oct 21, 2004. [http://www.outlookindia.com/article/i-hope-my-forced-silence-will-be-heard/225472]

22. Supreme Court of India. Judgement on Appeal by Guru. August 5, 2005

23. Anjali Mody, "Three sentenced to death in parliament attack case", *The Hindu*, Dec. 19, 2002. [http://www.thehindu.com/2002/12/19/stories/2002121905170100.htm]

24. Ifthikhar Gilani, *My Days in Prison*, Penguin Books India, New Delhi, 2005, and interview with the author

25. "Delhi parliament attack pair freed", Oct 29, 2003, BBC. [http://news.bbc.co.uk/1/hi/world/south_asia/3223183.stm]

26. Supreme Court of India, Judgement on Appeal by Guru, Aug. 5, 2005.

27. Sandeep Joshi and Ashok Kumar, "Afzal Guru hanged in secrecy, buried in Tihar jail", *The Hindu*, Feb 10., 2013. [http://www.thehindu.com/news/national/afzal-guru-hanged-in-secrecy-buried-in-tihar-jail/article4396289.ece]

28. Interview with the author.
29. Interview with the author, 2014.
30. Ibid.
31. Ibid.
32. "Qazi blames Jaish for attacks on India's parliament", March 7, 2004. PTI in *Deccan Herald*. [http://archive.deccanherald.com/deccanherald/mar072004/f5.asp]
33. Email to the author.
34. Praveen Swami, "Death of a terrorist", *Frontline*, Sept. 13–26, 2003, [http://www.frontline.in/static/html/fl2019/stories/20030926003702000.htm]
35. "JeM-linked site celebrates attack, calls it revenge for Afzal Guru", *Hindustan Times*, Jan. 10, 2016. [http://www.hindustantimes.com/india/jem-linked-site-celebrates-attack-calls-it-revenge-for-afzal-guru/story-fSrsoKhJaF6THblwOx3zCM.html]
36. Praveen Swami, "Indian consulate attack: Before dying, Afghan attackers scrawled 'Afzal Guru avenged' on walls", *Indian Express*, Jan 6, 2016. [http://indianexpress.com/article/india/india-news-india/mazar-e-sharif-consulate-attack-before-dying-afghan-attackers-scrawled-afzal-guru-avenged-on-walls/]
37. Muzamil Jaleel, "Afzal Guru and the Jaish's jihad project", *Indian Express*, Jan 12, 2016. [http://indianexpress.com/article/explained/afzal-guru-and-the-jaishs-jihad-project/]

7. PURSUIT OF VALOUR: THE INDIA-PAKISTAN MILITARY STAND-OFF, 2001–2002

1. *India at Risk*, p. 249.
2. Ibid.
3. Rear Admiral Raja Menon, "Nuclear Issues-Op Parakram: The Nuclear Threshold from a Conventional Crisis", Monterey Paper, Aug. 16, 2005.
4. General V.K. Singh with Kunal Verma, *Courage and Conviction: An Autobiography*, General V.K. Singh, Adelphi Book Company, New Delhi, 2013, pp. 240–2.
5. Gurmeet Kanwal, Lost Opportunities in Operation Parakram", *Indian Defence Review*, Dec. 13, 2011. [http://www.indiandefencereview.com/spotlights/lost-opportunities-in-operation-parakram/]
6. *India at Risk*, p. 249. p. 249
7. Background briefing to journalists. Author's notes.
8. Walter C. Ladwig III, "A Cold Start for Hot Wars? The Indian Army's New Limited War Doctrine", Belfer Center, Harvard University. International Security. Vol 32. No 3. 2008 [http://belfercenter.ksg.harvard.edu/files/IS3203_pp158–190.pdf]

9. *Courage and Conviction*, p. 243.
10. Shashank Joshi, "Indian Power Projection: Ambition, Arms and Influence" (RUSI Papers), Routledge, London 2015.
11. Brigadier (retd) Gurmeet Kanwal. "Lessons: Operation Parakram. Achievements and Lessons: Cold Start and Integrated Battle Groups", May 13, 2006.
12. "Indian Power Projection".
13. Steve, Coll, "The Stand-Off", Feb. 13, 2006, *The NewYorker*. [http://www.newyorker.com/magazine/2006/02/13/the-stand-off]
14. "US Crisis Management in South Asia's Twin Peaks Crisis", Sept. 1, 2006, Stimson Center. [http://www.stimson.org/books-reports/us-crisis-management-in-south-asias-twin-peaks-crisis/]
15. "Pakistan Boasted of Nuclear Strike on India Within Eight Seconds", Nicholas Watt, June 15, 2012, *The Guardian*. [http://www.theguardian.com/world/2012/jun/15/pakistan-boasted-nuclear-strike-pakistan]
16. Author's notes. Also see "A Blunt-Speaking General Says India is Ready for War", Celia W. Dugger, Jan. 11, 2002, *New York Times*. [http://www.nytimes.com/2002/01/11/international/11CND-INDIA.html]
17. Timothy. D. Hoyt, "Kargil: The Nuclear Dimension", in *Asymmetric Warfare* in South Asia, p. 166.
18. "US Crisis Management in South Asia's Twin Peaks Crisis". [http://www.stimson.org/books-reports/us-crisis-management-in-south-asias-twin-peaks-crisis/]
19. India's List of 20 most-wanted men. Jan 11, 2002. Dawn. [http://www.dawn.com/news/14410/india-s-list-of-20-most-wanted-men]
20. "Joint Press Availability with Indian Foreign Minister Jaswant Singh" US Department of State, Jan. 18, 2002. [http://2001–2009.state.gov/secretary/former/powell/remarks/2002/7341.htm]
21. Ibid.
22. Ibid.
23. *Courage and Conviction*, op. cit. p. 244.
24. Ibid., p. 244.
25. Brigadier General (retd)Gurmeet Kanwal,"Lost Opportunities in Operation Parakram", *Indian Defence Review*, December 13, 2011. [http://www.indiandefencereview.com/spotlights/lost-opportunities-in-operation-parakram/]
26. Interview with the author, 2002.
27. Author's notes. 2002.
28. Manas Dasgupta, "SIT finds no proof against Modi, says court", April 12, 2012, *The Hindu*. [http://www.thehindu.com/news/national/sit-finds-no-proof-against-modi-says-court/article3300175.ece]
29. "Pakistan's Musharraf: Bin Laden probably dead", Jan 18, 2002, CNN.

[http://edition.cnn.com/2002/WORLD/asiapcf/south/01/18/gen.musharraf.binladen/]

30. "Al Qaida Number 3 says he planned 9/11, other plots", Associated Press, March 15, 2007. [http://www.nbcnews.com/id/17617986/?GT1=9145#.V1mNuPkrKM8]

31. State Department. Declassified cable. [https://foia.state.gov/searchapp/DOCUMENTS/NEA/F-2009–01221/DOC_0C05323855/C05323855.pdf]

32. Background briefing for foreign journalists based in Delhi. Author's notes

33. "Kaluchak Massacre", 14 May 2002. Details on website of Indian Ministry of External Affairs. [http://mea.gov.in/in-focus-article.htm?18990/Kaluchak+Massacre+14+May+2002]

34. Praveen Swami, "Building Confrontation", May 25–June 07, 2002, *Frontline*. [http://www.frontline.in/static/html/fl1911/19110040.htm]

35. Author's notes.

36. "Indian PM calls for 'decisive battle' over Kashmir", May 22, 2002, *The Guardian*. [http://www.theguardian.com/world/2002/may/22/kashmir.india]

37. "Our patience is running out, says Vajpayee", May 26, 2002, *The Hindu*. [http://www.thehindu.com/thehindu/2002/05/26/stories/2002052605780101.htm]

38. Pakistan President General Pervez Musharraf's address to the nation. May 27, 2002. South Asia Terrorism Portal. [http://www.satp.org/satporgtp/countries/pakistan/document/papers/Pervez_May272002.htm]

39. "US Crisis Management in South Asia's Twin Peaks Crisis", Sept. 1, 2006, Stimson Center. [http://www.stimson.org/books-reports/us-crisis-management-in-south-asias-twin-peaks-crisis/]

40. Author's notes. See also, "Straw says Kashmir war not inevitable", *The Daily Telegraph*, May 29, 2002. [http://www.telegraph.co.uk/news/1395684/Straw-says-Kashmir-war-not-inevitable.html]

41. Background briefing to journalists. Author's notes.

42. US Crisis Management in South Asia's Twin Peaks Crisis. [http://www.stimson.org/books-reports/us-crisis-management-in-south-asias-twin-peaks-crisis/]

43. "20 million can die in N-war", June 5, 2002, *Tribune India*. [http://www.tribuneindia.com/2002/20020606/world.htm#2]

44. "India Rejects Putin's Effort on Kashmir", Michael Wines, June 5, 2002, *New York Times*. [http://www.nytimes.com/2002/06/05/world/india-rejects-putin-s-effort-on-kashmir.html]

45. "West ups alert over Kashmir", June 5, 2002, BBC. [http://news.bbc.co.uk/1/hi/world/south_asia/2027624.stm]

46. Ibid.

47. US Crisis Management in South Asia's Twin Peaks Crisis. [http://www.stimson.org/books-reports/us-crisis-management-in-south-asias-twin-peaks-crisis/]
48. Ibid.
49. US Crisis Management in South Asia's Twin Peaks Crisis. [http://www.stimson.org/books-reports/us-crisis-management-in-south-asias-twin-peaks-crisis/]
50. "Stand by your pledge. Stop infiltration, India, USA, tell Pak", *The Tribune*, Chandigarh. [http://www.tribuneindia.com/2002/20020625/main1.htm]
51. "India lifts Pakistan flight ban", June 10, 2002, BBC. [http://news.bbc.co.uk/1/hi/world/south_asia/2036357.stm]
52. Author's notes.
53. *In the Line of Fire*, p. 299.
54. "Comparative Fatalities in J&K, 2001 to 2009", South Asia Terrorism Portal. [http://www.satp.org/satporgtp/countries/india/states/jandk/]
55. *Between Dreams and Realities*, pp. 195–196.

8. IN THE NAME OF THE PEOPLE: A SHORT HISTORY OF THE KASHMIR DISPUTE FROM 1846 TO STATE ELECTIONS IN 2002

1. Details on the elections are from author's notes, unless otherwise stated, 2002.
2. Basharat Peer, *Curfewed Night*, Random House India, New Delhi, 2008, p. 7.
3. "Fatalities in Terrorist Violence 1988—2016", South Asia Terrorism Portal. [http://www.satp.org/satporgtp/countries/india/states/jandk/data_sheets/annual_casualties.htm]
4. "Voter turnout in Jammu and Kashmir, 2002 & 2008", *South Asia Terrorism Portal*. [http://www.satp.org/satporgtp/countries/india/states/jandk/data_sheets/election2008.htm]
5. Author's notes.
6. William Moorcroft George Trebeck, *Travels in India: Himalayan Provinces of Hindustan and the Punjab. In Ladakh and Kashmir. In Peshawar, Kabul, Kunduz and Bokhara from 1819 to 1825*, First published in 1841; p. 248 in edn republished by Low Price Publications, New Delhi, 2000, vol. II, pp. 123–124.
7. Ibid., pp. 123–124.
8. Ibid., pp. 293–294.
9. Sumatra Bose, *Kashmir: Roots of Conflict, Paths to Peace*, Harvard University Press, Cambridge, MA, 2003. p. 7.
10. *Kashmir, A Disputed Legacy, 1846–1990*, p. 90.

11. Christopher Snedden, *The Untold Story of the People of Azad Kashmir*, Hurst, London, 2012, p. 21.

12. Christopher Snedden, *Understanding Kashmir and Kashmiris*, Hurst, London, 2015, pp. 88–89.

13. British 1941 census quoted in Kashmir. *Roots of Conflict, Paths to Peace*, p. 16.

15. Text of UN Resolution. [http://www.un.org/en/ga/search/view_doc.asp?symbol=S/RES/47(1948)]

16. Wajahat Habibullah, *My Kashmir: Conflict and the Prospects of Enduring Peace*, United States Institute of Peace, Washington, DC, 2008, p. 6.

17. Interview with the author, 2014.

18. "Winning the battle but losing the war? 'Human rights abuses' and the Kashmir conflict", unpubl diss., Liz Harris, Department of War Studies, Kings College, London, 2012.

19. *Kashmir: Roots of Conflict, Paths to Peace*, p. 129.

20. Arif Jamal, *Shadow War: The Untold Story of Jihad in Kashmir*, Melville House, New York, 2009, pp. 141–144.

21. Ibid., pp. 155–156.

22. Interview with the author

23. *Kashmir: Roots of Conflict, Paths to Peace*, p. 161.

24. Ibid., p. 141.

25. Ibid., p. 146.

26. Annual Fatalities in Jammu and Kashmir, 1990–2016. South Asia Terrorism Portal. Graph. [http://www.satp.org/satporgtp/countries/india/states/jandk/data_sheets/jandk2016.htm]

27. Briefing to journalists. Delhi Jan. 11, 2002. Author's notes.

28. Background briefing to the author, Delhi 2002.

29. Interview with the author, 2014.

30. A.S. Dulat and Aditya Sinha *Kashmir: The Vajpayee Years*, Harper Collins, New Delhi, 2015, p. 118.

31. Ibid., p. 141.

32. Ibid., pp. 116–118.

33. Comparative Fatalities in J&K, 2001 to 2009. South Asia Terrorism Portal. [http://www.satp.org/satporgtp/countries/india/states/jandk/]

34. News conference in August 2002, based on author's notes.

35. *Kashmir. The Vajpayee Years*, p. 233.

36. Ibid., p. 183.

37. Interview with the author, 2002.

38. Voter turnout in Jammu and Kashmir, 2002 & 2008, South Asia Terrorism Portal. [http://www.satp.org/satporgtp/countries/india/states/jandk/data_sheets/election2008.htm]

39. Statistical report on General Election 1996 to the Legislative Assembly

of Jammu and Kashmir. Election Commission of India. http://eci.nic. in/eci_main/StatisticalReports/SE_1996/StatisticalReport-JK96.pdf

40. Kashmir elections "fair but not free". Oct 9, 2002. BBC. [http://news. bbc.co.uk/1/hi/world/south_asia/2313347.stm]

41. Anjali Mody, "Observers laud conduct of J&K assembly elections", *The Hindu*, Oct 10, 2002. [http://www.thehindu.com/2002/10/10/stories/2002101005311100.htm]

42. Shujaat Bukhari. "PM extends 'hand of friendship' to Pakistan. *The Hindu*, April 19, 2003 [http://www.thehindu.com/2003/04/19/stories/2003041905500100.htm]

43. *Neither a Hawk Nor a Dove*, p. 162.

44. Ibid., p. 584.

45. *Kashmir: The Vajpayee Years*, p. 151.

46. "We have left aside' U.N. resolutions on Kashmir: Musharraf", Reuters interview quoted in *The Hindu*. [http://www.thehindu.com/2003/12/19/stories/2003121908320100.htm]

47. India-Pakistan Joint Press Statement, Islamabad, Jan. 6 2004. Text on SATP. [http://www.satp.org/satporgtp/countries/india/document/papers/indo_pak-6jan04.htm]

48. *Neither a Hawk Nor a Dove*, p. 168.

9. THE NOBLE LIE: THE INDIA-PAKISTAN PEACE TALKS, 2004–2007

1. Interview with the author, 2011.

2. Transcript of the Q&A portion of the Prime Minister's Press Conference. *The Hindu*, Jan 4, 2014. [http://www.thehindu.com/news/national/transcript-of-the-qa-portion-of-the-prime-ministers-press-conference/article5537934.ece]

3. Summary based on author's interviews with retired diplomats from India and Pakistan. For further details, see also: G. Parthasarathy and Radha Kumar. *Frameworks for a Kashmir Settlement*. Delhi Policy Group (2006) and *Neither a Hawk nor a Dove*.

4. Interview with the author. 2011

5. *Letters of Iqbal*, Compiled and Edited by Bashir Ahmad Dar, Iqbal Academy, Pakistan, 1978.

6. Choudhary Rahmat Ali. "Now or Never; Are We to Live or Perish For Ever?", full text online at: [http://www.columbia.edu/itc/mealac/pritchett/00islamlinks/txt_rahmatali_1933.html]

7. Muhammad Ali Jinnah's first presidential address to the Constituent Assembly [http://www.columbia.edu/itc/mealac/pritchett/00islamlinks/txt_jinnah_assembly_1947.html]

8. *Pakistan Studies and Pakistan Affairs*, Professor Naushad Khan, Islamia College University Peshawar, 2012, pp. 293, 306.

9. Ibid.

10. "Highlights of Indo-Pak Joint Statement", April 18, 2005, Rediff. [http://www.rediff.com/news/2005/apr/18mush6.htm]

11. "Make Siachen a Peace Mountain: Manmohan", Shujaat Bukhari, June 13, 2005, *The Hindu*. [http://www.thehindu.com/2005/06/13/stories/2005061307000100.htm]

12. K.M. Arif. *Khaki Shadows: Pakistan 1947–1997*. Oxford University Press, Karachi, 2001 p. 177.

13. Interview with the author, 2015.

14. Interview with the author, 2014.

15. Raffaello Pantucci, *"We Love Death As You Love Life": Britain's Suburban Terrorists*, Hurst, London, 2015, p. 22.

16. Raffaello Pantucci, "A Biography of Rashid Rauf: Al Qa'ida's British Operative", July 24, 2012, Combating Terrorism Center. [https://www.ctc.usma.edu/posts/a-biography-of-rashid-rauf-al-qaidas-british-operative]

17. *"We Love Death As You Love Life"*, p. 69.

18. Ibid., p. 68.

19. Ibid., p. 196.

20. Ibid., p. 219.

21. Joint Statement between President George W. Bush and Prime Minister Manmohan Singh, July 18, 2005, The White House. [http://georgewbush-whitehouse.archives.gov/news/releases/2005/07/20050718–6.html]

22. Strobe Talbott, *Engaging India: Diplomacy, Democracy and the Bomb*, extract published Oct. 1, 2004, Brookings. [http://www.brookings.edu/research/books/2004/engagingindia]

23. The US India Nuclear Deal. Council on Foreign Relations. Nov 5, 2010. [http://www.cfr.org/india/us-india-nuclear-deal/p9663]

24. George Perkovich. Faulty Promises, "The U.S.-India Nuclear Deal", Carnegie Endowment for International Peace. (Sept. 2005). [http://carnegieendowment.org/files/PO21.Perkovich.pdf]

25. Interview with the author, 2014.

26. *Neither a Hawk Nor a Dove*, p. 744

27. Elizabeth Bumiller and Carlotta Gall, "Bush Rules Out a Nuclear Deal with Pakistanis", *New York Times*, (March 5, 2006). [http://www.nytimes.com/2006/03/05/international/asia/05prexy.html?n=Top%2FReference%2FTimes%20Topics%2FSubjects%2FT%2FTerrorism&_r=0]

28. *Pakistan Studies and Pakistan Affairs*, p. 313.

29. Pew Research Center. Global Attitudes and Trends. August 8, 2007 [http://www.pewglobal.org/2007/08/08/pakistanis-increasingly-reject-terrorism-and-the-us/]

30. Operation Enduring Freedom—iCasualties.org. Coalition Deaths by Year. [http://icasualties.org/oef/ByYear.aspx]

31. *Neither a Hawk Nor a Dove*, p. 348.

32. Robert W. Bradnock. Kashmir: Paths to Peace. Chatham House. (May 2010). [https://www.chathamhouse.org/sites/files/chathamhouse/public/Research/Asia/0510pp_kashmir.pdf]

33. Sanjaya Baru, *The Accidental Prime Minister: The Making and Unmaking of Manmohan Singh*, Penguin, New Delhi, 2014, pp. 190–191.

34. Interview with the author, 2011.

35. *The Accidental Prime Minister*, p. 187.

36. Interview with the author, 2011.

37. "A Possible Outline of a Solution," full text of speech by Satinder Lambah, May 14, 2014, *Outlook*. [http://www.outlookindia.com/article/a-possible-outline-of-a-solution/290718]

38. *Neither a Hawk Nor a Dove*, p. 302.

39. Comments to the author, 2016.

40. Interview with the author, 2015.

41. Version given to the author by Pakistani and Indian diplomats involved in the original talks over Siachen.

42. Interview with the author, 2015.

43. Interview with the author, 2014.

44. Interview with the author, 2015.

45. Ibid.

46. "Breakfast in Amritsar, lunch in Lahore, hopes PM", Jan. 9, 2007, *The Hindu* [http://www.thehindu.com/todays-paper/breakfast-in-amritsar-lunch-in-lahore-hopes-pm/article1780445.ece]

10. WAR BY OTHER MEANS: THE ATTACK ON MUMBAI

1. Interrogation report of David Coleman Headley, National Investigation Agency, Government of India. Based on interrogation from June 3–9, 2010. Copy of report with the author.

2. Paul Eckert, "Pakistan vote presents risks, some upside for US", *Reuters*, Feb 20, 2008. [http://www.reuters.com/article/us-pakistan-election-usa-analysis-idUSN1927237720080220]

3. "Zardari ready to set aside Kashmir issue", CNN-IBN, March 1, 2008. [http://www.ibnlive.com/news/india/zardari-ready-to-set-aside-kashmir-issue-284217.html]

4. Interview with the author, 2014

5. *Ce que je n'ai pas pu dire*, p. 408.

6. Ibid., p. 469.

7. Interview with the author. 2009.

8. Ibid.
9. Statement by US Department of Justice. April 9, 2004. [http://www.justice.gov/archive/opa/pr/2004/April/04_crm_225.htm]
10. Statement by US Department of Justice. [http://www.justice.gov/opa/pr/david-coleman-headley-sentenced-35-years-prison-role-india-and-denmark-terror-plots]
11. Interrogation report of David Coleman Headley. National Investigation Agency. Government of India. Copy of report with the author.
12. Ibid.
13. "Un djihadiste francais juge a Paris", Feb. 7, 2007, *L'Express* [http://www.lexpress.fr/actualite/politique/un-djihadiste-francais-juge-a-paris_462757.html]
14. Interpol official website. [http://www.interpol.int/notice/search/wanted/2010–44050]
15. Statement by US Department of Justice. [http://www.justice.gov/opa/pr/david-coleman-headley-sentenced-35-years-prison-role-india-and-denmark-terror-plots]
16. Interrogation report of David Coleman Headley. National Investigation Agency. Government of India. Based on interrogation from June 3–9, 2010. Copy of report with the author.
17. Ibid.
18. Ibid.
19. Ibid.
20. Ibid.
21. Ibid.
22. Details on Kasab are from Indian Supreme Court judgment unless otherwise stated. [http://www.nia.gov.in/acts/Ajmal%20Kasab%20-%20Supreme%20Court%20Judgment.pdf]
23. Ibid.
24. David Coleman Headley. National Investigation Agency. Government of India. Based on interrogation from June 3–9, 2010. Copy of report with the author.
25. Joby Warrick, "US Officials: Pakistani Agents Helped Plan Kabul Bombing", Aug. 1, 2008, *Washington Post*. [http://www.washingtonpost.com/wp-dyn/content/article/2008/08/01/AR2008080100133.html]
26. "Indian, Pakistani forces trade fire on border", July 10, 2008, Reuters. [http://www.reuters.com/article/idUSISL202936]
27. Bappa Majumdar,"India PM says Pakistan peace process under threat", Aug. 15, 2008, Reuters. [http://www.reuters.com/article/us-india-independence-idUSDEL12225520080815?sp=true]
28. Simon Cameron-Moore, "Doubts Pakistan can assert control over spy agency", *Reuters*, July 28, 2008, Reuters. [http://www.reuters.com/article/us-pakistan-spies-analysis-idUSISL27007420080728?sp=true]

29. Obama's Remarks on Iraq and Afghanistan, July 15, 2008, *New York Times*. [http://www.nytimes.com/2008/07/15/us/politics/15text-obama. html?pagewanted=print]

30. Ibid.

31. "Obama calls for better India-Pakistan ties", *Reuters*, July 22, 2008, [http://www.reuters.com/article/us-obama-afghanistan-situation-idUSL2293241120080722]

32. Indian Supreme Court judgment. [http://www.nia.gov.in/acts/Ajmal% 20Kasab%20-%20Supreme%20Court%20Judgment.pdf]

33. James Glanz, Sebastian Rotella and David E. Sanger, "In 2008 Mumbai attacks, piles of spy data, but an uncompleted puzzle", *New York Times*, Dec 21, 2014. [http://www.nytimes.com/2014/12/22/world/asia/in-2008-mumbai-attacks-piles-of-spy-data-but-an-uncompleted-puzzle. html?_r=0]

34. Bret Stephens, "The Most Difficult Job in the World", *Wall Street Journal*, Oct 4, 2008. [http://www.wsj.com/articles/SB122307507392703831]

35. Transcript: Barack Obama talks to Rachel Maddow 5 days before election. Oct 30, 2008. [http://www.nbcnews.com/id/27464980]

36. Voter turnout in Jammu and Kashmir. 2002 & 2008. South Asia Terrorism Portal. [http://www.satp.org/satporgtp/countries/india/states/jandk/ data_sheets/election2008.htm]

37. "There is a bit of India in every Pakistani: Zardari", Vinod Sharma and Zia Haq, Nov. 23, 2008, *Hindustan Times*. [http://www.hindustantimes.com/ india/there-is-a-bit-of-india-in-every-pakistani-zardari/story-gB4z ET8PlhmNHGZOxYYugP.html]

38. Indian Supreme Court judgment. [http://www.nia.gov.in/acts/ Ajmal%20Kasab%20-%20Supreme%20Court%20Judgment.pdf]

39. "In 2008 Mumbai attacks, piles of spy data, but an uncompleted puzzle".

40. All details of the attacks from Ajmal Kasab India Supreme Court judgment. [http://www.nia.gov.in/acts/Ajmal%20Kasab%20-%20Supreme %20Court%20Judgment.pdf]

41. Intercepts reproduced in Supreme Court judgment. [http://www.nia. gov.in/acts/Ajmal%20Kasab%20-%20Supreme%20Court%20 Judgment.pdf]

42. Ibid.

43. "India blames elements from Pakistan for attack", C.J. Kuncheria and Robert Birsel, Nov. 28, 2008, Reuters. [http://www.reuters.com/arti-cle/us-india-mumbai-pakistan-sb-idUSTRE4AR2GN20081129]

44. Supreme Court judgment. [http://www.nia.gov.in/acts/Ajmal%20 Kasab%20-%20Supreme%20Court%20Judgment.pdf]

45. Interview with the author. 2014.

46. *The China-Pakistan Axis*, p. 61

47. "Pakistanis Added to UN sanctions list after Mumbai", Louis Charbonneau, Dec. 10, 2008, Reuters. [http://www.reuters.com/article/us-india-mumbai-un-sanctions-idUSTRE4B97N620081211]

48. "Pakistan Cracks Down on Lashkar", Abu Arqam Naqash, Dec. 13, 2008, Reuters.   [http://www.reuters.com/article/us-india-mumbai-sb-idUSTRE4BC10E20081213]

49. Comments made to the author.

50. Stephen Tankel, *Storming the World Stage: The Story of Lashkar e Taiba*, Hurst, London, 2011, p. 237.

51. Ibid., p. 240.

52. Ibid., p. 243.

53. US Department of State. Rewards for Justice. [http://www.state.gov/r/pa/prs/ps/2012/04/187342.htm]. Briefing attended by the author, 2010.

55. US Department of Justice. [http://www.justice.gov/opa/pr/david-coleman-headley-sentenced-35-years-prison-role-india-and-denmark-terror-plots]

56. FBI/US Department of Justice. [https://www.fbi.gov/chicago/press-releases/2013/tahawwur-rana-sentenced-to-14-years-in-prison-for-supporting-pakistani-terror-group-and-terror-plot-in-denmark]

57. "Mumbai Case Offers Rare Picture of Ties between Pakistan's Intelligence Service, Militants", Sebastian Rotella. May 2, 2001, *ProPublica*. [http://www.propublica.org/article/mumbai-case-offers-rare-picture-of-ties-between-pakistans-intelligence-serv]

11. ANATOMY OF MURDER: PAKISTAN'S RELATIONSHIP WITH ITS NORTH-WEST FRONTIER, 1947–2011

1. "Dancing Girls of the Swat Valley", Shaheen Buneri, Sept. 13, 2001, Pulitzer Centre. [http://pulitzercenter.org/reporting/pakistan-mingora-dancing-taliban-pashtun-fazlullah] "The decline of Swat's celebrated dancing girls", M. Ilyas Khan, Sept. 10, 2011, BBC. [http://www.bbc.co.uk/news/world-south-asia-14415389] Details also given to the author by local journalists.

2. "Pakistan, the United States and the End-Game in Afghanistan: Perceptions of Pakistan's Foreign Policy Elite", Jinnah Institute. 2011. [http://www.jinnah-institute.org/images/ji_afghanendgame.pdf]

3. "Rethinking the Durand Line: The Legality of the Afghan-Pakistan Frontier", Bijan Omrani and Frank Ledwidge, First published in *The RUSI Journal*, Oct. 2009. [http://www.bijanomrani.com/?p=Rethinking%20the%20Durand%20Line]

4. Robert Nichols, *A History of Pashtun Migration: 1775–2006*, Oxford University Press, 2007, p. 4.

5. *Handbooks for the Indian Army: Pathans*, 1938.

6. *A History of Pashtun Migration*, p. 143.

7. Ibid., p. 145.

8. Jon Boone, "Musharraf: Pakistan and India's backing for 'proxies' in Afghanistan must stop", *The Guardian*, Feb 13, 2015. [https://www.theguardian.com/world/2015/feb/13/pervez-musharraf-pakistan-india-proxies-afghanistan-ghani-taliban]

9. US Department of State. [https://foia.state.gov/searchapp/DOCUMENTS/9-FY2013/F-2010–03784/DOC_0C17522039/C17522039.pdf]

10. Interview with the author, 2014

11. "Living in Fear of Pakistan's new 'Taliban' regime", David Blair, Feb. 17, 2004, *The Daily Telegraph*. [http://www.telegraph.co.uk/news/worldnews/asia/pakistan/1454611/Living-in-fear-of-Pakistans-new-Taliban-regime.html]

12. Asad Durrani, Pakistan section of *PSI Handbook of Global Security and Intelligence*, Ed. Stuart Farson, Peter Gill, Mark Phythian and Shlomo Shpiro, Praeger, 2008, p. 235.

13. "Whose side is Pakistan's ISI Really On?" Declan Walsh, *The Guardian*, May 12, 2011. [https://www.theguardian.com/world/2011/may/12/isi-bin-laden-death-pakistan-alqaida]

14. "Five Years After 26/11, Intelligence Agencies Still Crippled By Staff Shortage", Praveen Swami, *The Hindu*, Nov. 26, 2013. [http://www.thehindu.com/news/national/five-years-after-2611-intelligence-services-still-crippled-by-staff-shortage/article5391698.ece]

15. "Launch Covert Action", Brig-Gen. (retd) Gurmeet Kanwal, Centre for Land Warfare Studies, Nov. 28, 2011. [http://www.claws.in/936/launch-covert-action-brig-gurmeet-kanwal.html]

16. Interview with the author, 2015.

17. Interview with the author, 2011.

18. "Pakistan, the United States and the End-Game in Afghanistan: Perceptions of Pakistan's Foreign Policy Elite", Jinnah Institute, 2011. [http://www.jinnah-institute.org/images/ji_afghanendgame.pdf]

19. "Haqqani Network Financing: The Evolution of an Industry", Gretchen Peters, July 31, 2012, Combating Terrorism Center. [https://www.ctc.usma.edu/posts/haqqani-network-financing] See also Vahid Brown and Don Rassler, *Fountainhead of Jihad. The Haqqani Nexus, 1973–2012*, Hurst, 2013.

20. "Looking for Taliban equivalents", Ali Arqam, May 2, 2012, *Pakistan Today*. [http://www.pakistantoday.com.pk/2012/05/02/comment/columns/looking-for-taliban-equivalents/]

21. Interview with the author, 2009.

22. This version offered to the author by locals from Swat.

23. Ibid.

24. Syed Saleem Shahzad, *Inside al Qaeda and the Taliban: Beyond bin Laden and 9/11*, Palgrave Macmillan, Basingstoke, 2011, pp. 166–68.

25. Author's notes, based on visit to Swat in 2011.

26. "US envoy weighs Afghan challenge", Lyse Doucet, March 23, 2009, BBC. [http://news.bbc.co.uk/1/hi/world/south_asia/7958603.stm]

27. Official website of Pakistan's Inter Services Public Relations (ISPR). [https://www.ispr.gov.pk/front/main.asp?o=t-press_release&date=2009/10/7]

28. Stanley McChrystal, Letter to Secretary of Defense, Aug 30, 2009, *Washington Post*. [http://media.washingtonpost.com/wp-srv/politics/documents/Assessment_Redacted_092109.pdf?sid=ST2009092003140]

29. "Obama sets Qaeda defeat as top goal in Afghanistan", Ross Colvin, March 27, 2009. Reuters. [http://www.reuters.com/article/us-afghanistan-idUSTRE52P7CO20090328#KuuMqsUJaiLRzwjj.97]

30. Comments to journalists, including the author.

31. Interview with the author, 2010.

32. "Afghan talks gain pace; US engages: sources", Myra MacDonald and Emma Graham-Harrison, Oct. 14, 2010, Reuters. [http://www.reuters.com/article/us-afghanistan-talks-usa-idUSTRE69D3KI20101014]

33. Senior Pakistani diplomat to author. 2010.

34. US Department of State. Full text of comments by Hillary Rodham Clinton at Asia Society. Feb 18, 2011. [http://www.state.gov/secretary/20092013clinton/rm/2011/02/156815.htm]

35. Operation Enduring Freedom iCasualties.org [http://icasualties.org/oef/]

36. Visit by the author in 2010, accompanied by the Pakistan Army.

37. Abubakar Siddique, *The Pashtun question: The Unresolved key to the Future of Pakistan and Afghanistan*, Hurst London, 2014, p. 96.

38. Ibid., p. 97.

39. Briefing to foreign journalists including the author, 2010.

40. *Pakistan, the United States and the End-Game in Afghanistan*. [http://www.jinnah-institute.org/images/ji_afghanendgame.pdf]

41. "Pakistan media publish fake WikiLeaks cables attacking India", Declan Walsh, Dec. 9, 2010, *The Guardian*. [http://www.theguardian.com/world/2010/dec/09/pakistani-newspaper-fake-leaks-india?INTCMP=SRCH]

42. "Leaking Away", Café Pyala, Dec. 9, 2010. [http://cafepyala.blogspot.co.uk/2010/12/leaking-away.html]

43. "Massaging Public Opinion", Cyril Almeida, Dec. 16, 2010, *Dawn*. [http://www.dawn.com/news/591570/massaging-public-opinion]

44. "Spy For a Spy: The CIA-ISI showdown over Raymond Davis", C. Christine Fair, *Foreign Policy*, March 10, 2011. [http://foreignpolicy.com/2011/03/10/spy-for-a-spy-the-cia-isi-showdown-over-raymond-davis/]

45. *The Way of the Knife: The CIA, a secret army and a war at the ends of the earth*, Mark Mazzetti, Penguin, 2013, p. 265.

46. "Pakistani Role is Suspected in Revealing US Spy's Name", Mark Mazzetti and Salman Masood, Dec. 17, 2010, *New York Times*. [http://www.nytimes.com/2010/12/18/world/asia/18pstan.html]

47. "US Drone Strikes in Pakistan" Amnesty International, Oct. 22, 2013. [http://www.amnestyusa.org/research/reports/will-i-be-next-us-drone-strikes-in-pakistan]

48. "Report exposes 'the hands of cruelty' in Pakistan's tribal areas", Amnesty International, Dec. 12, 2012. [https://www.amnesty.org/en/latest/news/2012/12/report-exposes-hands-cruelty-pakistan-s-tribal-areas/]

49. "Public Opinion in Pakistan's Tribal Regions", New America Foundation, Terror Free Tomorrow, Sept. 2010. [http://www.terrorfreetomorrow.org/upimagestft/FATApoll1.pdf]

50. "Most of those killed in drone attacks were terrorists: military", March 8, 2011, *Dawn*, [http://www.dawn.com/news/611717/most-of-those-killed-in-drone-attacks-were-terrorists-military]

51. "Drone Blowback In Pakistan Is A Myth", Aqil Shah, *Washington Post*, May 17, 2016. [https://www.washingtonpost.com/news/monkey-cage/wp/2016/05/17/drone-blow-back-in-pakistan-is-a-myth-heres-why/]

52. "'Living Under Drones': the anti-drone campaign can do damage too", Myra MacDonald, Oct. 3, 2012, Reuters. [http://blogs.reuters.com/pakistan/2012/10/03/living-under-drones-the-anti-drone-campaign-can-do-damage-too/]

53. Pakistan IDP Figures Analysis, Internal Displacement Monitoring Centre, July 2015. [http://www.internal-displacement.org/south-and-south-east-asia/pakistan/figures-analysis]

54. *Pakistan, the United States and the End-Game in Afghanistan*.

55. "Document: Pakistan's Bin Laden dossier", Al Jazeera, July 8, 2013. [http://www.aljazeera.com/indepth/spotlight/binladenfiles/2013/07/201378143927822246.html] "In Hiding, Bin Laden Had Four Children and Five Houses", Declan Walsh, March 29, 2012, *New York Times*. [http://www.nytimes.com/2012/03/30/world/asia/on-run-bin-laden-had-4-children-and-5-houses-a-wife-says.html?pagewanted=all&_r=0]

12. PURSUIT OF PARITY: THE CLOSING YEARS

1. Visit by the author, 2010.

2. Visit by the author, 2010.

3. "Floods give renewed clout to Pakistan Army", Myra MacDonald, Sept. 5, 2010, Reuters. [http://www.reuters.com/article/us-pakistan-floods-army-idUSTRE6840CA20100905]

4. Comments made to the author, 2010.

5. "Pakistani children haunted by floods", Myra MacDonald, Reuters, Aug. 31, 2010. [http://uk.reuters.com/article/uk-pakistan-floods-children-idUKTRE67U4SJ20100831]

6. "What's really going on with income trends in India and Pakistan?", Farrukh Iqbal, July 15, 2015, Brookings. [http://www.brookings.edu/blogs/future-development/posts/2015/07/15-income-india-pakistan-iqbal]

7. International Human Development Indicators, United Nations, 2015. [http://hdr.undp.org/en/countries]

8. "Which are the world's fastest growing economies?" World Economic Forum, April 18, 2016. [https://www.weforum.org/agenda/2016/04/worlds-fastest-growing-economies/]

9. South Asia Regional Update, April 2016, International Monetary Fund. [http://www.imf.org/external/]

10. World Economic Forum, *The Global Competitiveness Report 2016–2017* [http://reports.weforum.org/global-competitiveness-index/]

11. Ibid: Regional Highlights South Asia. [http://reports.weforum.org/global-competitiveness-index/regional-highlights-south-asia/]

12. "US says Pakistan's ISI supported Kabul embassy attack", Missy Ryan and Susan Cornwell, Sept. 22, 2011. Reuters. [http://www.reuters.com/article/us-usa-pakistan-idUSTRE78L39720110922#sGXCqgGHbS6xLtoo.97]

13. U.S. Aid to Pakistan, 2011–2017, Chart, *Reuters*. [http://fingfx.thomsonreuters.com/gfx/rngs/USA-PAKISTAN-AID/010021DY3EE/index.html]

14. "Death of Mullah Omar Exposes Divisions Within Taliban", Joseph Golstein and Taimoor Shah, *New York Times*, July 30, 2015. [http://www.nytimes.com/2015/07/31/world/asia/taliban-confirm-death-of-mullah-omar-and-weigh-successor.html?_r=1]

15. "US drone strike in Pakistan kills Taliban leader Mullah Mansoor", Jon Boone and Sune Engel Rasmussen, *The Guardian*, May 22, 2016. [https://www.theguardian.com/world/2016/may/21/us-airstrike-taliban-leader-mullah-akhtar-mansoor]

16. "China Readies $46 billion for Pakistan Trade Route", Saeed Shah and Jeremy Page, *Wall Street Journal*, April 16, 2015. [http://www.wsj.com/articles/china-to-unveil-billions-of-dollars-in-pakistan-investment-1429214705]

17. For a detailed analysis of Indian military power, see Shashank Joshi's *Indian Power Projection*.

18. Ibid.

19. "Enclaves swapped in landmark India-Bangladesh border deal", BBC, July 31, 2015. [http://www.bbc.co.uk/news/world-asia-india-33733911]

20. "Difa-e-Pakistan: Religious right delivers verbal punches at rally", Sabia Imtiaz, Feb. 13, 2012, *Express Tribune*. [http://tribune.com.pk/story/335663/difa-e-pakistan-religious-right-delivers-verbal-punches-at-rally/]

21. Pakistan's Federal Budget 2014–2015, official data. [http://www.finance.gov.pk/budget/Budget_in_Brief_2014_15.pdf]

22. *Military Inc. Inside Pakistan's Military Economy*, Ayesha Siddiqa, Oxford University Press, Karachi, 2007.

23. "Election in September, CJ will favour us and government will fall", Hashmi quotes Imran, Sept. 1, 2014, *Express Tribune*. [http://tribune.com.pk/story/756506/election-in-september-cj-will-favour-us-and-govt-will-fall-hashmi-quotes-imran/]

24. "Fatalities in terrorist violence in Pakistan 2003–2015", South Asia Terrorism Portal. [http://www.satp.org/satporgtp/countries/pakistan/database/casualties.htm]

25. "I44 Stories. Remembering Lives Lost in the Peshawar School Attack" [http://www.dawn.com/news/1223313]

26. "Imposing Silence. The Use of India's Laws To Suppress Free Speech", Pen International, May 20, 2015. [http://www.pen-international.org/news-items/writers-and-human-rights-experts-call-on-india-to-repeal-laws-that-threaten-free-expression-in-worlds-largest-democracy/]

27. "Academic Freedom is Under Threat in India", Amartya Sen, Sagarika Ghose, *Times of India*, Feb. 21, 2015. [http://timesofindia.indiatimes.com/india/Academic-freedom-is-under-threat-in-India-Amartya-Sen/articleshow/46318446.cms]

28. "The Modi Phenomenon", Pew Research Center, Sept. 17, 2015. [http://www.pewglobal.org/2015/09/17/1-the-modi-phenomenon/]

29. These included a meeting between Prime Minister Singh and President Zardari in Yekaterinburg, Russia in June 2009 and talks between Singh and Pakistan Prime Minister Yousaf Raza Gilani in Sharm el-Sheikh in Egypt in July 2009. For Yekaterinburg, see "India, Pakistan leaders hold first talks since Mumbai", Reuters, June 16 2009 [http://www.reuters.com/article/idUSLG668165] and for Sharm el-Sheikh, see joint statement [http://www.reuters.com/article/idUSLG668165]

30. Briefing attended by the author, 2010.

31. These included an attack on an Indian air base in Pathankot, Punjab in January 2016 that India blamed on Masood Azhar and the Jaish-e-

Mohammed. See for example, "India, Pakistan Talks Deferred after Pathankot Air Base Attack, Reuters, Jan 14, 2016. [http://uk.reuters.com/article/india-pakistan-talks-idUKKCN0US18520160114]

32. "Indian Military Modernization and Conventional Deterrence in South Asia", *Journal of Strategic Studies*, Walter C. Ladwig III, Vol. 38, No. 4, May 2015.

33. *Indian Power Projection.*

34. *A Cold Start for Hot Wars?*

35. "A Conversation with General Khalid Khidwai", Carnegie Endowment for International Peace, March 23, 2015. [http://carnegieendowment.org/files/03–230315carnegieKIDWAI.pdf]

36. David E. Sanger and William J. Broad. "In Hacked Audio, Hillary Clinton Rethinks Obama's Nuclear Upgrade Plan", *New York Times*, Sept. 29, 2016. [http://www.nytimes.com/2016/09/30/us/politics/hillary-clinton-obama-nuclear-policy.html?_r=0]

37. "Voter turnout in Jammu and Kashmir", 2002 & 2008, South Asia Terrorism Portal. [http://www.satp.org/satporgtp/countries/india/states/jandk/data_sheets/election2008.htm]

38. "Kashmir: Paths to Peace", Robert W. Bradnock, Chatham House, May 2010. [https://www.chathamhouse.org/sites/files/chathamhouse/public/Research/Asia/0510pp_kashmir.pdf]

39. *Understanding Kashmir and Kashmiris*, p. 34.

40. Visit by the author, 2014.

41. "Trends of violence in Jammu and Kashmir", SATP. [http://www.satp.org/satporgtp/countries/india/states/jandk/data_sheets/trendsofviolence.htm]

42. Shakir Mir. "It's Time to Bring Kashmir's 'Miserable Guillotine' Out from the Shadows", *The Wire*, September 26, 2016. [http://thewire.in/68602/kashmirs-miserable-guillotine/]

43. *Letters of Iqbal*, Compiled and edited by Bashir Ahmad Dar, Iqbal Academy, Pakistan, 1978.

EPILOGUE: A JAW FOR A TOOTH

1. Naveed Iqbal, "A town called Uri—how the Sept 18 attack may now change it", Indian Express, Sept 25, 2016. [http://indianexpress.com/article/india/india-news-india/uri-attack-baramulla-army-headquarters-kashmir-loc-india-pakistan-3048498/]

2. Vivek Chadha, Rumel Dahiya, Neha Kohli and Shruti Pandalai, "Uri, Surgical Strikes and International Relations", Institute for Defence Studies and Analysis, New Delhi, Oct 4, 2016. [http://idsa.in/issuebrief/uri-surgical-strikes-and-international-reactions_041016] See also, Shiv Kunal

Verma, "The Uri Fiasco". [http://bharatkalyan97.blogspot.co.uk/2016/09/the-uri-fiasco-shiv-kunal-verma.html]

3. Statement by NSC Spokesperson Ned Price on National Security Adviser Susan E. Rice's Call with National Security Adviser Ajit Doval of India. The White House. Sept 28, 2016. [https://www.whitehouse.gov/the-press-office/2016/09/28/statement-nsc-spokesperson-ned-price-national-security-advisor-susan-e]

4. "Militants attack Indian army base in Kashmir, 'killing 17'", BBC, Sept 18, 2016, [http://www.bbc.co.uk/news/world-asia-india-37399969]. See also "India mulls response after deadly Kashmir attack it blames on Pakistan", Reuters, Sept 19, 2016. [http://uk.reuters.com/article/uk-india-kashmir-idUKKCN11P0DC]

5. "Uri attack: Ram Madhav wants 'jaw for tooth'". Indian Express, Sept 19, 2016. [http://indianexpress.com/article/india/india-news-india/uri-terror-attack-pakistan-involvement-ram-madhav-indian-army-pm-modi-3038298/]

6. Shashank Joshi, "The Line of (out of) Control. Summary of reports of previous Indian raids." Oct 4, 2016. [https://shashankjoshi.wordpress.com/blog-2/] and Dexter Filkins, "Kashmir Border Duels, Rhetoric Heat Up", Los Angeles Times, May 27, 1998. [http://articles.latimes.com/1998/may/27/news/mn-53885/2]

7. "Pathankot Attacks: Pakistan, India Reschedule Peace Talks", BBC, Jan 14, 2016. [http://www.bbc.co.uk/news/world-asia-india-35309559]

8. Saeed Shah, "Despite Crackdown, Some Pakistani Militants Walk the Streets", Wall Street Journal, April 25, 2016. [http://www.wsj.com/articles/pakistans-crackdown-on-islamic-militants-looks-selective-1461565803]

9. "South Asian summit uncertain as India, others pull out in snub to Pakistan", Reuters, Sept 28, 2016. [http://uk.reuters.com/article/uk-saarc-summit-idUKKCN11Y1MX?il=0]

10. Sanjeev Miglani, "After military raid, India looks at more ways to pressure Pakistan," Reuters, Sept 30, 2016. [http://in.reuters.com/article/india-pakistan-idINKCN12002W]

11. Statement by NSC Spokesperson Ned Price on National Security Adviser Susan E. Rice's Call with National Security Adviser Ajit Doval of India. The White House. Sept 28, 2016. [https://www.whitehouse.gov/the-press-office/2016/09/28/statement-nsc-spokesperson-ned-price-national-security-advisor-susan-e]

12. Transcript of Joint Briefing by MEA AND MOD, Sept 29, 2016. [http://www.mea.gov.in/media-briefings.htm?dtl/27446/ Transcript_of_Joint_Briefing_by_MEA_and_MoD_September_29_2016]

13. Shashank Joshi, "The Line of (out of) Control. Summary of reports of

previous Indian raids." Oct 4, 2016. [https://shashankjoshi.wordpress.com/blog-2/] See also Vijaita Singh and Josy Joseph, "Operation Ginger: tit-for-tat across the Line of Control", *The Hindu*, Oct 9, 2016. [http://www.thehindu.com/news/national/operation-ginger-titfortat-across-the-line-of-control/article9202758.ece]

14. Statement by Congress spokesman R.S. Surjewala, Oct 4, 2016. [https://twitter.com/rssurjewala/status/783288273930063872]

15. Sushant Singh, "Inside the Surgical Strike: Choppers on Standby, 70–80 Soldiers", *Indian Express*, Oct 1, 2016 [http://indianexpress.com/article/india/india-news-india/surgical-strikes-india-pakistan-loc-jammu-and-kashmir-indian-army-3059059/] and Praveen Swami, "Surgical strikes: Bodies taken away on trucks, loud explosions, eye-witnesses give graphic details", *Indian Express*, Oct 6, 2016. [http://indianexpress.com/article/india/india-news-india/pakistan-border-terror-camps-surgical-strikes-kashmir-loc-indian-army-jihadist-3065975/]

16. Sandeep Unnithan, "Crossing a Red Line", *India Today*, Oct 6, 2016. [http://indiatoday.intoday.in/story/surgical-strike-indian-army-loc-uri-attack-pakistan/1/781369.html]

17. "Past operations were covert, not surgical strikes: Manohar Parrikar", *Indian Express*, Oct 13, 2016. [http://indianexpress.com/article/india/india-news-india/manohar-parrikar-surgical-strikes-pakistan-indian-army-3079225/]

18. Cyril Almeida, "Exclusive: Act against militants or face international isolation, civilians tell military." *Dawn*, Oct 6, 2016. [http://www.dawn.com/news/1288350/exclusive-act-against-militants-or-face-international-isolation-civilians-tell-military]. See also Andrew Small, "As Indo-Pak Tensions Simmer, China Adopts Diplomatic Balancing Act", *The Wire*, Sept 30, 2016. [http://thewire.in/69943/as-indo-pak-tensions-simmer-china-adopts-diplomatic-balancing-act/]

19. "Security Council Condemns Nuclear Tests by India and Pakistan", June 6, 1998. [http://www.un.org/press/en/1998/sc6528.doc.htm]

INDEX

Abdullah, Farooq: family of, 158, 163; leader of National Conference, 160–1, 163

Abdullah, Omar: 166–7, 200; background of, 164; family of, 163, 183; Indian Minister of State for External Affairs, 164; visit to Pakistan (2006), 183

Abdullah, Sheikh: 156–7; family of 158, 183; imprisonment of (1953), 158, 164

Advani, Lal Krishna: 73, 80; Indian Home Minister, 41, 78, 121; protest march led by (1992), 37; visit to Pakistan (2005), 174

Afghanistan: 12–15, 29, 74, 83–5, 89–90, 94, 96–7, 99–101, 114–15, 122, 129, 148, 172, 199–200, 211, 217, 230–2, 240–1; borders of, 13, 93–5, 107, 137, 221, 225, 239; Civil War (1992–6), 17, 92; coup d'état (1973), 86; Durand Line, 85–6, 92, 211–12, 218, 223, 231; government of, 116, 215; Herat, 215; Jalalabad, 86, 88, 98, 215; jihadi training camps in, 94–5, 98; Kabul, 9–11, 85, 88, 90–2,

96, 99, 186, 190, 197, 210, 215, 222, 224, 239; Kandahar, 11, 13, 15, 19, 23–4, 26, 84, 95, 215, 257, 260; Kunar Province, 225; Kunduz Airlift (2001), 116–17; Mazar-e-Sharif, 95, 131, 215; National Directorate of Security (NDS), 98, 216; Operation Enduring Freedom (2001–14), 29–30, 67–8, 99, 105, 109, 114–17, 130, 134, 137, 174–5, 179–80, 192, 194, 198, 210, 214, 218, 221, 225–6, 239; Panjshir Valley, 11, 92; Pashtun population of, 85, 113–14, 214; Saur Revolution (1978), 86; Soviet Invasion of (1979–89), 5, 8, 13–14, 36–7, 83, 86–7, 91–3, 111, 113, 122, 160, 174, 191, 197, 213, 216–17, 226; Tora Bora, 114

Agra Summit (2001): 78–9, 181–2; attendees of, 71, 73–4, 77, 80–1; establishment of, 74–5; failure of, 80–3, 99, 129

Ahl-e-Hadith sect: 191

Ahmad, Afaaq: suicide bombing conducted by (2000), 76

INDEX